Inventive Thinking through TRIZ

Michael A. Orloff

# Inventive Thinking through TRIZ

## A Practical Guide

Second Edition

With 232 Figures

Springer

Author

Professor Dr. Dr. Sc. techn. Michael Orloff

Modern TRIZ Academy International
Europe-Center
D-10789 Berlin
Germany
*e-mail: michael.orloff@modern-triz-academy.com*
*www.modern-triz-academy.com*

ISBN 978-3-642-06980-2 e-ISBN 978-3-540-33223-7



Springer is a part of Springer Science+Business Media.

springer.com


Printed in Germany



Cover design: E. Kirchner, Heidelberg

*Dedicated to my son Alexey*
*with love and respect*
*for his hearty generosity,*
*purposefulness*
*and*
*courage*

A heuristic program is necessary for effective solutions to the requirements of inventing at a higher level that replaces the continuously new selection of variations with a goal-oriented movement into the area of the solution.

*Genrikh Altshuller*

*Algorithm of Inventing*
*Moscow, 1973*

# TRIZ at the Beginning of the 21st Century

## Author's Foreword

*It is never too early to think about tomorrow.*
*Federico Mayor**

*Humanity developed on the stepping stones of inventions.* Brilliant inventions brought humanity to breathtaking heights. Millions of other inventions made these stepping stones and the entire construct of civilization secure. The rise of civilization accelerated continuously.

But, the process of inventing remained the same throughout the ages. There was intellectual torture about a problem, a search in all possible directions, countless unsuccessful attempts, stumbling, total loss in a labyrinth, circular movement in fog, and - very rarely - unexpected ideas shone like a light in the deepest darkness, like the realization of our dearest dreams or a cure for an incurable disease. This is how we invented. Sometimes inventors searched their entire lives long.

There were many enthusiasts who attempted to uncover the secret of the birth of inventing. Brilliant scientists tried to develop theories of creativity. Great pragmatists collected hordes of useful suggestions to stimulate the development of ideas and put them to use. However, all of this was only marginally successful in praxis.

***It was impossible to learn how to invent!***

This was only because it was impossible to explain and pass on individual and historical experience while inventing. Well-known descriptions of inventive creativity were written down in metaphors with emotional language and individual suggestions and recommendations. This was not done scientifically: there were no laws or methods. It was also not possible to treat inventing like an art because even art can be learned and taught to a great degree.

Despite this fact, civilization rose steadily. Enthusiasm about the progress exemplified by automobiles, aircraft, space rockets, by the Internet and cellular phones was so great and so universal that very few people in the 20th century also recognized the deadly threats that these devices in their complexity represent for humanity.

Even the shocking truth about coming global catastrophes caused by the destruction of nature by industry and technology was not sufficiently sobering. Lack of responsibility and egotism in many technocratic structures, the lack of critical knowledge about questions of global survival, and the lack of globally coordinated institutions, not to mention problems in the consolidation of the efforts of all industrialized countries - all of this has to be changed from the ground up as quickly as possible.

---

* Federico Mayor – former General Secretary of the UNESCO (2002)

A secure future has to be the goal and motivation of every attempt at progress and of all politics. Engineers, teachers, and scientists can assume a part of their personal responsibility in such attempts. We should all search for organizational and technical possibilities individually and with our fellow professionals that can help avoid technogenic - and therefore - sociogenic catastrophes.

When we consider the extremely short time for inventions and the practical application of essential ideas, it is not enough to rely on the methods for finding new ideas that our wonderful, yet so imperfect civilization has created. Perhaps this civilization is sometimes so deficient because the methods that have shaped it are imperfect.

Who controls the development of humanity? Can we really make a reliable prognosis about our best way into the future? How can sociogenic, geogenic, and cosmic catastrophes be avoided? How can we insure the progress and security of coming generations?

***TRIZ teaches us how to make inventions!***
***TRIZ teaches us how to construct the future!***
***TRIZ changes your thinking, i.e., all of civilization, too!***

Rational decisions about the problems above cannot be made today without the use of TRIZ.

TRIZ will be an invaluable part of all the possible sciences and learning processes that remain from the $2^{nd}$ millennium AD. What could be more valuable than a science about *how we can learn to think effectively, to become an inventor, or even a genius!*

The following are the essential concepts of TRIZ in its modern form:

1. All systems (not only technical systems) are developed to fulfill a certain function, the system's so-called useful primary function. Systems are developed according to the certain laws that can be perceived and used to shape the development of systems.
2. All systems strive to enhance their effectiveness during their life cycle. Effectiveness can be understood as the ratio between positive factors from the implementation of useful functions and negative factors - such as compensation for harmful effects on the environment - that arise from the development, use, and application of the system.
3. All systems and components develop differently in comparison to other systems in their environment. This is the main cause of slow growth in the effectiveness of systems and of technical problems.
4. Contradictions between incompatible characteristics and requirements that prevent the achievement of the useful primary function of the components and the system create the basis for all technical problems.
5. A solution for such a contradiction with technical means is then an invention.

6. The number of different types of contradictions is limited. This allows us to perceive them precisely in real problems and to evaluate them with adequate methods for a solution.
7. Adequate methods for the solution of contradictions can be developed by investigating a sufficient number of a representative selection of real inventions along with patent descriptions and technical literature.
8. Methods for the solution of contradictions can be developed along with procedures for the development and stimulation of memory, attention, associative thinking, imagination, and various useful characteristics of the intellect and psyche.
9. Methods for the solution of contradictions can be applied along with other methods used to shape the development of complex systems - economic, system-technical, cultural-educational, and even political methods.

everal thousand inventions were examined for the development of the first navi-itors in TRIZ for the solution of contradictions. The number of investigated in-ntions is now more than 2.5 million. TRIZ navigators have proven effective for any years and continue to be applied successfully.

At the beginning of the 21st century, TRIZ is the only constructive theory of invention and, based on its essence, of engineering creativity. TRIZ has in no way been developed fully. It must be further developed, structured, and supplied with axioms. Special and combined theories and methods can be developed along with TRIZ, such as the integrated theory **CROST – Constructive Resource-Oriented Strategy of Thinking & Transforming** that was developed by the author of this textbook. In accordance with the model of TRIZ, still more patents and scientific-technical literature should be examined. However, the main principles of TRIZ are still invariable, just like with every other effective theory. They can therefore be considered as classical principles.

Although time and a special praxis are required for a study of the basis of TRIZ, this theory will prove itself in your future activities, regardless of your profession. The methods of TRIZ allow you to find valuable solutions more quickly and with less effort. TRIZ is simply irreplaceable for solutions to extremely difficult problems. In my almost 40 years of TRIZ praxis since 1963 when I read my first small book [1] by Genrikh Altshuller, I have heard of no one who had abandoned it after studying its methods and models. At this point, I would like to quote a statement by the author of TRIZ:

***"TRIZ supports thinking, it doesn't replace it".***

I would like to thank many specialists who have supported my idea to write the first textbook on the principles of classical TRIZ. Conversations with Prof. H.-J. Linde (FH Coburg) and Dr. R. Thiel, Dr. D. Zobel as well as Dr. M. Herrlich were especially helpful.

Meetings with Prof. W. Beitz and Prof. G. Seliger (Technical University Berlin) helped me become familiar with the creative components of university education in Germany. Prof. G. Ropohl's (J. W. Goethe-University, Frankfurt am Main) ideas about the problems and the role of technocracy in the maintenance and further development of civilization - impossible without environmental protection and humanistic social ethics - and his supportive letters reinforced my plans.

I cannot mention everyone here who helped enable us to live and work in Germany. However, my special thanks go to Udo Matusch (engineer and entrepreneur, head of the firm AMT Automatisierungstechnik GmbH, Essen) who was the first person to invite me to Germany and who allowed me to work on an adaptation of the TRIZ methodology for Germany at his company for 2 years.

My heartfelt thanks go to the engineer and inventor Katharina Koterewa, head of the firm ZWEK Vakuumtechnik GmbH in Apolda, who provided ideal conditions for me at her home in Thueringia's mountains to order my thoughts and maintain hope and optimism in a very difficult situation during my move to Berlin. I would like to thank my friend Heinrich Kochs (recently specialist at VOLKSWAGEN) for the many days for thought and discussion, for my first introduction into the German everyday, and for the use of his garden house with a large library and the best conditions for my work in a wonderfully quiet region in the woods near Hannover. My great thanks go to Dr. Lydia Dessau, the manager of Innovation Centre IGZ-OWZ Berlin, who allowed me to work in her firm and who worked together with us to deal with the difficulties in establishing my first German firm. I would like to thank her husband, Hartmut Dessau, an employee at SIEMENS who always supported us with his constructive criticism. I thank both of them that they offered us their idyllic weekend house on the river Dahme for a long time.

My thanks also go to my colleagues Harald Lemanski and Siegfried Helling. And I hope that the translation of this textbook into English in creative cooperation with Dr. Cary Henderson - a translation that reproduces the spirit of TRIZ - helps my readers connect positively with the book.

I am especially thankful to Prof. Dr. Martin Moehrle (University Bremen) whose energetic and timely support first made it possible for me to continue working in Germany and to publish my most important works.

I am extremely thankful to the Springer Publishers, especially to Mrs. Eva Hestermann-Beyerle, Editor of Textbooks Engineering, who made the suggestion to write a textbook on the essential principles of classical TRIZ.

I am hearty thankful to my son Nikolai for contribution to improvement of this book, for subtle understanding TRIZ and belief in TRIZ future.

I wish success to everyone who is not afraid to search for new ideas in the creation and development of technical systems and who remembers that all of our solutions changes humanity in some way.

Michael A. Orloff
Berlin, November 2002 – December 2005

# Table of Contents

The methods of inventive creativity are not a recipe for inventions. They can also not replace technical knowledge.

But, it helps to apply the methods called knowledge very effectively.

To study these methods does not guarantee that an inventor will surpass Popov or Edison.

On the other hand, university seminars don't guarantee that a student will exceed Newton or Einstein with time, either.

*Genrikh Altshuller*

*Wings for Icarus*
*Petrosavodsk, 1980*

# Introduction

*NATURA NIHIL EST CALLIDIUS*[1]

## 1 Invention of Civilization

This is a textbook about inventiveness in technical creative work. Above all else, it is about the highpoint of technical creative work - invention. Humanity has developed on the stepping-stones of inventions[*].

Today, discoveries and inventions move humanity forward faster and faster, as we stood on a great escalator.

If we assume that today the productive age of an individual is up to 40 years and we then consider the number of generations that have lived through this span of time, we will then be able to correctly assess the developmental speed of civilization for the first time.

Of **1000** generations in the last 40,000 years:

NB:
- more than **800** generations lived without artificial shelters in woods and caves;
- only **120** generations have known and used the wheel;
- about **55** generations have known and used the Archimedes' law;
- about **40** generations have used windmills and watermills;
- about **20** generations have known and used timepieces;
- about **10** generations have known printing;

NNB:
- **5** generations have traveled with ships and trains;
- **4** generations have used electric lights;
- **3** generations have traveled with automobiles, have used telephones and vacuum cleaners;
- **2** generations have traveled with aircraft and used radios and refrigerators;

NNNB:
- **only today's generation** has traveled in outer space, has used atomic energy, PCs and notebooks, and uses artificial satellites to transmit audio, video and other information around the globe.

**90 % of the knowledge and all material values that have been arisen in the history of humanity were developed in the 20th century!**

---

[1] Nothing is more inventive than nature / Marcus Tullius Cicero (106-43 BC), Roman rhetorician, philosopher, statesman

[*] my favourite metaphor from book by Vikentiev I.L. and Kaikov I.K. "The stair of ideas" (in Russian), 1992

It is interesting to note that, as a biological object, the human brain has not changed in the last decades, not in many thousands of years (!). The organization and apparently the working principles of the brain are the same as they were, say, 50,000 years ago.

We can assume that the human brain is supplied with a huge "functional over-capacity" like many biological objects in nature. We can also recognize that nature uses this principle generously to maintain life on the planet, either through the distribution of seeds or through the maintenance of a bio-population of the necessary size. But, the purely biological over-capacity of the brain does not lead to **quality thinking.** This probably explains why the number of really valuable inventions does not exceed 1% of the total number of patents!

Quality thinking can change in many ways and depends on the quality of learning and the subjects learned. Modern technology and the subjects learned by individuals are not without essential faults. Along with the influence of the respective social milieu, this explains why humanity is still developing today according to "biological", stochastic laws. However, this is an unacceptable waste of potential today. It increases the probability that intellectual mediocrity will be reproduced and certainly does not support genius.

We can also see that the wealth of information, the standards, and the meaning of the problems to be solved have changed significantly. Is the human brain still capable of dealing with the continuously growing body of knowledge? Is humanity capable of dependably avoiding or successfully stopping possible catastrophes, some of which are hidden or have developed very slowly? Can humanity shape its future towards harmony and progress? Can humanity invent (or rediscover) the actual criteria for harmony and progress? Doesn't it seem that the only way that humanity can move from it current phase as ***homo sapiens technologicus*** to a phase as ***homo sapiens progressus*** (Latin: *rational, evolving, developing human*) is to create its own ideals for progress and harmony?

But, how do people find ideas for inventions? How do people find creative solutions for non-technical problems? The English philosopher Karl Popper[2] suggested that the correct question would be:

**Where do good ideas come from?!**

In the 20th century, someone was ready to tell the entire civilized world that it cannot think. This means that people waste their intellectual potential because of poorly organized thinking. Not only do people not learn to think, they also don't suspect that they think ineffectively!

Someone once said the following about his idea: Today, just like thousands of years ago, the method of *try and error* is the basis of thinking. This method is an unstructured guess for some kind of solution. Very few of these ideas are successful, and most of these are abandoned later. This person also said: *Wouldn't it be more logical to learn from success?!* It would be even better to condense the experience gathered from the best solutions into concrete rules and to develop a methodology with complete models or even as a practical theory.

---

[2] Karl Raimund Popper (1902-1994) - English philosopher

This person's name was **Genrikh Saulovich Altshuller (1926-1998).** In the middle of the 20th century, he developed the "Teorija Reschenija Izobretatel'skich Zadac" that he then called TRIZ (Russian acronym). In English this is a "Theory of Inventive Problem Solving". This is how he outlined new possibilities to learn inventive creativity and its practical application.

TRIZ has established itself more and more since the end of the 20th century. However, a complete textbook on the essential principles of classical TRIZ that everyone can understand has never been written until now. The book you are now reading is just such a textbook.

I hope that TRIZ will help you find the path to new possibilities and success!

# 2 Reinventing – the Key Concept for the Study of TRIZ

Among other things, this express study and self-taught study of TRIZ uses the following methodological procedure: Before you learn all of the necessary concepts and models, the practical functions of the theory will be demonstrated using simple examples as if you were already familiar with the essential principles of TRIZ.

These examples have been selected and are presented in such a way that they make a movement in thinking clear from the simple to the complex, from the external to the internal, from the concrete to the abstract, and from model to theory. In other words, this express study undertakes a kind of experiment with the objects that are essential factors in the theory. Students of TRIZ can then derive the key concepts of the theory from the experiments on their own.

The objects of classical TRIZ are inventions, technical systems, and their components. The essentials of the initial learning experiments are as follows:

1) Presentation of the key problem that was solved with a concrete invention;
2) Definition of the main procedure that was used to solve the problem with this invention.

The following methodological procedures will then be used later:

1) Generalization and classification of the models of the key problems and of the main procedures used to solve problems with inventing;
2) Presentation of laws for the creation of problems, prognosis, and the controlled and systematic solution of problems.

**The process of inventing is the movement of thinking from "what already exists to what is coming*". It is the construction of an intellectual bridge between what is and what is supposed to exist.**

Every "bridge" is based on a certain theory. Clearly the "reliability" of a bridge also depends heavily on the theory that provides the basis on which it is built. Classical brainstorming is an example: very few rules, essentially unlimited space to search, lots of enthusiasm and noise. Another example is classical TRIZ: systematic investigation of a task, controlled application of adequate procedures for a

---

* I am interpreting a well-know expression and the title of a book by a Nobel Prize laureate, the Belgian bio-physicist Ilya Prigogine (1917-2003)

solution, and directed movement into the useful areas of especially successful solutions.

The basis of the teaching experiments in this study of TRIZ is a methodological procedure that I call "reinventing".

**Reinventing** – is a demonstration of the process of inventing. It works as if the users already knew the principles and procedures for a solution to the problems that their inventions then address. Reinventing then functions later as a means to strengthen skills for investigating and solving problems after the essential principles of the theory have been mastered. Finally, quick reinventing can be extremely helpful when working with the analogies that are also offered for problem solving in our software (see section 21.3).

This methodological procedure stimulates associative thinking and ensures emotional acceptance and a positive perception of the theory. The student's intuition can then connect extant knowledge, skills, and experience with the key concepts of the theory on its own.

***TRIZ is a qualitative theory, not a mathematical or quantitative one.*** The theory's formal ideas and concepts are like categories, patterns, and metaphors. The procedural methods to solve tasks - methods that consist of several steps - are called algorithms. This is also a metaphor, although it has been shown that this is a completely correct definition in the context of modern constructive mathematics.

When my colleagues reflect on TRIZ as a theory based on the above, they might suggest that it is a conceptual, phenomenological, and finally a psychological theory. In any case, the concepts of the theory reflect its axiomatic and structural principles in a more understandable, non-formal way, even if these concepts are not specifically described in scientific articles or monograms. This mode of description is the point here. The content used for qualitative models (metaphors) is also of interest. As opposed to other procedures, the models of TRIZ are constructive and can be reproduced and taught by its users.

In this textbook, we will avoid the use of formalized constructions, although we have to create and rely on just this kind of construction in our software. It is not our goal to construct formal principles for this theory. Instead, we want to model thinking qualitatively and apply practical models from this theory to real tasks. However, we will certainly not change the terminology of the theory, although we expect you to be just as critical and suspicious of this terminology as for example of words such as *assignment, departure data, solutions, result.* In most practical cases, we also don't need to define exactly which theoretical axioms and formal associations are hidden in the background of these words. Intuitively we understand completely the qualitative essence and content of these words (that is - metaphors and images) with reference to certain concrete tasks.

But let's now examine the fundamental concepts of the theory.

According to its definition, reinventing is the following process (fig. 2.1).

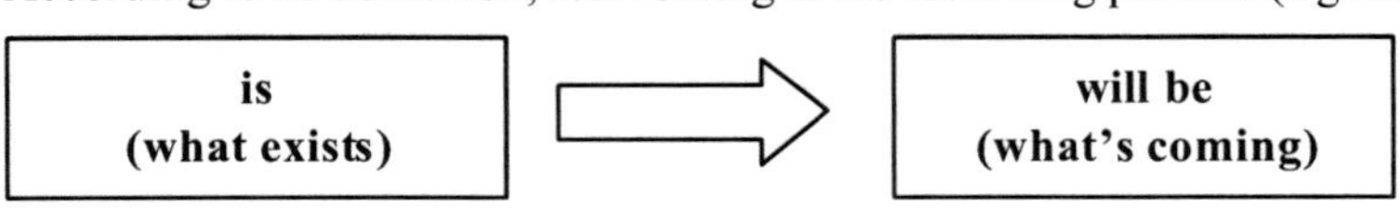


**fig. 2.1.** Movement of thinking from "what is" to "what's coming"

The arrow above shows thought processes - the *"flow of thought"* and the *"generation of ideas"* – in accordance with the theory's suggestions. Of course, reinventing in the sense of brainstorming reflects the process of brainstorming in solving tasks and assignments. TRIZ reinventing reflects the process of TRIZ in solving tasks and assignments.

How reliable do you think the following suggestions are from one of the versions of a "theory of brainstorming", an example of which is shown in figure 2.2?

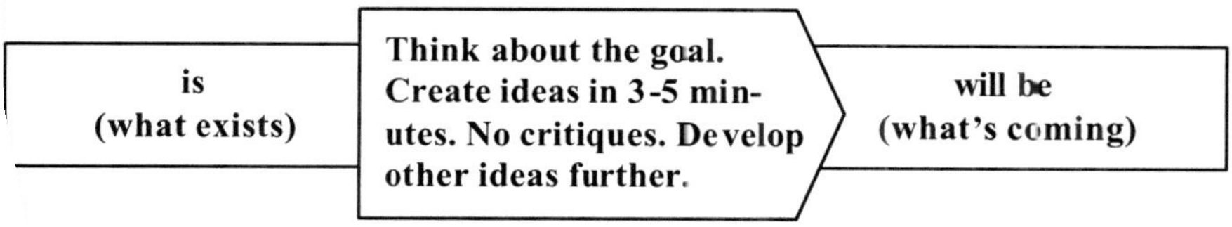


g. **2.2.** Scheme of reinventing based on brainstorming

n't you also think that it almost seems in this scheme that the entire body of ory from military schools can be reduced to Caesar's[3] somewhat laconic thod:

**VENI, VIDI, VICI**
**I came, I saw, and I conquered.**

Do you believe that this "method" teaches you to solve problems that require creativity?

What do you think about when you continue to read and see what the "stream of thought" of TRIZ is about (figure 2.3)?

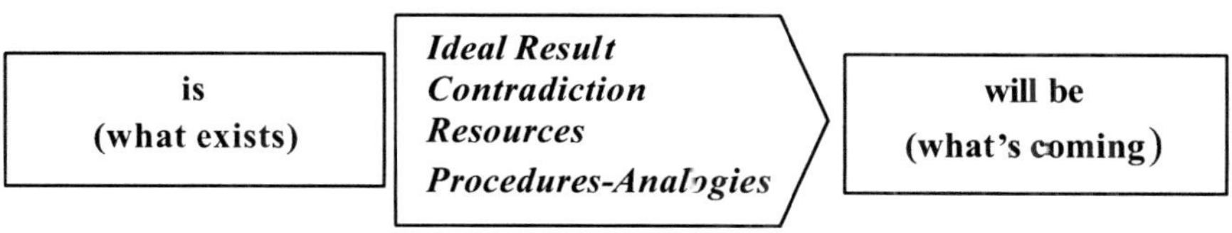


**fig. 2.3.** An example of reinventing based on TRIZ

Don't you associatively combine these concepts into a chain like the following one:

***Using available or newly transformed resources, procedures, and analogies, you remove the contradictions that prevent the achievement of the ideal result.***

I certainly think that this chain looks like a more secure bridge for the movement "from what is – to what's coming"! Usually I demonstrate the principle of reinventing by using a simple example, the "tip of a feather". This is an example of the development of the *working organ* of writing instruments that work with liquids.

[3] Gaius Julius Caesar (102 or 100 - 44 BC) - Roman statesman, military leader and author

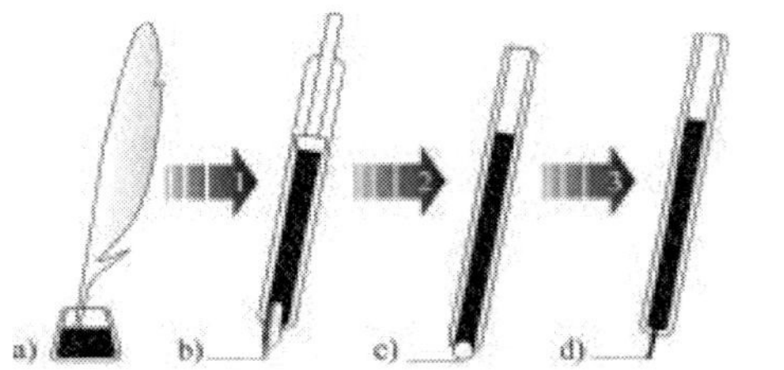


**fig. 2.4.** Evolution of ink writing tools: a) goose feather with ink; b) fountain pen; c) ball point pen; d) felt-tip pen

Of course, a goose feather with ink (figure 2.4a) was the most widely used means to record and transmit knowledge for ca. 2.5-3 thousand years (!) until the end of the 18th century, when the servant of the mayor of Aachen Janson devised a metal tip for the goose feather of his boss.

Then these tips called pens underwent a long construction-technical evolution.

However, the essence of writing with a pen did not change: the tip had to be dipped into ink and it could then write on paper until the ink on the pen ran out or dried out. The development of writing instruments that led to the first fountain pen (figure 2.4b) did not begin until the beginning of the 20th century (1). 50 year passed until the ball point pen spread rapidly (figure 2.4c). Then the mass use of felt-tip pens (figure 2.4d) started 25 years later. This is two times more quickly - and truly a rapid acceleration.

Let's now use TRIZ reinventing to reconstruct the evolution of writing instruments with liquid.

**Example 1. 1st transition: 3000 years from goose feather - to fountain pen.** Goose feathers - even when they are equipped with a metal tip - have a major problem in that they don't transmit ink evenly and smoothly onto paper. Either they dry out directly at the tip or they cause spots and puddles. The ink at the tip ran out quickly and the feather had to be accurately dipped into ink and carefully transferred to the paper in such a way that there were no drops.

*The useful primary function* of a pen as a work organ of the entire writing device is to leave an ink track on paper. Let's call the pen an *instrument* (or even an *actor* or *inductor*, meaning the thing that initiates action). Then the track is the *product* of the pen (or even a *reactor* or *receptor*, meaning the thing that receives or takes in the action, or is produced by the inductor). The ideal track is smooth and has the necessary width. But, what happens in the pen? When there is too little ink on the pen, the track quickly becomes too thin and the pen has to be dipped in ink often. When there is too much ink on the pen, the track can get too wide or spots can occur. This is a clear contradiction between too "little" and too "much".

Let's formulate the *ideal functional model:* there should be so much ink on the tip of the feather that it is possible to create a track of any length and there should also be no ink on the tip so that it cannot dry out or cause drops that then lead to spots.

The requirements presented in this kind of formulation are incompatible! But, this is reality!

There has to be as much ink available as possible during the creation of the track. We call this time when the feather completes its primary operation the *operational time*. At all other times until then, we don't need any ink on the tip of the pen! Doesn't it seem to you that the contradiction has disappeared somewhere?! Somehow we have *solved the contradiction in time.*

It is now time to formulate the clearest version of the ideal functional model: ink moves *by itself* to the tip of the feather when the feather is supposed to create a track. There is no room at the tip of the pen to store a large amount of ink or for a mechanism to regulate the flow of ink. In other words, there are too few *spatial resources.*

Is there an empty space near the tip of the pen? Certainly there is, for example in the hollow space in the goose feather or in a special container that can be attached to the writing instrument. Then this container can be filled with ink and connected to the tip of the feather with a tube equipped "with a small valve".

We can also say that we have *solved the contradiction in space*: it is possible hat there is no ink at the tip, but there is a lot of ink nearby! This idea for a solu-ion can also be represented as a *solution to a structural contradiction*: there is a t of ink in the *entire* fountain pen and in the entire technical system, even though ere is no ink in a small *part* of the fountain pen other than during the operational ne!

But, how should we approach the requirement that the ink may move *by itself* the tip of the pen only when a track is to be created?

Let's formulate a concrete version of the ideal functional model: the pen regu-lates the amount of ink that moves to the tip *by itself*! This means we need a fountain pen with a locking device.

This is how it happened in reality: the tip of the pen was formed in such a way that it consists of two parts. There is a fine canal along the pen to the point where it is connected to one or more thin tubes coupled to a container that stores ink (figure 2.5).

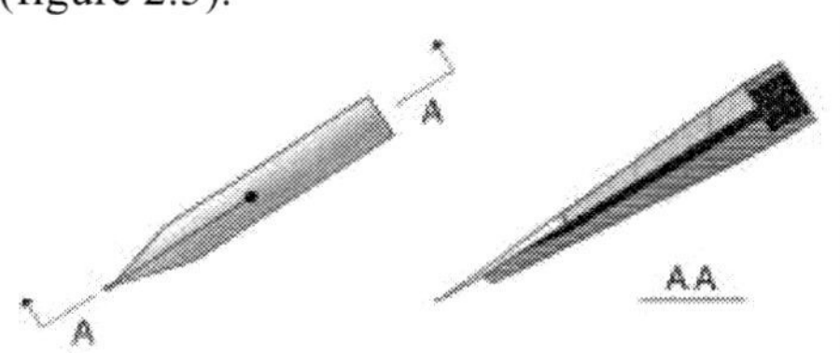


**fig. 2.5.** Essential construction of a pen

When the fountain pen is not in use, the canal is closed to prevent the movement of ink because both halves of the tip are very close to each other. When the pen is pressed onto paper, the parts of the tip spread and ink flows into the canal that ensues. That's it!

In short, we found an *ideal solution, an ideal final result* in the form of a tip with a locking mechanism. The energy needed for this work comes from the hand that presses on the fountain pen. When we start to write, pressure is transmitted to the tip - the locking mechanism opens. When there is no pressure, it closes!

Here we also see a *solution to a material contradiction*: *resources in construction and in the internal energy of the materials* of the pen (movable properties) and the *energy of an external source* (the resources of the hand) were used to ensure that the canal at the tip has two states (closed and open).

At first this explanation seems very long and not really clear. You are absolutely correct. There is also something else that is problematic. First, several new concepts have been introduced simultaneously. Second, there are many technical solutions to the problem of a fountain pen that can all be described with different versions of reinventing that differ in the depth of their analysis. But, you will soon be able to automatically construct similar explanations on your own for real assignments, not just for teaching examples.

**Example 2. 2nd transition: the ball point pen arrives 50 years after the fountain pen.** It is easy to perceive that the slightest inconsistency in production or simply with time the ink can flow spontaneously and therefore can cause spots. The ink can flow by itself when the atmospheric pressure changes, especially when there's not much ink left. Air is not completely pressed out of the reservoir when the pen is filled with ink and there is therefore always a bit of air and a bit of pressure left. When the external pressure is lower than this remaining air pressure, pressure pushes the ink out of the fountain pen. This happened often in planes. The clothes and documents of the passengers suffered.

Let's remember again the last ideal functional model that we just formulated for a fountain pen: ink moves *by itself* to the end of the pen only when it is supposed to produce a track.

We can now analyse the resources. Ink is a liquid like water that can therefor easily flow from the container to the pen. If the ink were thicker, it would no flow. But, this is a new contradiction: the ink *should be thicker* so that it doesn't flow too readily, but it should also *not be too thick* to flow easily through the work organ.

We will investigate this considerable contradiction in a *first strategic direction*: the use of "thickly flowing ink". For 50 years, there seemed to be no way to solve this problem with normal ink.

The use of "thickly flowing ink" leads specifically to the idea of the installation of some kind of valves for the movement of ink. But, we could then no longer maintain that the ink moves to the end of the work organ *by itself*.

Here it would be logical to ask about a change in the work organ. We would need an energy source that enables us to transfer "thickly flowing ink" or paste onto paper. The use of a valve would then clearly mean an interrupted operation and a partial transfer of paste. But, we need an uninterrupted and smooth transfer here.

We would need a few "tiny people" who could take the paste from the reservoir and transfer it smoothly in small portions onto the paper. These "tiny people" could then take past from the reservoir with their "shovels", pass these on to each other towards the paper, and then pass their empty shovels in this kind of chain back to the reservoir, for example. This would cause a circular movement of full shovels from the reservoir to the paper and empty shovels from the paper to the reservoir. This is similar to the functional mode of typographical machines that use a roller to bring thickly flowing ink from one side of the roller to paper. Could we not build a writing instrument that functions like a miniature pressure machine? This is a very constructive idea!

We don't know whether the inventors of the ball point pen, the Hungarian brothers Biro - the journalist Ladislas and the chemist Georg, thought this in 1938. Still they used this kind of printing ink as their first "thickly flowing ink". But, they used a ball instead of a small roller (like a miniaturized printing roller).

# Before It's Too Late

Vicky de Cervera

Pen Press

First published in Great Britain by Pen Press

All paper used in the printing of this book has been made from wood grown in managed, sustainable forests.

ISBN: 978-1-78003-211-5

Printed and bound in the UK
Pen Press is an imprint of
Indepenpress Publishing Limited
25 Eastern Place
Brighton
BN2 1GJ

A catalogue record of this book is available from the British Library

Cover design by Jaqueline Abromeit

*This book is dedicated to my brother John*

*(Sub-Lieutenant John Gerald St.Leger Weldon)*

Giving all my thanks to lovely friends, who have helped me through this last year, of sweat and tears. Having had the stroke, while building my last house, in Tanzania. I had to write the whole book with my left hand. Not very funny.

All my praise and congratulations to Clement Wilson, Miles's flat mate in Edinburgh. His patience with me at the beginning was remarkable. Twice he has been here to the house, and slaved away correcting my texts. Also all my deepest thanks to my friend Sarah Henderson, Lizzie Titley, my adorable neighbour, Clare Redfern who filled in for the others when they were busy, and last but not least, Eliza Deacon, who scanned all my photos with infinite patience. Repeating them sometimes four to five times.

# *1. Tanzania*

6th July 2006, a sunny Sunday in Hortansia, the pretty little cottage I was renting on a flower farm. The dogs woke me up as I left the cottage back door open for them; I leapt out of bed and let them into my room, thinking, *bliss it's Sunday, I can lie in, I certainly need the rest.*

Threw myself back onto my bed, and suddenly my right leg went numb, my right arm landed up on my left side, and I felt very odd. There is never a good time or place to suffer a stroke but as a 68-year-old widow, in the middle of building a dream home in Africa, it is definitely far from ideal.

I lay still, to think to myself, and tried to remain calm. Eventually I rang Martina, a nearby friend who owned the Rivertrees Lodge, explained what had happened and described the symptoms.

'Vicky, stay still, I will be over in a minute, but don't move.'

After a while Yussuf, the Indian manager of Hortansia, arrived; the dear little man was too shy to come into my room, but followed my instructions to open the front doors and to unplug the alarm. Moments later Martina came with a qualified nurse, Cathy Stubbs, who I knew vaguely. She asked me to repeat everything I had told Martina, to describe exactly what had happened. She listened intently, and then spoke, confirming my worst suspicions.

'Vicky, you've had a stroke.'

It was not a difficult diagnosis; I was totally paralysed down the right-hand side. I was speaking with a slurred voice, unusual for a Sunday morning, though thank the lords, I did not have a twisted face.

All hell broke loose, people rummaging for my passport and dollars before turning to the telephone, calling an ambulance and notifying the 'Flying Doctors'; I was on my way to Nairobi, the capital of Kenya, and the nearest place in Africa with the medical expertise to deal with the situation.

More friends arrived, Lizzie and Hugo turned up promptly, and she accompanied me in the ambulance; Vegas, my Labrador, wanted to come too, but the paramedics said no. Hugo followed us in his car. Bizarrely, I kept thinking how lucky I was; I had recently moved from France to Africa, and the friends one has here are simply adorable, what a change from the damn frogs!

The Flying Doctors were already on the runway to meet the ambulance at Arusha, the little airport; a charming pilot and a medically trained male nurse who kept offering me oxygen, which I pushed away apparently. Saying goodbye to dear Lizzie, I still did not know exactly what was happening. Looking through the portholes, I saw the sky was all blue and said to myself, 'That's funny, there were some clouds at Usa River, our local village.'

We cleared the police arriving at Nairobi, retrieved my passport and then another ambulance took me to the Aga Khan University Hospital. In the emergency check-in, I was met by the doctor on duty, Dr Nadeem Sheik, attached to the heart specialist, Dr Majid Warshow.

They performed hundreds of tests, and left me for the night. I kept asking them for something to eat, I was starving, having had nothing since the day before, but they just fussed over my medical insurance. Once they had my card and had phoned my medical insurance in Denmark, they relaxed.

Sarah Henderson, another lovely friend and neighbour from Usa River, came to see me the next day. I don't know what I looked like, or behaved like, but she was looking worried, and kept asking me who from my family was coming. I had no intention of letting anybody know a thing. I really had no idea what a stroke was, and if it was serious or not. Four years down the line, I know only too well, the side affects are simply horrendous. I was in the Aga Khan for three weeks, spending my time in physiotherapy, learning to walk with a gammy leg.

To my horror, Dr Warshow had insisted that my next of kin should contact him. I informed him that I have no real next of kin, my parents are dead, and my brother too. What I consider my two children, Miles and Caroline Craig, are actually the children of a cousin. Martina and Lesley de Koch had already come to Nairobi and the doctor told them to contact Miles.

Miles arrived, poor bugger, very upset, and I was shocked as I had not even realized he was aware what was happening. They all thought I could kick the bucket at any minute. Well, it's four years later and I'm still here. I do though get very depressed in the early mornings, wondering how it will happen and when.

Miles stayed a few days, then went back with Martina to see how the house building was surviving in my absence. Adorable of him to have come, but I was mad at Dr Warshow for telling him. One of the reasons for coming to live in Africa was not to bother the kids, as there is nothing more ghastly than having to look after elderly relations. Darling Caroline had said, 'Vicky looked after us when we were young and took care of all our problems with Daddy, now it's our turn to look after her.' I don't agree, it's my fate, and I want to leave them alone to get on with their own lives.

I was in hospital for three boring weeks, and miserably cold; Kenya is much cooler than Tanzania. I kept asking for a heater in my room. I was surprised one day when Homer and Sheila Combes, the owners of Hortansia came to see me with a huge bunch of flowers. Very kind of them, as I did not know them well. Most embarrassingly, they came a second time, but by then I had stuck a polite but firm notice on my door, saying 'No visitors between 14hrs and 16hrs', as they woke you up so early and I needed my Spanish siesta.

Finally, when allowed out, Philip Ashby, who was assisting me in building the house, came to pick me up, bless his heart, and brought with him Elizabeth Patterson, who kindly offered to come and help. We stayed the night at the Serena Hotel, and Maggie von Lekow invited Philip to her house. I was shy to be alone with him, as knew I could have problems on the way home; the bladder, being on the right side, was as paralysed as the muscles. A good four-hour drive plus an hour at the border, always a hassle.

Returning to the cottage, my dear little maid, Asha, crying and whispering, 'Mama Vicky, Mama Vicky,' when she saw me struggling to get out of the jeep. It was lovely to be back with the dogs, Napoleon and Vegas, and little Minouche, my Siamese cat, but naturally I was frightened of falling over them.

Now it was August. I was supposed to carry on with physiotherapy; my bad luck, the only one I knew then was Theo, a Dutchman, who was on holiday in Europe. Lesley suggested I should go back to Europe and get professional help; she phoned Dr Warshow and told him so. He replied confidently, 'No, it is better for Vicky to relax with her dogs, rather than go to a strange hospital where she knows no one.'

Looking back I think he was wrong, as you make good progress at the beginning, whilst now, four years later, it is worse and I never seem to improve, despite sessions of physio nearly every day.

Having built and developed properties all over the world, lived in Malta, New York, Paris, Spain and Provence, I had a gloriously wild future in Africa to look forward to. The beautiful house with the thatched roof in the African bush is now complete for me to hobble around in. I walk with a stick for balance, always frightened I will fall over after a few glasses of white wine; I'm not allowed any hard stuff. I have twisted my feet and fallen badly twice. It's so sad, as all my plans to travel Africa are now down the drain.

When I moved here I thought it would be very similar to the eccentric community of El Cuarton, with nutty, funny people, all wandering in and out of each other's houses, planning picnics in the bush, riding their horses and all dining together in the club restaurant.

Sadly this is not the case, my friends and neighbours in Africa are from a different generation than those in Europe. Everyone here is working, there are no playboys, no farting around, all are far too serious and the majority just too broke to properly enjoy themselves. Maybe in another few years, they will relax and start having fun.

Or it is just me?

Perhaps I have got too old and, after everything I have been lucky enough to experience, maybe now I am just too bored to even try to make an effort.

# 2. *Childhood*

The 1st April 1938, as increasing rumblings of discontent spread through Europe, I announced my impending arrival with urgency and energy, kicking my mother during a dinner, one week early.

'GERRY!' Daddy's nickname. 'Help! The baby is coming, fetch the doctor, please hurry.'

In those days home births were a necessary evil rather than the fashion statement they have since become. The doctor arrived and administered an anaesthetic, and when Mummy awoke, she was a mother for the second time.

'Doctor, what time is it?' was her first reaction.

'Ten minutes past midnight, Isabel, don't panic, it's a girl, and she's no April Fool.'

Years later, she suggested the doctor had lied, such was her belief that I am quite mad.

I was born in the Royal Naval Hospital Haslar, as my father was a serving officer and a doctor. Both parents were Anglo-Irish, descendants of the English awarded lands and titles in Ireland by the Crown. Daddy was the nephew of the Viscount Doneraile, Algernon St Leger; the St Legers were an old family, with a proud history who could trace their lineage back to Sir Robert de St Leger, William the Conqueror's knight-in-attendance at the Battle of Hastings in 1066.

The future did not look so bright. Some years later Algernon tried to pass on the title and the family seat, Doneraile Court in County Cork, as well as its attendant problems, to my father and brother. Later still the Dowager Viscountess would encourage me to become the roving ambassadrice for the family and keep up the name, and stay in contact with the French cousins.

Daddy was a young surgeon lieutenant commander and had been posted to Hong Kong where Mummy, I, a new born baby, and my brother, John, a three-year-old, were meant join him, though war was finally declared a few months later. As the official news was broadcast, it was announced that no more women and families were allowed to travel. Our family's possessions had already been sent ahead, so not only were we separated from Daddy for the next four years, but all my parents' precious belongings, furniture and wedding presents were torpedoed in the Indian Ocean.

With Daddy in Hong Kong, we went to Wales to live with our grandparents, where my maternal grandfather, Surgeon Captain James McAlister Holmes, had retired from the navy to a private medical practice in the country town of Llandovery, Breconshire. Shortly after we arrived, as an officer with wartime experience he was called up to rejoin the navy and operate in the highly dangerous surroundings of the underground hospital at Grimsby on the East coast; he had already served in the Battle of Jutland, First World War, where he was awarded the DSO for bravery.

Growing up in wartime, many of my early memories are mixed. I was terrified by the tin hats of the local Home Guard, and as Christmases came and went I refused point blank to let any old bearded man down the chimney, insisting stockings were hung in the corridor. We were issued with Mickey Mouse gas masks, and squabbled with the ghastly little evacuees who we were to house offering refuge from the east end of London and the Blitz; they were dreadfully rough children who broke our toys. I developed double mastoids and poor Grandfather had to come back to operate on me in the local cottage hospital, as there were no surgeons left; I can still taste and smell the chloroform that was poured over cotton wool and stuck to my mouth. I was four.

One day a total stranger with a big black beard suddenly appeared at the front door. I was terrified by him, with no idea who he was.

'Gerry, oh heavens! My God, thank goodness you're safe,' shrieked Mummy at the sight of this man.

I realised this man was my father, and it took me a long time to get used to him. He was suffering badly from tuberculosis, having spent too many hours in the claustrophobic confines of the submarines off the Greek coast, saving our soldiers from the catastrophe in Crete. After only a few days reunited with his family, the poor man was hurried off to Midhurst in Hampshire, a TB sanatorium.

After his cure we were posted back to RNH Haslar in Portsmouth where we had a delightful house in Alverstoke. Although the war was not quite over, conditions were improving, and Johnny and I were growing up fast, getting ourselves into all sorts of scrapes and colourful escapades; running round the garden naked, falling into the fish pond, and sticking kitchen scissors up the fat bottoms of some old farts in deck chairs. John also put the scissors to good use, cutting the whiskers off our black cat. An aunt of ours arrived one day sporting the most enormous hat. We kids stifled our giggles, watching our cat, minus its whiskers, creep along the mantelpiece before pouncing onto the brim of this ridiculous creation. Screams from the horrified aunt, who stormed out vowing never to return, accusing us of planning the attack.

I particularly remember two air-raid shelters, one in the garden and a huge steel one inside the house. When the air raids sounded, signalling Hitler's last pathetic attempt to take England with his doodlebugs, we had to climb inside the shelters. On one occasion my mother displayed incredible cruelty by locking Johnny in the garden air-raid shelter, cross because he had filled my toy pram with stones to make a tank and turned the willow tree into a submarine. My brother was an amazing little boy and I worshipped him. I sat outside crying with him, calling Mummy every rude word we knew.

After three years in Portsmouth, and the end of the war, Daddy was promoted again and posted to RNH Bighi, Malta. John, poor little bugger, was sent to board at prep school, while I accompanied Mummy on a troopship from Southampton to the Mediterranean. We spent a night in London before our departure, and as she had social plans for the evening, she locked me in our hotel room. In an act of defiance, I vomited all over the room incurring furious anger on her return! Sailing to Malta we encountered the worst storm in 30 years in the Bay of Biscay; everyone on board was seasick, and trunks floated around the cabin.

We finally arrived in the Grand Harbour, Valletta, basking in gorgeous sunshine as the battlements and old forts made of sandstone glowed burnished yellow in the light. What a change from grey old England, and the pouring rain. I remember hundreds of brightly painted open boats, called *dhiasas*, rowing out to greet us, as our anchor chains rattled over the bow into the deep blue, glistening sea.

Daddy, minus his beard, very smart in his white uniform, was waiving to us from a small barge, and grinning from ear to ear. He was surrounded by little brown Maltese boys, diving under the hull for pennies, some even surfacing on the port side. The scene is etched on my mind, as if it was yesterday.

The Royal Naval Hospital Bighi, off our port bow, rose majestically above us, built during Napoleon's era, Doric colonnades of sandstone and terraces with covered walkways. Ahead of us loomed Fort St Angelo and the dockyard, and away over to our right, Valletta, the capital, with her cathedral, St John's, the Bastille and army headquarters surrounded by bastions and moats as far as one could see. I just gazed in wonder as a little girl, not knowing then how much this island would affect me in later life.

There followed three years of school and learning to swim; playing with other little girls on the flat roofs of the Maltese buildings, picnics on hidden beaches and visiting Gozo and her tamarisk trees, Catholic fiestas that seemed to last for ever, punctuated with their noisy fireworks.

John came out now and again on holiday, whenever my parents could afford it; one day to their horror they caught me bashing his head in, crashing it onto the stone floor of our apartment. I was hauled off him and given a good beating. John was tiny for his age, and he was teased mercilessly at his school, suffering hell as the bullies and prefects were ghastly to him. Arriving in Malta his ambition was to take his revenge out on me…but I was tough and retaliated. He had spent all his shorter holidays with our grandparents in Wales, and to this day I think this was a huge mistake, as naturally he grew up very jealous of me, comparing my idyllic times in Malta with the misery of his boarding school. My parents weren't to blame, they only had Daddy's pay to live on, and he had no idea about finances, but to send their son to a good school was important in the circle of their Naval friends.

My first three years in Malta came to an end when Daddy was posted to Plymouth. Typical navy, they moved you around from one posting to another. He was due a long leave so my parents decided to make a holiday out of the return journey to England. For the long drive home they bought one of the first cars on the market, a hideous green thing called a Standard Vanguard. They persuaded a good friend of theirs, the army general of the island, to ship her across to Sicily on his converted MFV (Motor Fishing Vessel). With the car strapped to the stern deck, we sailed for Catania amidst rough seas and brewing storms, and a whole bunch of naughty officers for company.

The men proceeded to live it up below decks, whilst Mummy and I took one look at the darkening sea, and wisely laid down on the deck with some blankets huddling together, and laughing as each of the officers surfaced on deck and threw their dinner overboard, including Daddy. MFVs were renowned for their round hulls, and had the most appalling yawl.

We landed next morning at Catania, Sicily, in the most brilliant sunshine, and much to the amusement of the local kids, swung the car onto the quay. We were bombarded with questions and paperwork from the Carabinieri, and when finally they were persuaded we were not some ruffians, smuggling booze, we were allowed to say our goodbyes to our hosts and hungover friends. We took off, jostling and bumping along the cobbled streets out of the town driving east, leaving the mountains including Mount Etna the volcano on our left. My parents had already planned to spend the first night at Taormina, which I discovered then as a young teenager, to be the most beautiful little town nestled on the cliffs. We stayed at the Villa San Pacracio, unforgotten to this day.

After crossing the Strait of Messina, we headed north east and began the long haul up the shoe of Italy, staying with friends at Naples, bypassing Rome and headed for Florence. There were no *autopistas* in those days, so map reading was essential. Sitting on the centre arm between them both, I can remember Daddy saying, 'Heh, Isabel, she is not so thick. That is twice Vics has corrected our map reading.' I felt very proud. He had noticed me at last. They dragged me round the art galleries and museums but my only interest was in the magnificent police horses. I was too young to appreciate art; that came later.

On our way to the border with Switzerland, we stopped and camped beside Lake Como always eating tinned tuna fish or corned beef as everyone was still so poor after the war. We slept out under the stars beside the car, but not for long. At three o'clock the whole lake became alive and moved towards us, as a thousand croaking toads marching in formation descended upon us. Mummy and I were terrified, not knowing what we were seeing and jumped into the car as fast as we could, while Daddy just laughed, a veteran of many more unimaginable sights.

We passed Lugano, ascended the Gothard Pass and finally arrived into France where we headed for the Channel ferry. The ferry staff were on strike. Daddy was bored and, needing some exercise as well as a diversion from the long wait, he suggested a visit to the local fair where we spent the night having fun on the bumper cars.

Arriving back in England, we went straight to Fernden, John's prep school, and took him out for a picnic. It was a joyful reunion and initially very relaxed, but before long we found out that he was very unhappy at school; so much so that the following week he ran away. Knowing my mother as I grew up, she probably boasted to him about all the gorgeous things we had seen in Europe on the drive home, and he must have become very lonely and depressed after our visit. Even Daddy who was a highly intelligent man did not sense it; in the '50s no one had any idea about psychology.

They did not think about people's feelings, unhappiness, depressions, not being suitable for certain jobs or even schools. Relationships between children and their parents were just beginning to develop from the Victorian era; my father was born in 1900, during Victoria's reign and lived through to Elizabeth II; he was brought up with a rod of steel, and it never entered his head to be soft with his children.

Daddy went straight to Plymouth and Mother went to see her parents who were still in Wales. I ended up in Plymouth at a convent day school. They were persuaded to take me on as a boarder, as Daddy could not find the time to house hunt. This was a difficult time for me, with evenings totally on my own, and sleeping up in a tower. The food was awful, so bad I would take it out of my mouth and stick it under the table ledge. This had to stop when one day a fierce old nun came to reprimand me about the terrible smell from the place where I sat. There they found the stale food and I was in trouble once again.

At last my parents found a home for us on the edge of Dartmoor, in the most delightful wooden cottage at Sampford Spiney. The higgledy-piggledy garden had rhododendrons and azaleas and a river at the bottom, and I was able to keep my first pony, Paddy, a lovely stocky dark bay. We bred Muscovy ducks, which flew around the house and made it shake with their wing beats. George the drake was huge, and produced at least three lots of ducklings a year, dear little yellow fluffy creatures which followed their mothers from one stream to the next. It was a total change from the Mediterranean, but lovely in its own way, except for school, which was a horror. John by now had gone to public school, Bradfield, and was doing very well, and seemed happy.

Sadly for him, he was either persuaded by my social-climbing mother, or he was affected deeply by the sinking of the submarine, Affray, in the channel, where we could hear the officers and men gasping for their last breaths, but he became determined to join the navy. It was the last thing he should have done, too small and too sensitive; but off he went to Dartmouth at the age of 16. He had made his mark at Bradfield and become a prefect, but at this age in the navy he was junior of juniors among the cadets, and again teased unmercifully, hung by his jacket on a peg with all the brutes mocking him.

Life in Devon as a teenager, when not at school at the convent, was the typical round of pony club events, hunting, and excursions over Dartmoor, in and out of the bogs; frightening nights lying awake, as the alarms went off, warning that a prisoner had escaped from the famous prison, wondering whether he would turn up at our back door. One horrific storm turned the river into spate; Caio, our adorable big thick cocker spaniel was out walking with Daddy, and as he did his usual flying leap onto the stones he knew so well to cross the river, he slipped on the flooded surface and disappeared. Daddy, who adored his animals, went berserk, shouting and running, he tore down river. Heartbroken, he could not find him. Three days later Caio's body was found five kilometres down stream.

We have always been animal lovers, but the loss of Caio, a Welsh breed of cocker, was horrible, as all losses to our animals were deeply felt; as with all my future animals, dogs and Siamese cats, they had human qualities, though horses I am not so sure about, but I have had some who were unique and definitely had brains and memories.

One day I was coming back from a ride over the moor, and down the drive saw my parents standing, looking ashen faced. What on earth can have happened? They asked me to dismount very carefully, and I felt a panic set in as they drove me back towards the Naval hospital, where Daddy was now the chief pathologist. We, as his kids, were always x-rayed regularly, as he was in touch with sailors who had tropical diseases, and he had had tuberculosis. You can imagine the fright and horror my parents had, when they heard the results of my last x-ray, indicating TB of the spine.

Months in hospital with tests non-stop, I was tested with millions of grammes of TB vaccines, always negative. In desperation they called in a civilian bone specialist, who diagnosed osteochondritis of the spine, or softening, of the fourth/fifth vertebrae. A result of having grown too quickly, with too few nutrients, during the war years. The several months that I subsequently spent in hospital were made tolerable by only one thing; my father raising our new cocker spaniel, Honey, to the window of the ward and having him wave his paw to me through the glass.

My parents wanted to keep me close, as I was in a plaster cast for four months and then a steel and leather brace, so instead of going to the naval school for girls in Surrey, I was sent to Sydenham House, an old Elizabethan manor near Okehampton, close to home and the most beautiful building. The school had been in London and was moved to the country to escape the blitz. The whole place was full of Van Dycks and Gainsboroughs, with oak panelling throughout, four-poster beds and a grand staircase, which as a sixth-former one had to decorate at Christmas. My lifelong passion for antiques, old furniture, decorating and art, stemmed from the influence of this lovely old house.

A major event, and memory of my childhood, was Queen Elizabeth II's coronation in 1953. An estimate of three million people lined the streets of London but I was lucky enough to have a VIP seat with Daddy at Admiralty Arch, as Mummy had kindly given up her seat to look after Jose, my grandmother. I was 15.

It was a captivating time watching the whole procession and photographing, with my first little camera, the carriages and the horses, and all the pictures I could get of Prince Philip, whom I already adored, with my desk at school covered with his photos.

I was fascinated, walking past St James's Palace, to see the Coldstream Guards spring to attention and presenting arms, and Daddy saluting in return, looking gorgeous in full dress uniform. Johnny, now a Midshipman, was standing guard in front of Westminster, with a posse of young sailors, who kept on fainting; they weren't allowed to move, poor buggers, while John as a very young officer was marching up and down in his gaiters, looking very important!

The ceremony of the occasion, coupled with seeing my father and brother proudly wearing the Queen's uniform with such dignity, filled me with enormous pride.

# *3. Daddy's Death*

At home during these teenage years, I began to become aware of my parents' quarrelling, often bitterly. Daddy was a great flirt causing Mummy to be very jealous, as he had the Irish charm for the opposite sex and was very naughty, with the most wicked eyes. All the nursing sisters were at his beck and call! Whatever my father's failings, when he was awarded his CBE, it made it easier for my snobbish mother to stomach.

On the day of his investiture he was accompanied by his mother, Josephine St Leger, who instructed a footman that the ceremony was of secondary importance to her. She wanted to see a portrait that she knew was hanging in the Queen's Gallery!

One of our ancestors, John Hayes St Leger, as a young aristocrat living in the late 1700s, struck up a close friendship with the Prince of Wales, who described him as 'one of ye best fellows who'd ever lived', and chose him to be a groom of the Royal Chamber. To mark the occasion, in 1782 the Prince commissioned Gainsborough to paint two portraits, one of himself, the other of John. When they were completed the Prince presented John with the one of himself whilst retaining the one of his friend, which still hangs in Buckingham Palace today.

Meanwhile, as Daddy was waiting in the queue to be received by the Queen, he got tired and wanted 40 winks so he sat down on a sofa, which gave way and he fell through it to the floor. The following time he went back to Buckingham Palace to be appointed QHP (Queen's Honorary Physician), low and behold, same sofa, same place, same hole!

At this stage of his career my father wanted to retire to Ireland to shoot and fish, but he was promoted to Rear Admiral with the post of Chief Medical Officer in the Mediterranean and head medical officer to NATO at Naples, with his base at RNH Bighi, Malta. Mummy was, of course, thrilled, but he got so worried over his promotion, he developed ulcers in the stomach. Of course, she won the battle, and off they went back to Malta again, for him to take up his new post. I had just finished my A-levels and a business course in Plymouth, so was left with the job of packing up our house and shipping out our latest cocker, Honey, and Siamese cat, Twing Ling. It turned out to be an impossible task. I had to leave the latter with a neighbour, with butter on her paws, to stop her straying. It did not work. She came back to the cottage at least three times, crossing two main roads and a river. Eventually I left her there with the new tenant, Admiral Troubridge. The cocker was given to my mother's parents, who by then had retired properly this time to a cottage nearby. Both my parents missed the pets terribly in Malta, and were very cross with me, not having brought them. They had no idea what the paperwork was like, and I was only 17, damn it.

This time I flew back to the yellow sandstone of Malta and the glorious Mediterranean, but now to an admiral's residence, on the Bighi creek, with our own barge and crew, official car and driver, petty officers running the house, and a glorious garden at the back. Huge ceilings with fans in all the rooms, and balconies giving onto the creek. Later we learned it was full of ghosts, and Mummy, with her Irish imagination, saw them often!

It was a glorious time, and a welcome change from the post-war misery of England. We took the barge round the island every weekend, with mad picnics at Peter's Pool, Comino and the Blue Lagoon; at non-stop parties my parents were introduced to all the aristocratic Maltese, and the NATO VIPs. I had my choice of polo ponies at the Marsa, as well as the gorgeous young ADCs, who flirted like mad but were always very correct. I developed a passion on one that was more sophisticated than the rest, and owned a Riley Pathfinder. It was nothing serious as it turned out, just a girl's first crush. They leave one very weak and stupid, never having been taught how to deal with the emotions. I had only learnt the facts of life from Daddy a year earlier, and was totally unsophisticated. No idea that oestrogen was swarming around one's blood cells in millions, and apparently I had far more than normal.

To stop me from charging round the island in the Riley Pathfinder with a dashing lieutenant, my father instructed me to find a job and I ended up working in St Luke's, the civilian hospital, where a cheerful pathologist used to ask me to turn my back and take notes from behind a screen, if I couldn't stand the site of stillborn babies in test tubes.

After finishing a working day I rode back to Bighi, the other side of Grand Harbour, on my Vespa. I always left it with the friendly police at the gate, but on one particular day no one was smiling, all very dour and none would look me in the eye.

'Heh, fellows, what's going on? You all look so miserable.'

No reply. *Bizarre*, I thought, wandering my way down through our garden and in through the French windows; there was Mummy looking very sour, talking to one of the senior doctors, so I left them alone and went to my bedroom.

The Surgeon Captain followed me and said straight out, 'Vicky, I am sorry to tell you this, but your father died this morning.'

I looked at him as if he was mad.

'What on earth do you mean; we had breakfast together a few hours ago?'

I rushed back to my mother, crying and repeating non-stop, 'Say it's not true—'

She looked straight through me, with her usual cold stare, and told me to go and have a quick lunch and change, and at that moment Daddy's steward walked down the corridor carrying his uniform. I howled, realizing it was the one he was wearing that morning. A horrible sensation, I felt quite sick.

We were accompanied up to the actual hospital, an old fort under the Knights of Malta, where we were ushered into a room in the officer's wing. There Daddy was laid out, very grey and very dead. I was crying my heart out, never had I seen a dead person before. My mother snapped at one of the doctors.

'Take her out, there is nothing she can do.'

Hard as nails, no affection towards me at all. I was only 18 and realized all the sad things about Daddy, and that we never really clicked. I was going to miss him badly, but at that time it was pure shock.

The house was a whirlwind as everyone came to call, and the garden filled with Maltese workers, all of whom adored him. We discovered it had been a massive heart attack, stretching and yawning, he fell backwards off his office chair to the floor. He was about to be promoted to Vice Admiral and Medical Director general of the navy, but just because he died three days short of his time as a rear admiral, his widow was not allowed a full Admiral's pension. Staggering.

Johnny arrived that night, poor little bugger, looking small, tired and white. He looked at us both seriously.

'I will take care of you now.'

My mother looked at him with total disdain.

'You little twit, you couldn't look after us for all the tea in China,' she sneered.

*

Our charming neighbour, the Flag Officer of Malta, Admiral Sir Charles Madden, offered my mother to arrange the whole funeral. Daddy was buried in the military cemetery after a service in the hospital church, which was packed not only with all the island's VIPs, the Governor General, Sir Robert Laycock, the Commander-in-Chief, Sir Charles Lambe, and Maltese ministers, but also all the local workmen and gardeners, crowded into the church courtyard in their hundreds. It was so moving to see how much these people loved him, a charmer who charmed every last man, as well as the nursing sisters!

John was marching in the cortège, carrying Daddy's medals behind the coffin; poor little fellow he looked so tired and distraught, so small and young following the pall bearers, who were all very senior officers. The music of the buglers, the last post and the rolling of the gun carriage and stamping feet of the sailors who pulled it was heart wrenching. I still cannot go to a military funeral in full pageantry without crying my head off.

John stayed a week in Malta, and as country lovers, we spent our time walking in the wildest part of the island near Dingli Cliffs, the highest point of Malta, taking in the view towards the uninhabited Filfa island, as we tried to relax and get over the shock.

Everything had happened so quickly. It was winter; cold, windy, grey and very depressing. Mummy was flooded with mail and documents to sign, but now, of course, without a secretary. Daddy had died with the bills for our Christmas presents in his pocket and his mess bill was enormous. The other officers clubbed together and paid it off. The poor fellow was never good at business, being very Irish he felt anything to do with money was vulgar.

The navy allowed us to stay on at the admiral's residence for three months. In the meantime, Sir Charles Lambe invited Mummy to go on a cruise on HMS Surprise, his official destroyer, to visit the Pope in Rome. She said thank you, but that she couldn't leave me alone. John by now had gone back to Greenwich, where he was doing his sub-lieutenant's course. Friends of Mother's arranged for me to join the naval skiing trip to Austria, in Obergurgl, a little village in the Ötztal Alps; a welcome break, heaven and great fun. I fell in love with the Alps and made long-lasting friendships with many Austrians. They say the Austrians are to the Germans, as the Irish are to the British; naughty, funny and wild. Friendly, but totally unreliable.

After skiing I went back briefly to Malta, simply to pack up before leaving for England on a troopship, together with the whole regiment of the Gordon Highlanders. As we sailed from the Grand Harbour, Sir Charles Lambe came out of his office on the Barracca Cliffs and saluted us. Very touching.

# *4. Return to the UK*

The ship was awful, tiny cabins and still filthy from the war. Imagine today sending back an admiral's widow and child under such conditions? I really think Mummy was so horrified at the way she was treated, she became quite rebellious. One night we passed the Straits of Gibraltar and I saw the rock from our porthole, looming out of the darkness like a huge monster, it rose straight out of the sea on the north eastern side, imposing but I had no sense of its future significance.

We docked ten days later in dirty, cold, wet Liverpool where we were met by an aunt, strangely in full battle dress. She was the wife of Mummy's brother John, but thank goodness we did not hang around, instead heading straight to Bath to the home of George and Kathleen Weldon, and their daughter Sheila.

We were staying for Sheila's wedding. She had met her fiancé, Hugh Balfour, in Malta while staying with us. He was a future captain of the Royal Yacht Britannia, but back then was a young lieutenant. I was one of the bridesmaids in what was a great wedding, marred only by Mummy's disappearance in the middle, after she became bored and slipped off for a drink in the local pub, with a good looking fellow from the party. George was furious.

Mother declined a grace and favour house at Windsor offered by the Queen saying, 'What do you want me to do with all these old age pensioners?' as she was then only 46. She went back to stay in Devon, near her parents, where we lived before, and from where I was sent up to London to get a job; fine for a young girl if you have a large family there, or been brought up in the city amongst friends. Neither was my case and I hated it. I found a job through my medical connections at the Royal Society of Medicine helping young doctors who were invited to England from behind the communist constraints of the Iron Curtain.

I was responsible for sorting out their papers, arranging accommodation for them, setting up their lectures, and eventually finding them jobs in hospitals.

I shared a flat with three other girls in Kensington. It was hideous but I was at least able to invite John to spend the odd leave he had, sleeping on a camp bed in the drawing room. On one of these occasions we were both shocked to the core, receiving a telegram from Mummy, out of the blue, informing us she was in Cornwall on her honeymoon! She had married a retired wing commander, Richard Smythe, who we knew as Winco, our neighbour in Devon who had looked after Twing Ling. John took it very badly, as did I at the time, but I soon realized how lonely she was and how very broke living on a captain's pension. I went to see them out of curiosity. He was obviously besotted with my mother; after years of Daddy being unfaithful, he gave her security, which she needed.

They first lived at Foxhams, near Horrobridge, a lovely old farm, where Winco had a good dairy herd. Later he bought an Elizabethan manor with a lovely garden, Sortridge, for a song. It had a separate wing that was rented by the local Member for Parliament, a young Michael Heseltine, whom we all came to know quite well.

I stuck London out for a year, but was miserable, earning peanuts whilst yearning for adventure. I became friendly with a girl who had been to Vaduz in Leichtenstein for a summer job the previous year, and she talked me into going there with her in her old MG. I readily agreed. It sounded adventurous so I jumped at the chance, leaving London with the thrilling expectation of going skiing again on the Arlberg Pass en route. We broke the back axle in the middle of France, slept in the Zurich train station, and nearly killed ourselves as we were so tired, falling down non-stop the next day.

We were working for a white Russian, Baron Edouard Alexandrowitsch von Falz-Fein, who had opened up tourist shops in Leichtenstein, peddling local wares to the first waves of post-war organized holiday makers.

I settled into the life in Europe; what a difference, very romantic evenings in the mountains and skiing at the weekends. Our boss was a very handsome fellow with a colourful past. He was a member of Liechtenstein's bobsled team competing in the 1936 Winter Olympics and initiated their Olympic movement. Aside from his sporting endeavours he was an accomplished womaniser and I realized he was trying his best to flirt with me. I looked twice and got goosebumps all over. The beginning of the end.

I was just the new, young, innocent idiot, Edouard was in his 40s, but I was totally infatuated for this charismatic Russian. So charming, so desperately good looking and sexy, and he knew it, as well as every trick in the book to seduce one; jumping in the window at night, and the famous first time up in the mountains of Vaduz, in the old *rathaus* of the Treis Sweisters, playing romantic gypsy music where we both knew and felt every fibre in our bodies, stretching their cords to breaking point. I lost my virginity and my soul in one night; total childish love, unforgiving and unassuming. I was hooked.

The summer madness was short lived. I was one of six girls working for Edouard, and in the end I discovered he was sleeping with another girl as well, keeping himself busy on alternate nights!

Heartbroken, I called my cousin David from Ireland, to get me out of trouble, and with two other friends, set off for the South of France: St Tropez, Cannes, Antibes, Villefranche and Monte Carlo, falling in love with the country, the coast and the culture. The French then did not like the English, so both being Irish we changed our passports in Nice to our original Irish ones. The Gaulles loved the Irish!

In Monte Carlo we met up with old friends of my family, the Spicers, a South African paper millionaire and his wife, whom my parents had become friendly with when they wintered their boat in Bighi Creek.

Mrs Spicer was a very jazzy lady, tremendously chic, and at the centre of the social life. They introduced me to Onassis, the Niarchos, and the Livanos and many other of their mad Greek friends. Terribly elegant parties were mixed with childish pranks, spending evenings in the casino and hotels, but also peeing in the Rolls Royce of that fat nouveau riche clown, John Mills, a 21-stone former Polish army officer done good, who owned Les Ambassadeurs nightclub in London.

By day we would explore the length of the Cote d'Azur, and my interest in boats took me to the port of Menton, where the Riviera meets the Italian border, and where I first saw M.Y. Sable. She was an old Air Sea Rescue boat, with very fast engines used to pick airmen from the drink after bailing out during the battle of Britain.

Her current English owner was in deep debt and had escaped the UK, using Sable to cross the channel and heading south via the French canals. Now she was under lock and key, impounded and up for sale by the order of an English judge.

Looking beyond the tired paint and cracked varnish, I could see her strong lines and spacious decks. Most importantly, her shocking state of disrepair meant she was going for a song.

Seeing my enthusiasm, the Spicers jokingly said, 'Come on, Vicky, put in a bid, buy the old lady, do her up and charter her in Cannes!'

It may have been mad but the idea sunk in. I returned to England, determined to make enough money as fast as possible to buy Sable.

Back in London I landed up working three jobs, one of which was in a very chichi restaurant in Knightsbridge, poorly paid by the hour but making a fortune in tips. The well-heeled, but newly wealthy clientele could not believe that a young Anglo-Irish aristocrat was working as a waitress.

I stored away some good savings before the owners sent me down to a new restaurant in Kingston-on-Thames. There I met an elderly English businessman and two young Portuguese boys, who were D'Aurey Pinheiros, an old, upper-class family from Estoril. During the course of conversation it quickly became clear that the businessman was seeking a little glamour and excitement in his old age, and was impressed by the aristocratic Portuguese and the idea of an admiral's daughter working in a restaurant, who was focused on making quick cash to buy an old motor yacht on the Cote d'Azur.

He immediately said he would employ all of us, as he was setting up a tourist business in Portugal. He would finance my purchase of M.Y. Sable; I was to fit her out as a floating office, and bring her around from the South of France to Estoril where he needed an offshore office for his water skiing and speed boat project, which the two young Pinheiros would set up and run.

Of course he was crackers. He had no idea how to start the business nor of the bureaucratic horror of setting this kind of thing up in 1960s. We were young, unsophisticated and naïve. We wanted to believe this old fellow, and to profit like mad with no shame whilst having as much fun as possible.

With all expenses paid, I flew back to the Spicer's announcing that I had sufficient funds, and was off to make an offer for M.Y. Sable!

They were delighted and enthusiastic and came with me back to Menton where Sable was still waiting for a taker. We made the offer, put her on the slip and had a survey done; there was no rot, her hull was in good shape but the old Perkins engines were tired. She was also hideous inside but I knew I could fix that in a moment. Three days later she was mine.

I am not sure if I felt a proud owner, or worried stiff, or too young to know the difference, but it felt magnificent to be a boat owner on the Riviera. Anything was better than working in London in a boring old office from nine to five.

I sailed Sable to Cannes, and rang David and Anna, our friend in Château d'Oeux and said, 'Come quickly, I have bought the boat!' Then I chatted up the local marine agency, Glemot, who are still there after 40 years. They were speechless and could not believe the Irish girl who just showed up with an old ASR for an overhaul, requesting new engines in readiness for a trip to Estoril!

'Not just a pretty face,' they remarked.

# 5. *M.Y. Sable*

After three months of hectic work, she was almost ready, and new engines installed, all electrical wiring renewed, Sable was painted and varnished inside and out.

In the interim I met the owners of the new Club Castellaras, an exclusive village a few miles from Cannes with houses grouped around a beautiful hilltop castle that formed the members' club. Wining and dining there, I met many new friends, who again were fascinated with the idea of the yacht-owning admiral's daughter.

I struck a deal that the club would charter Sable on a long-term basis for the benefit of the members' entertainment. It was a popular service, accommodating intrigues, as half the married couples used the boat as a hideaway from their spouses.

The organizers of the Cannes Film Festival also chartered her to take out VIPs. The parties during the festival in those days were unbelievable; stars and directors, Louis Jordan, Alain Delon, Robert Hossein, and American playboys all lying around Eden Roc, thousands of journalists; a milling mass of humanity all trying to be more important than their neighbours.

Amidst the bizarre, on one charter I landed up with the ambassador to the USSR and his clipped and stuttered English.

'How are you an English young lady with a yacht, surely you are a capitalist?'

'Yes,' I replied. 'Do you own a bicycle or a car in Moscow?'

'Both,' he answered.

'Then surely you are just as much a capitalist as I am, albeit at a somewhat lower stage of development?'

Judging from his reaction to the boat, the Russian may have taken exception if he had seen my first car, which I bought that summer in Cannes: an Aston Martin in cream and pale blue.

It was the former racing car of an Oriental royal, who, as a miserable shit, had given it as a divorce present to his Irish-Brazilian wife. The poor thing couldn't drive, and did not have the cash to fill up the tank, as it sucked up petrol just looking at a pump. I took it off her and offered to drive to the only dealer in Europe, in Bern. She was thrilled, but when I arrived they took one look at the chassis and said it was a total mess, one whole welded mass of broken metal from so many accidents, and they would not touch the car. When I rang to deliver the verdict the poor woman broke down, so I offered to keep the Aston, and pay all the expenses from then on. She was delighted to get rid of the damn thing.

As the summer drew to a close we concentrated in the early autumn on getting Sable to Portugal, where our sponsor was waiting, running into bureaucratic difficulties, and trouble with the Portuguese lads, who were not being very serious. The Angolan War of Independence with Portugal was starting in full force, and we had to fly over to arrange the whole business, as they were being called up into the army. The water in Estoril was freezing, and no one saw the hope of a water skiing tourist business taking off at that time. With the boys off to Angola our old man told us to leave Sable in Cannes for the winter, and we would talk again in the spring. I was thrilled; with many fun friends on the Cote d'Azur now, the idea of living in Estoril with very dour Portuguese, who looked at a woman in those days from head to toe as a total foreigner, did not appeal to me at all.

Also I was wary of navigating her via the coast of Spain through the Straits of Gibraltar, and around Cadiz to Lisbon and the Atlantic coast. She had lived through a war, and was not in her first youth, despite her overhaul.

I had found a skipper for the boat, an ex-Royal Air Force officer, who seemed to good to be true and turned out exactly so; the first and last time I was taken in totally by a crook. He said if I put her on the slip, he would pay the costs and go half and half over the future charter gains or the profits in Portugal, when and if we went there. With Sable on the slipway, he ordered new parts and services that we did not need, and then left, leaving me with a whopping great bill. We found out much later he was being looked for by Interpol. Never again would I take anyone on trust value alone.

Wintering in Cannes, one morning, who turns up out of the blue, but my old love the Ruskie, dear Eddie, looking as naughty as usual in the most divine drop-head Ferrari.

'Get away from me, you bastard, let me forget about you!' I laughed.

'Ha ha, Vics, what are you up to? I heard through the bush telegraph you had a yacht in Cannes!'

This time I was tough, and told him, he was never to look me up again, or I would shoot him! Agony, but I stuck to my guns, and he drove off looking maybe sad, maybe not, who knows. I met him again years later in St Moritz. We were racing our cars on the frozen lake, and he was giving the prizes away. As he gave me mine, he whispered in my ear, 'You're one of the best lovers I've known, gosh you were great,' or some such silly remark. If looks could kill, he would have dropped through the ice there and then.

Forty years after I first met him the Russian came to my attention again, this time as a venerable old man: receiving a medal from Vladimir Putin, for returning stolen Nazi works of art to the Hermitage. I rang to offer my congratulations. As I spoke to him the years fell away to reveal a connection, however faint, that had endured over time. I felt a minor vindication, that the man whom I thought only wanted me for one thing, might not have after all.

Naturally during the time of youthful inexperience, to try and forget him, I played around with various young men that were available, using them, having been so hurt to have been used by him. This is the way we all get tough, it's a hard lesson, but eventually we learn to separate the wheat from the chaff.

As well as the romantic liaisons of the Riviera, the reality of the Sable business was beginning to become clear. Inevitably the whole Portugal fiasco fell through, and I put the yacht up for sale. An acquaintance from Paris, Regis de Ramel and a friend of his who was a conductor of the Brussels Symphony Orchestra, thought it would be great fun to own a boat and invite their business associates on board. They bullied me down on her price, saying she was unseaworthy, which they promptly proved by sinking her off a Greek island. Crooked shits, but I'd had enough fooling around in the south, so I clinched the deal, and headed off for Paris, with enough cash to start a serious bank account and have fun for a few months.

# 6. *Paris*

I loved Paris, which was wild and great fun, I took to the city like a duck to water, zipping around the streets in a dark blue fiat convertible, living in an apartment on the Rue Bayard with three friends, partying at Regine every night, as I slowly tried to forget Edouard the Russian.

As much fun as wintering in the city was, I soon yearned for the sea and I was back in the south again by the springtime to take a job for Bruce Campbell, the powerboat designer. It was not a serious job, I was simply showing off his boats to all and sundry, but as I knew the very closed circle of foreigners living on the coast, it was a ball. Powerboat racing was then a burgeoning sport attracting a myriad of gentleman amateurs including Sir Rocco Forte, the hotelier, Gianni Agnelli, the Fiat boss, and Johnny Bingham, who was soon to become the infamous Lord Lucan.

I was staying in Biot, the village famous for hand-blown glass, in a lovely old farmhouse full of dogs, which belonged to a lady called Peggy Colling. I met her the previous summer when introduced to her by Jack Abrahams, the De Beers diamond magnate.

With a similar sense of humour, we got on like a house on fire, and Peggy and Jack quickly began trying to match me up with some fellow. One evening Jack announced he was going to introduce me to a Frenchman, supposedly an ideal beau for me. We arrived at this person's flat on the Croissette overlooking the casino, and the door was thrown open by an abnormally tall frog, dressed in white and very tanned. In the background his daughter was jumping up and down on a sofa, giggling.

'Daddy, this is the ideal English girl for you!'

'Irish,' I replied, rather snootily.

After brief introductions Jack conveniently disappeared, and Jacques Michoud, as this man was called, took me to dinner at Mougins. He was very sophisticated, and I felt very in awe of him. When we parted, he said he was returning the next day to Paris and would I come and see him off at the station? Returning to Peggy's house I thought, *Oh! La! La! What an attractive fellow!* but I realized then and there he was another womaniser and, of course, much too old for me. His daughter must have been more or less my age.

For these reasons I did not go to the station, and neither did I phone him once I was back in Paris the following September. Apart from my doubts about his suitability, I was more immediately concerned with checking up on the job that I had been offered by a character I had met at the boat show studying new designs with Bruce Campbell. He was Compte Guy de Roquemaurel, a Parisian with his own bank and he wanted my assistance in organizing the details for his future boat-chartering business plans in Mallorca. He offered me my own office and a Swedish secretary, and my hours were very free to come and go as I wished. I had to set up a base in Palma de Mallorca, very close to the Club Nautico, a prestigious yacht club, and flew out there every month, backwards and forwards to Deia and Valencia on the mainland. We rebuilt the Arcoa motor cruiser, a French-built cabin-cruiser, especially designed for the new middle-class bourgeois, who had just enough capital to own a boat, but the builders had no idea how to make them look elegant and racy. I redesigned the outline and the cabins. The new style is still used today.

The new designs were sent to Mallorca. Guy loved the island, and his passion was to have a fleet of boats and ship chandlers to service them, and then charter out other bigger yachts on the free market.

Whilst they were ambitious plans, it was all great fun; the Swedish secretary fell in love with Eugenio Jaudenes, the President of the Club Nautico whilst Guy was making gooey eyes at me, but I never had any interest.

In 1963, Guy was with me in Mallorca when Kennedy was assassinated. He was in the next room and came to tell me with just a towel around him. We were both horrified, and sat glued to the box all evening. He tried everything in the book to seduce me but I held him off and never even flirted with him.

On that same trip I met Sol de Portago, the racing driver's sister, and her man friend on their most wonderful old sailing boat. They played gin rummy, betting for thousands each round. She laughingly said, 'Vicky, don't play with us, we will take you to the cleaners!' The next yacht along the quay belonged to Jean de l'Epee with his piano welded into the hull!

I was enjoying my professional and social life enormously but there was a deep black cloud on the horizon. My brother Johnny's personal happiness had been in a state of constant deterioration for sometime. With grim inevitability he had been invalided out of the navy for his psychological problems, as they had concluded that he was not officer material; something I could have told them years earlier. Tragically, he was scarcely better suited to civilian life, and I am not sure if he would have been entirely happy in any place or role. As well as being bullied in every institution he had passed through, Johnny had fallen unhappily in love with an eastern woman in Singapore and never truly recovered from the rejection.

Although the warning signs were present, it was, of course, a devastating shock to receive a phone call from Mother's second husband, telling me the horrific news that Johnny had committed suicide, shooting himself through the head with his naval pistol in the solitude of London's Putney Heath. I found out later that Johnny had recently been to visit Mummy, and she had been so beastly to him and so unsympathetic over his problems, that he walked out, vowing never to return.

Poor little bugger, Mummy made the various obvious excuses, local medical friends calmed her down, saying he suffered from schizophrenia, but it was all nonsense in reality; the simple truth was he was lost without any family love. He had been such a lovely child, and so brilliant in many ways. He finished up loathing our mother. What a terrible disaster.

*

Back in Paris, eventually out of curiosity I rang the Frenchman Jacques Michoud; he was furious that I had not contacted him earlier, and I agreed to see him again. A fatal mistake. Got the goosebumps once more, as he was very sexy, and had not felt like this since I had told Edouard to bugger off. It was always the older man who dominated me that I fell for. I hung on for as long as possible, sussing out the situation: divorced with two children, Sabine and Jean Paul, both about my age. He owned a huge apartment on Avenue Foch, one of the most prestigious streets in Paris, and one of the most expensive addresses in the world. Sabine lived with her father and Jean Paul had his own flat in the 16$^{th}$ arrondissement; he was a typical spoilt French playboy, arrogant and misogynistic, who locked girls into his car to fiddle with them!

Jacques was full of earnest charm and yet there was no doubt about it, just from his manner I could tell he was pure danger yet still I lacked any residual caution. One evening after dinner, he took me back to his luxurious pad. That was it. I was hooked physically by him then. He did not offer to drive me home; I should have realized there and then what a selfish person he was and totally unsuitable for a 25-year-old.

Right from the outset he had me by the scruff of the neck in a way that even at the time I recognised as unhealthy, if not slightly sick. I certainly tried as hard as I could to keep up a separate life, as I had no great interest in Jacques's nakedly aspirational circles that consisted largely of the bourgeois. It did not take long, though, for my worst suspicions regarding my new lover to be confirmed, in a classic case of catching a rat in the act.

Rather oddly, Jacques announced in advance that he would have a sore throat the following day, thereby cancelling our dinner date. Of course, I could tell that this excuse was garbage, so the following evening I arrived unannounced, much to the surprise of dear Leone, the housekeeper, who opened the door, shocked to see me.

'Mademoiselle, I thought you were Madame Roux, who should be here now at any time.'

'No problem, I'll only be a minute,' I replied, but shaking at the knees went through to his room to find his lordship in bed, a scarf wrapped round his neck, looking ridiculous, protesting ill health with the vigour of an Olympic athlete. Naturally panicked, he insisted I sat on a chair, so as not to get the bug, before telling me to leave. I was terrified but stuck my ground, long enough to tell him what a shit he was. I left the tawdry scene in tears, without ever meeting Mme Eliette Roux, a very high-powered Dior saleswoman, but vowing to sever my ties with this lying, conceited bastard once and for all, a sentiment that all my friends heartily agreed with. Underneath my resolve was a fear of the inexplicable force that attracted me to this unsuitable fellow.

Like a twit, crying my eyes out, I went and had dinner with friends Patsy Schryver and Michael Parker, one of the Duke of Edinburgh's best friends, previous Private Secretary, who could offer sound advice as he was no stranger to the mindset of a philandering male. Poor them; I was a pain in the arse, blubbing like a baby. They encouraged me that I needed to get away from Jacques, to get out of Paris.

Though very unhappy, I did not answer the phone next morning, made my excuses to Guy and the *banque*, before driving to the coast, back to Peggy Colling's in Biot, vowing to have nothing more to do with him, but feeling wretched. Peggy was very kind and took me everywhere to distract me, introduced me to Freddie Heineken, the beer magnate and Bobby Cunningham-Reid, among others. Bobby was a hoot with his died hair and getting us girls to accept cigars under the table, and then pass them to him, to augment his supply. One day out on Freddie's yacht, in the bay of Cannes, we were chased by a fast speedboat, that sidled up to our port side, and lo and behold, there was Jacques looking bashful and for once, quite shy.

'Fancy seeing you here, Jacques, is it not a bit early for the season for the likes of you?' It was only June.

Then he followed me round the little streets to the back entrance of Camper & Nicholson's, the yacht designers and charterers, but never came up to say hello. Or give me a hug. What an extraordinary individual.

I knew he was hooked, but so proud. He had this weird character that actually hated women and only wanted to use them. He never came sentimentally close enough, to either get hurt himself or be put in the weaker position. Years before, he had a very pretty girlfriend; long, blond and slender, but he completely refused to marry her, and eventually married her off to one of his friends, but went back to bed with her on their first night of the honeymoon. Sick.

At the end of that summer, Guy wanted me to go to New York to market his yachting business to wealthy Americans. He thought it was an ideal time for me to get out of Paris, as he was possibly a bit jealous of Jacques, and wanted me to get over him. Bizarrely, I still actually craved that Jacques would propose to me. So to America I went; a dear friend Vanessa McConnell agreed to lend me her apartment in New York, and in November 1965 I set sail across the Atlantic on the SS France.

# 7. *New York*

It was a very stiff and rather boring crossing, except the thrilling anticipation of arriving at 5.00 am off the coast when we slowed down to take in the Verrazano Bridge, only opened a year earlier, and the Statue of Liberty.

Something was obviously wrong. There was a sudden silence on the deck. Whispered rumours started circulating; the tension rose and we all thought, like the Titanic, we had struck something. Finally, the tannoys started working, announcing that there was a strike in the docks and we could not get a berth until much later, and eventually at 10.00 am we slowly came into a still New York harbour. No dockhands, no moorings and the quayside empty. It would normally be a teeming mass of people.

We found out slowly that there had been an enormous power cut on the entire east coast, from the Great Lakes to Florida. Over 30 million people were left without electricity for up to 12 hours.

The whole of New York was in a black-out. People stuck on the top floors of skyscrapers, in lifts, in the underground, everywhere. Finally, when we got a taxi, and that took hours, we made our way across the city, stopping every five minutes to let people come up and out of the manholes as the steam expired from the underground pipes. They had been caught there all night in the dark. Nine months later the birthing rooms in all the city hospitals were full! Arriving at Vanessa's flat, 56th East, the doorman had just arrived and had found two terrified couples caught in the lift. They had never seen such mayhem in the city. Astonishingly it is said to be the lowest amount of crime on any night in the city's history since records were first kept.

The aftermath was discussed in every bar and restaurant, and the Mayor's office and the Senate. It took six days to locate the supposed cause: a single faulty relay in Ontario, Canada, which triggered a sequence of power surges, shutting subsequent power plants down in a domino effect.

Myself and many other friends were convinced it was the after effect of two very large UFOs sighted, described as fast, bright fireball-like objects hovering over the main grid just before the black out. Of course, people pooh-poohed the theory, but why should our planet be the only life form? Perhaps there are thousands of planets and satellites out there in space, full of humanoids and their friends!

New York at that time was amazingly social; I was invited everywhere by the Europeans who were living there, a jet-set element and playboys that simply don't exist today. Prince Alfie von Auersperg, a young, handsome blond known as a top sportsman and lady-killer. Alfie, an Austrian, had little except his title, as his family estates were on the wrong side of the Iron Curtain, annexed by the Socialist East German Democratic Republic. He appeared to be fortunate to have enough relatives who still retained wealth, which perhaps kept him in the style to which he was accustomed. Peter Salm was known as one of the most eligible bachelors in America. His home was a 1,000-acre estate near the Hamptons, called the 'Port of Missing Men', where he started the only English-style driven shoot in the USA. He was madly in love with Jacqueline de Ribes, generally agreed to be the most beautiful woman in Paris. When they were skiing in Gstaad, the whole mountain came to a halt just to admire them.

I was asked to be a guest on *What's My Line?*, a television programme on which contestants would quiz a combination of 'celebrity' guests and members of the public to try and discern the nature of their employment or speciality. I have no idea how they found me, but I accepted readily, thinking Guy would be delighted, as I was supposed to be in New York to promote the yacht-chartering business. Nervous, I arrived at the studio at the requested hour. One of the technicians ran me through their questions, and then somebody slapped make-up on me, and before I could think straight, I was shoved before a panel of tough New Yorkers. It was a nervous and slightly intimidating experience. Really bitchy women, though the men were more pleasant. They were absolutely furious, as they could not guess 'my line'. Although they quickly ascertained it was transport related, none had the sense to think of boats. They were most disgruntled when I finally had to tell them that it was chartering yachts in the Mediterranean.

Buzzing around New York with new-found friends was fun but, as always, I enjoyed getting out of the city. Hugh and Sheila were stationed in a lovely Naval residence in Bermuda, and I flew down to stay with them and their two wee daughters, Louise my god-daughter and Catherine, then toddlers, today pushing 50, crikey! Hugh was now a captain, and Sheila enjoying the sun, as we shared gorgeous picnics on their beaches. A great respite.

My Achilles heel has always been the weather, which I take far too personally and in New York it veered towards the extreme. In 1966 the coldest ice storm on record was the breaking point for me; I contacted Guy in Paris, to tell him I'd done everything I could in New York and now would like a three-month sabbatical to go south to the sun. At that time of year, all the big money interested in chartering yachts would be in the Caribbean, and I offered to work there unpaid. Of course, he said yes.

First I headed for Miami Beach, where I had contacts, and was fascinated to see what it was like. I met up with Jimmy Kimberly, the yachtsman about town and owner of Kleenex, a sophisticated pirate with one earring. I also became friendly with David Naylor-Leyland, an Englishman, of course, but married to an American heiress, Dita Douglas, whose mother was said to have coined the phrase, 'A woman can never be too thin or too rich.' There were many more fleeting friendships in Miami Beach, but so superficial, so temporary, and so terribly American.

I flew on to Jamaica. On landing, I looked around, breathed deeply and thought to myself, now we're talking. Clear blue sea, gentle tropical breezes, mountains on the skyline, yellow beaches to the right of the runway, and a tin band to welcome us; Montego Bay with the world at one's feet.

1966, the mid-'60s, when Jamaica was still the playground of the rich and happy, the world and his wife had all built houses at Round Hill. Negril was then still a huge white beach with no one on it, but a lonely shark cruised the waters. The blue mountains were wild and inaccessible and the black river was full of crocodiles, but today sadly full of boats and people. Ocho Rios was to the east, where there were fabulous, huge waterfalls and the home of Ian Fleming, writer of all the James Bond books. It is a small place, and within a few days I knew everyone, and especially became good friends with Sarah Spencer Churchill, spending many happy times in her beautiful home above Montego Bay and the yacht club. The daughter of the Duke of Marlborough and granddaughter of Consuelo Vanderbilt, she was a huge character not to be daunted by, charmingly and disarmingly direct. I had first met her shortly after arriving in New York, where she had taken me under her wing, so to speak.

After divorcing her previous husband she had recently married a beautiful Chilean boy called Guy Burgos, nearly 20 years her junior. Sarah very kindly invited me to stay, joining a huge house party, with polo matches, barbecues, swimming naked at Negril, shark watching; it was heaven after dirty old New York. To my surprise all the young men were obviously gay, and I realised pretty quickly that her new husband was as well. This was not a surprise to Sarah, and for this reason the marriage turned out to be short-lived but she and Guy remained friends for the rest of their lives.

In Montego Bay I had a quick fling with a polo player, Charlie Browne, a Jamaican of the two bloods; frivolous stuff. After some time I booked a flight back to NYC thinking I ought to go back to work, but as I walked onto the flight, I had a change of heart and walked out again on the other side of the plane. Quite nuts; I was still in love with Jacques, but a flirt was good for me and Charlie was very attractive, he kept me sane and we laughed a lot. I found out through the chattering Caribbean grapevine, that Jacques was in Barbados. What a sick fellow, he did not have the guts to come and get me, but he wanted to make sure I knew he was around.

After a long talk with Guy, we both decided it was time for me to go back to Europe, and although this time I caught the flight, I was very sad to leave the island. I knew it was time to stop playing and get back to my apartment in Paris and the job. Also, I had made the decision never to sleep with Jacques again. I was going to be tough, either we got married or he could bugger off.

Back in Paris I made the conscious decision to draw a line under Jacques and not leave myself open to the pain he invariably bought in his wake. At 27, I knew I could ill-afford to continue in the rut I had allowed myself to fall into, my personality needed space to expand and in spite of my achievements, I craved a stronger sense of self.

It was tough, but I stuck to my guns and refused to have anything to do with him, ably supported by good friends. The international cast of Marcia Donnelly, another Anglo-Irish girl in Paris, and my best friend, Vanessa, Anne Robinson, a Swedish girl, and Sophia Bertelsen, a very clever Dane, managed to keep me resolved.

# *8. Marriage to Jacques*

Jacques's response was to literally throw his toys out of the pram, not so much because he loved me, more that he had never experienced rejection before and obviously found the sensation more than his delicate male ego could bear. Trying to get me back became a kind of contest for him, and for four months he bombarded me with letters and phone calls, desperately trying to claw his way back in. I was steadfast and determined. Perhaps he second-guessed this as in the end he did what I most desired but needed the least; he asked me to marry him.

Very stupidly I said, yes.

He really was not marriageable and he must have known this. As he was a divorced Catholic, but as he had not got an annulment from the pope, we could only get married civilly. He chose the date to correspond with the day before a pre-arranged trip up the Nile with a whole bunch of his friends. A bit odd to say the least.

Sometime after his proposal, I suggested, rather shyly, that traditionally the man offered his bride-to-be an engagement ring. He looked rather horrified at the thought but went to Winston's, the famous jewellers on Avenue Montaigne, to an old friend Paul de Rosiere, and made some deal. Surprisingly he actually bought me the most beautiful sapphire and gave it to me at a lunch at the Relais Plaza, then an elegant restaurant, today full of celebrities.

'Vicky, you can design the ring as you like when we come back from Egypt, but for now here is the stone; only you must give it back to me before we leave.'

It was some tax dodge!

We arranged a wedding lunch with our closest friends at his apartment, and the night before, good old Jeanne Marie Lubomirski, known in Paris as the Triple Duchess, gave a dance for us. Mummy had arrived from Malta – Winco had sold Sortridge and bought a farm in Gharghur, obliging Mother to return to the island as a retired wing commander's wife. She was sick and hated it as a sixpenny settler.

We were married at the Mairie of the 16th arrondissement with my mother, his children and a dozen or so friends, including Paul and Harriette de Rosiere, Lola Dudley, Anne Robinson and Vanessa. On the flight to Egypt the next day, he started flirting with the most sleazy female across the aisle. Disgusting.

In our Cairo hotel we had a huge room, with beds miles apart, so I told Jacques to call someone and put them together.

'What for?' he asked.

'What for? Hell, it's our honeymoon, no?'

I started having very grave doubts about him, but thought, well, you twit, it's now too late. I can be tough, but, wow, would I need all my wits about me to get through this marriage. Egypt was spectacular, slowly Jacques relaxed and we had some good laughs. His friends were actually very nice but obviously all much older, and I think they were fascinated watching him behave as he did. Towards the end of the cruise, he started to *vous voyez* me.

'What's the problem now?' I asked.

'Oh! It's normal, many husbands address their wives as "*vous*"—'

'Well, not to me, Jacques, I'm not a stuffed shirt and only French from my ancestors.'

There were more obstacles to overcome back in Paris when we discovered that Sabine had not moved out of his flat. He told her to leave immediately, as he had bought her a very nice small apartment and she had been too lazy to do so. When we arrived quite late, he told me to go and sleep in Sabine's room at the back, and if and when I wanted him to come and find him. Shocked to the core, I cried myself to sleep. The next morning the housekeeper asked what the matter was. I just replied that he was sick.

I don't know how I did it, but somehow I got the strength to stand up to him and said, 'Well, if this is how you want to live, very well;

Sabine's room is where your wife is sleeping, so it is the main room of the house. If you want me, you will have to move.'

Once we were 'legal' we hardly ever made love again.

'What does it matter?' he said one day. 'Society and friends don't know.'

I was puzzled, wounded and humiliated. Our life was totally superficial, one great social round of the nouveau riche. If I was feeling horny, he called me the nymphomaniac of Avenue Foch. I later found out that he was having multiple affairs, which started during our honeymoon in Egypt. My situation had become insufferable.

I realized that I could not spend my life as a chattel to such a man and that I must make some changes. Dear Marcia advised me to go out and pursue my own business in real estate.

'Vicky, for heavens sake, you have brains and guts; go and borrow capital from Guy and buy up ruined old apartments in the Marais. You have fabulous taste, use it!'

I took her advice and have never looked back.

Straddling parts of the 3rd and 4th arrondissements in Paris, the Marais was beginning to become fashionable in the late 1960s. I bought up old apartments, knocked down walls, found 16th century beams, old fireplaces and staircases to the roofs hidden behind plaster. I transformed the poky little rooms into elegant apartments and sold them on, returned my loan to Guy and did the same thing again. The turnaround became so fast that I was buying two or three at a time. Jacques thought I was quite mad but I had found an excellent distraction from the unhappiness of my marriage.

Another friend, Vanessa, herself an artist and designer, was looking for land for one of her own projects. Bouyed by my success in Paris, we flew down to the Straits of Gibraltar to look at land in a 200-year-old cork forest El Cuarton with magnificent views over the columns of Hercules and Morocco.

As it happened, Jacques and I had been looking for a house and land of our own in the South of France. Our two apartments, one in Paris and the other in Cannes were too much for me, an Anglo-Irish country lover. Until then we had found nothing we wanted to buy. The visit to the cork forest area changed all that and Jacques and I fell in love with Spain. We bought one hectare above Vanessa's, high up the mountain with spectacular views across the straits towards Jebel Musa in Morocco.

El Cuarton was an intriguing prospect, but we decided to wait a couple of years to see how the *bon viveurs* turned developers, Dominic Elwes and Hugo Millais, proceeded with their plans.

Vanessa built her house straight away, and one day she rang up saying, 'Listen! You love the sun, both of you. Don't build up there where you have bought. There is thick fog on your land even in mid-summer!' This was the first we heard about the infamous *levante* winds, created by the heat over the Iberian land mass, which blows to the east and funnels down through the Strait of Gibraltar, creating a funnel. This meets the cooler air of the Atlantic and it blows up north west to redo the same cycle, and can continue non-stop for two weeks.

We spent our summers in Marbella and visited El Cuarton from time to time, seeing the village grow and many plots sold to friends. Finally we discovered the perfect place down the mountain below the road, in the most beautiful valley where we bought our own plot near to a stream. The view was not as good, but there was much less wind and no fog.

In 1969 we decided to take the plunge and start building, drawing up plans with the architect, Philip Jebb, as we lay on the grass, swilling down the local jerez. I wanted a real Spanish *cortijo* with an arched terrace, and full of antiques. There was to be a big gravel patio with a cork tree in the middle and a pool out to the west, surrounded by the guest wing. The building was to be as long and as low as possible. A huge amount of earth had to be excavated as the land was on the mountain, sloping down to the valley. Having struck a deal with a local contractor, I now started building in earnest. I have in me a desire to create and build and design, perhaps I should have been an architect. There was no point in leaving Jacques, and I was thrilled with the distraction of building this house, and found the atmosphere in Spain to be divine.

I took my Spanish cook, Pepe, with me from Paris on my next trip to El Cuarton. We combed the countryside of Baja Andalucia, Antequera, Jerez de la Frontera, San Lucar de Barrameda and Seville, buying up old grilles, doors, 16th century beams and ceilings, trucking the whole lot back in two lorries. Another huge consignment, which I bought for an absolute song, was the whole of the convent on the left of the cathedral in Seville; 12th century gothic windows and doors and ceiling tiles as thick as your thumb. All the tiles went into an old American car, which as a result had very little ground clearance, and we had to drive through the night to avoid the Guardia Civil.

There was also fun to be had away from the building site. At a party in El Cuarton, Dorine, who was handling public relations for the development, introduced me to a devastating Spaniard, very good looking and very tall, with the naughtiest eyes, even more so than Daddy's and with a head like a Roman senator. I danced with him in front of a fire outside on the terrace, and in a slightly inebriated moment, I asked him to a party that we were giving a few days later. He turned up at 11.00 pm, well after it had started. I had totally forgotten inviting him and said rather flippantly, 'You're so late, there is no more room, you'll have to sit with the nannies down there.'

Although he was quite miffed, and his aristocratic nose had been put out of joint, Joaquin Cervera was an absolute gentleman, a charming and attentive Spaniard, and his wife Maria Rosa was a lively and intellectual woman. Jacques and I quickly became friends with them, socializing a lot together.

Just before leaving Spain at the end of that summer, Jacques was trying out the recently finished Sotogrande golf course and I took off to the stables to find something more interesting to do. I asked them if there was any particular horse I should ride and was told, 'There's a very young four-year-old mare, but she's huge and very skittish.'

Fascinated, I went to see her and instantly fell in love with Fabiola, a lovely dark bay with intelligent eyes, standing a good 17 hands. Some up-country people had sent her to Sotogrande to be sold as a polo pony but at 17 hands she was, of course, far too big for this. I rode her away from the bulldozers and we clicked immediately on the most glorious ride through the cork trees.

I set a deal in motion straight away, and two weeks later, Fabiola was mine. There were no horse boxes in those days, so we put her in a cattle lorry and took her to my local gypsy, six kilometres from the house. My career with horses in Spain had started.

In the spring of 1970, finally the house at El Cuarton was finished. An often frustrating but immensely satisfying experience. My Spanish was certainly not fluent in those days but continuous conversations with the builders and an occasional visit from the Spanish engineer improved it rapidly. The house was built to the dimensions of the antiques I had found all over Andalucia, each room accordingly was the width of the beams and the size of the windows and the grills. Each window space had a Roman number and each door an Arabic one. It was almost impossible for them to understand that the more irregular the lines, the more authentic it would look. My satisfaction was final after it was finished nine months later, complete with the first ever central heating in the south of Spain, when some Americans came to see the house and exclaimed, 'Wow! Vicky, what a heavenly old *cortijo* you've found and all with Roman pillars!' I laughed and said nothing, knowing those particular pillars were drainpipes full of sand, and rubbed down with lava and mud from the mountains. We moved in for Easter using with packing cases and upturned doors as tables before the antiques that Pepe and I had hunted for, all round Andalucia were eventually put into place. The bathrooms had cork tiles on the floors and walls which had to be imported from France, despite the fact that we were in a cork forest.

I moved Fabiola over from her stables and made a corral in amongst the cork trees in the garden. It was heavenly, just jumping on and riding all over the mountains, though some boring friends from Paris thought we were quite mad, living so far away, it had taken them four day's driving to get there. Cuarton was developing and other friends started building houses. A girlfriend from London, Antonia Cole, had the next plot along the valley; the interior designer Milet Delme-Radcliffe built her house amongst three huge rocks halfway down the hill.

It was an amazing place, and characters abounded, not least Hugh Millais and Dominic Elwes. The village was 60-odd apartments and a pool in the centre, a Roman restaurant on top of the mountain, and monks making bread down in the valley. Their imaginations were out of this world, but totally impractical; the mountain belonged to the army for a start! There were complaints about the inadequacy of the restaurant until they put up a notice saying, 'The service is non existent, the food is disgusting, but thank God it's expensive.'

The village flats were almost full and everyone knew everyone. There was no flight around the world where one could not meet somebody from Cuarton. Nicholas and Elizabeth Luard, the writers and part-owners of Private Eye, built their modern *palacio* up the hill, with Dutch people around the corner, and then the main house, designed by Dominic Elwes, The Muneca was bought by our friends Bruno and Rosalinde D'Oncieu de Chaffardon from Geneva.

*

We decided to have a house warming, and set the theme as Arabic, asked some good friends from Marbella, and put them all up for the night. By then we knew all the fun relations of Joaquin and his wife, Maria Rosa. Anichi and Santi Cordoba, Josele and Clemencia Nunez, and Maria Luisa and Juaca Alvarez, his younger sister, to name just a few. They were a huge family.

I made a *sangria loca*, a secret recipe laced with vodka, for sipping to flamenco music by local gypsies. Down through my patio came a donkey with Mary and Joseph and the three shepherds; he came into the house and the poor fellow did the splits, sliding on the spilt vodka. It was Milet, of course, playing pranks with her daughters.

Summers were great fun and very hot; all my family came and my best girlfriends from Paris joined us, especially Marcia and her adorable baby Edward, as well as Hugh and Sheila Balfour and their children, cousin David and his wife Jane. And, of course, Jacques's children, Jean Paul and Sabine.

We were also invited to the Cerveras's non-stop: to their farm on the other side of Algeciras, on their boat M.Y. Marigalante I, bullfights, up to Jerez to see the Arabian studs and pure-bred Spanish horses. One day on the boat, I asked Joaquin and Maria Rosa why they had never sailed up the Guadalquivir to the Feria at Sevilla, which is always on just after Easter. They laughed and scratched their heads, replying, 'Don't know, Vicky, we have just never thought about it!'

Dorina, as we called her then, heard about my proposition and laughing her head off, said, 'They have never had such fun since they met you.'

Some of our foreign friends in El Cuarton were very jealous, and asked me, 'How do you and Jacques get invited to the Cerveras's so often?'

Later I was to learn why. After I had snubbed Joaquin for arriving late to my party, he made enquiries to the Spanish shareholder of El Cuarton, Alfredo Molinero.

'How can I get to know that girl better, Alfredo?'

'Joaquin Cervera! Watch it! She has a very tall French husband and what's more, he is arriving tomorrow!' Alfredo replied.

I was totally naïve, and never realized the invitations were all part of a plan that Joaquin was setting up to try and seduce me.

Thankfully, neither did Jacques.

*John and I playing Indians, 1942*

*Paddy, my first pony, and me in a plaster cast, 1952*

*Daddy greeting the Mountbatten's on their arrival in Malta, 1955*

*Daddy and the Duchess of Kent, 1955*

*My first ball, Malta, 1955*

*John, Malta, 1955*

*My brother John, carrying Daddy's medals in the funeral cortege, 1956*

Daddy's Funeral,
1956

Edouard von Falz Fein,
1959

M.Y.Sable,
Cannes, 1960

*Powerscourt, Dublin 'Bal des Petits Lits Blancs' with the Lobkowitz's, 1964*

*What's your line? New York 1965*

*Honeymoon on the Nile, Egypt, 1966*

*Jacques and Sabine at Cuarton, 1969*

*Le Cortijo del Molino Viejo, nearly finished, Spain, 1970.*

*Alambique, the antique shop and rastro, 1972*

*Feria de Jerez de la Frontera, 1972,*
*me on Fabiola, Alvaro Domecq and Natallie de Noaille.*

*Vicky and Joaquin at the Feria of Sevilla, 1973*

*Drinks at the Marbella Club, 'Maxims Business Club', 1974, Me in the middle with Prince Alfonso Hohenlohe, Vanessa McConnell and Count Rudi von Schonberg*

*Marbella with the Duc de La Rochefoucauld, 1974*

*Vicky at the Feria de Jerez, 1974*

# 9. Falling in Love with Joaquin

Back in Paris, it was quieter that winter. There was a change of government and new politicians, but the social round carried on as usual. My professional life had not raised my status with Jacques, I was still cut out of his cosy circle of trust, that he enjoyed with his children, forced to sit with dull wives as he held business meetings in my own home with their husbands. Superficial lunches with his phoney children, yakking away about their shallow and meaningless preoccupations, hour upon hour on end. Desperately bored by it all, I bought another horse, Delacio, and went stag hunting twice a week, which got me out of the apartment and kept me fit. I was no longer converting the Marais apartments as they had priced themselves out of the market and I escaped to Spain whenever I could, to work on the house there.

As Easter approached, Joaquin said he was willing to go to Seville, and started making plans, but as usual it was all very last minute, very Spanish. The Marigalante I did not have many creature comforts and there was just room for them and us, so our guests from Paris would have to sleep in a hotel when we arrived in the city. They were actually the lucky ones, as showering on board was extremely difficult and it was cold and damp. I found motoring up the river quite boring and we had to take a pilot, following the twists and turns through the protected nature reserve of the Coto Doñana, an area I came to know very well later from the saddle on Fabiola.

We were wined and dined, in and out of the *feria* ground, bullfights and the old elegant Hotel Alfonso XII. Jacques had to fly back to Paris as there were problems in his insurance business. I was totally blind to Joaquin trying to flirt, and actually spent all the time talking to Maria

Rosa, who was highly educated and very well read. I had no way of knowing then, but it was a tradition in the family that if you start a cruise then you stay until the end. I had seen a superb four-poster bed at Jerez and wanted to collect it so thanked the family graciously and left in a friend's car to collect it. I was extremely embarrassed when I discovered my unintentional rudeness. They were furious and we did not see much of each other for a while.

Back to Paris and the spring, putting up with Jacques and his children, making the best of it all. There did not seem any point in leaving him having built the most glorious home in Spain, the *cortijo*; I created her, every single little detail, from the door locks to the garden. Jaques knew by now he could not treat me like dirt.

I had also bought a little village house in La Virginia, a most amusing and artistic development, built by Juan Manuel Figueras behind Marbella, mainly thinking of my mother, to give her a fun place to live, surrounded by foreigners, and somewhere I could rent out, while she made up her mind to leave Malta. She had returned to the island with my stepfather, Winco, and they had built themselves a very nice modern farmhouse. I wanted them to come and live in Spain, but never won her over to the idea. She never could cope with another language, despite everyone in Marbella speaking English.

My little house was painted yellow on the outside, and I again found old doors and grills up in Ronda and a marvellous marble fountain. By this time, I had converted an old lorry into a horse box. Two of my nieces on holiday came with me and we loaded her up with all the things I had bought, and quite mad, I drove her laden to the roof, swaying on all the curves in the dark, down the horrendously dangerous road to San Pedro de Alcantara on the coast. We arrived in La Virginia at 3.00 am; exhausted we fell into each other's arms, saying, 'Wow! We've made it.' I think they were terrified but didn't dare admit it.

*

We had a great summer and lots of fun with the Cerveras, without any mention of my previous rudeness. I was invited to ride over to their farm Las Pilas to show them Fabiola. I arrived at what I thought the normal time, 1.30 pm, to find Joaquin not there. It was a very hot September day and Maria Rosa was busy. Unsaddling Fabiola, I tied her to a tree and went to the pool for a swim. Joaquin arrived home a bit later and Maria Rosa came and said he had not shaved and to have a drink, which I certainly needed by then. Joaquin came for a swim; tanned and laughing, he swam up to the wall and sat very close to me. Nothing entered my head, until, maybe on purpose, our legs touched. It was like an electric shock. I looked at him in amazement and he just laughed and looked rather shy.

Finally we had lunch, and another Spaniard came and inspected Fabiola. There were compliments all round and some envy too.

Some days later Clara Larios, daughter of Pepe, the Duque of Lerma, turned up at my house grinning.

'Guess what Daddy's just heard? Joaquin Cervera has the most enormous crush for Vicky.'

I could not believe my ears. Went to bed amazed, and thought, well, this is food for thought; he is very attractive, but married, Catholic, and head of this enormous family. My stomach started fluttering again and remembered the physical shock at his pool.

The following night, I persuaded a friend, Françoise Marque, to accompany me to the yacht club, where I knew he spent most evenings. We met dear Manolo, his brother, at the bar, and asked for him. He grinned, as if he knew why, and said, 'Stay in the corner, Vicky, he is outside taking his wife fishing. I will tell him you're here.' It seemed as if everyone knew except for yours truly.

Joaquin arrived and squashed me into the corner, and whispered, 'At long last you have understood.'

There were people all around us.

'Meet me at the Cigaron at one o'clock,' he urged.

It was then only 9.30 pm. Against my better judgment, we went for dinner, met up with Juaca and, as normal, on to the Cigaron, a *boite* belonging to a friend of Joaquin's. We were sitting around the bar chatting with Pepito Lerma and others when there was a sudden silence. Joaquin appeared out of the dark, the others just melted away. I felt everything had been preparation for this moment, learning about life with Edouard, the ghastly marriage with Jacques; paving the way for this amazing relationship. Joaquin just held me between his knees, as he was sitting sideways at the bar and I was still standing. We did not have to talk, it was all there in his eyes. I was still very confused but totally smitten and realized then how deeply his feelings were, and how blind I had been for so long. Talking of electricity, it was so strong, no one in this world could have stopped the power that it had over us from that moment on. Wrong, sinful, whatever it might appear, but we were made for each other, and both needed love desperately.

My car was close and he jumped in and taking me in his arms, kept on repeating, 'Why did it take you so long? Why?' A conversation that followed was drowned out by our closeness. We went to my house El Molino; his strong footsteps echoed across my gravel entrance, a sound I can still hear today. God forgive me for my sins, as I loved his wife very much, and vowed there and then, that she would never know. We kept it secret, thanks to his lovely nephews and nieces, and never flirted with each other in public.

The following day while I was having a siesta, I heard the front door opening, but no further sounds. Later I found a bale of hay at the entrance, and a sweet note saying, 'For Fabiola, all my love, Joaquin.'

I could not believe that he had not come upstairs to find me; he admitted he was afraid I had second thoughts and was terrified of a rebuttal.

We managed to meet in secret whenever we could and I kept a very cold front in public. He put Marigalante I up for sale, and insisted I should be on board when he signed her away to a friend from Mallorca. I was horrified he let her go without a full payment, so trusting he was with his friends. The summer was drawing to an end and very soon I had to go back to Paris. Never would I have believed it possible to be in bed with my husband, and dreaming of another.

One of Joaquin's nephews was sick and he found this excuse to bring Maria Rosa to Paris, so naturally we asked them to stay. By this time I had converted Jacques's bedroom at the front of the apartment into a large double bedroom for us, so we offered them his daughter's room, where previously I had been installed as the young wife.

The Paris boat show was on, giving us another excuse to be together, as Maria Rosa went shopping while we went to see the new hulls that were on show. Joaquin was determined to order a fibreglass hull for a 20-metre motor yacht from Thorneycroft. Laughingly, I told him, 'You may get champagne and lobster at Cowes from Thorneycroft, but you won't see a finished boat in years.'

I knew all these yachting people backwards, and took him to meet Camper and Nicholson's instead. Joaquin was thrilled with their latest design and ordered his new hull to be built by them in Southampton. Afterwards we celebrated with champagne at Sylvia Piper-Fleming's apartment. We only made it back to Avenue Foch just in time, feeling very guilty.

The next night, Jacques and I had been invited to a sit-down dinner hosted by the Prince Ali Khan, where we knew the Infante, Don Jaime, was going. We arranged for the Cerveras to be invited afterwards. He was thrilled to meet him again, as Don Jaime was the uncle of Juan Carlos, the present day king, but had been disinherited in the succession for being deaf and dumb, missing out a whole generation of Bourbons: Don Juan who should have been king and Jaime, his elder brother.

Winter dragged on interminably, until we could not wait any longer, so Joaquin and I arranged to meet in Estoril. He took me to a gorgeously romantic place called Cintra, and got the fright of his life when the phone rang in the middle of the night, saying it was the golfer, Trent Jones. Poor man, I knew then how guilty he felt, and decided it was not worth carrying on the affair. I tried desperately through the spring of 1972 not to see him and to finish it once and for all.

His young family did not help as they were having such fun, and always somehow managed to get us together; they arranged an apartment in Seville for the *feria* in April the following year, as the new Marigalante II was now in Bilboa getting her engines installed. Of course, it was a piss-up from morning to night. I remember riding Fabiola in the Plaza España and she slipped on the paving stones and fell over onto her side. I just slid off her, totally pie-eyed on jerez. Joaquin, who was walking behind, was terrified we were both hurt. Thankfully, we were unscathed.

At this stage my building projects in Paris were finished, El Molino in El Cuarton was finished, and the little yellow house in La Virginia, Marbella, which I'd done for my mother, was complete. However, the marriage to Jacques was becoming more and more impossible, compounded by the fact that I was madly in love with Joaquin, constantly wishing to get back to Spain and be with him.

One day in September, the end of the summer, I was still in Spain, always staying long after Jacques had left for Paris, Joaquin, Maria Rosa and a friend of mine from Paris, Jacqueline Colliere all went on the Marigalante II to Marbella, with the idea of driving up to Ronda for the famous Goya Corrida of Ordonez. In the port, Jacqueline disappeared with David Naylor-Leyland, and I begged her to be back before dawn. Of course she never turned up!

I took a taxi at 5.00 am and went looking for them, very cross; I found them in one of Terry Pantz's apartments. I was very worried because she let me down *vis-à-vis* Maria Rosa, who I was very fond of and had enormous respect for, and did everything possible to hide my relationship with Joaquin from her. That morning in Marbella, she announced to him, that she felt sick and wanted to go back to Madrid; of course, he felt terrible, and even his brothers had offered to take her the week earlier, as they knew he was in love with me and wanted to stay in the south.

So we abandoned the Goya festival and sailed back to the home Port Algeciras. They left for Madrid, and slowly I returned to Paris. In a matter of weeks Joaquin wrote to me that darling Maria Rosa had cancer of the peritoneum. Inoperable and she had only six months before her. Of course, I felt terrible and guilty as hell. Is cancer brought on by stress? Did she know about our affair?

I found out years later, that one of Joaquin's sisters had told her, the bitch.

Back in Paris I took the tough decision to leave Jacques and go and live in Spain permanently, but not before I had planned it properly. I started by moving my odd pieces of furniture to Jacqueline's apartment on the left bank, and packed my things in boxes when Jacques was in his office. Another girlfriend came with me, and we left bloody old Avenue Foch at 3.30 am, the dead of night, in my Fiat sports car, with the antlers of my stag strapped onto the roof. We drove south, non-stop until we crossed the Spanish border to the Costa Brava.

Exhausted but still laughing, we arrived on the coast as the hotels were opening their doors, picking a small but pleasant little place to finally get some sleep. Refreshed, we continued south, finally arriving in Tarifa, the southern-most tip of Europe, and my village, home to El Molino. Greeted by the staff and guardian, Domingo, with open arms. *Bien entendu*, they had not understood anything!

There were no mobiles in those days, so we had not heard a word from Paris, nor Madrid.

The peace did not last long. Jacques announced he was coming for Easter, and what the hell did I think I was doing? Poor Joaquin was doing his best in Madrid surrounded by family, 12 brothers and sisters. His poor mother never stopped.

My friend flew back to Paris, and Jacques arrived. I told him straight out that I was not going back to Paris, that he was a lousy husband and miserable to me. I did not want any alimony from him, just wanted the *cortijo*, as I had built it from the ground up. It was actually Joaquin who had told me it was the least he could give me, after using the best years of my life. I did not quite agree, but went for it via a friend, who was a lawyer in Paris. We worked it out not too painfully.

I satisfied Jacques's negative curiosity, when I told him that I intended to set up a *rastro*, and collect antiques for future houses in Cuarton. I had already made an offer for El Alambique, a little old cottage off the main road; a still in Spanish is *alambique*. Gorgeous garden of black earth, large patio and bracken and fresh water, with the cork forest below and spectacular views over Tangiers to the west.

He simply said, 'You're very brave to set up a business on your own in Spain,' and went straight back to Paris to start the divorce proceedings. In the meantime, I bought the cottage, cleared out the junk, added on a wing, planted a palm tree in the patio and put in a reservoir. I had included a bar with tapas, so the opening was fun, but having leased it to a local Spaniard, I got furious with the way they threw all their mess on the floor. I would not have run it myself so just had to put up with it.

I had arranged for Maxime's Business Club from Paris to come out for a long weekend to El Cuarton. This was a collection of young businessmen in their thirties and forties, and their girlfriends or wives. It was a huge organisation; arranging buses to pick them up at Malaga airport, drinks at the Marbella club, dinner at Cuarton, sleeping 28 of them between four houses, and the village. Hmmm. A great deal of bed-hopping went on, which of course was shushed up! Riding over the mountains, golf in Sotogrande, flamenco on the beach and some of us even made it to the *feria* in Jerez. I lent one of my horses to Nathalie de Noailles, and to another couple, with the correct *traje corto*, boots and *zajones*; they fitted into the scene as if they were Spaniards.

# *10. Joaquin's History and the Civil War*

Joaquin was an extraordinary man, with an amazing strength of character and unmistakable presence, and by the time he entered my life he was a man of vast experience and had already passed through a number of affairs.

Coming from the proud lineage of the Cervera clan, descendents of Austrian warriors who had fought the Moors and even had a town named after them, Joaquin followed his illustrious father into the navy. If this gives the impression that he was as prim as he was dutiful, then it would be misleading. From the off Joaquin's rogue-like nature was all too apparent. Whether it was spending a very active night in a brothel in Spanish Morocco, having failed to secure other accommodation for the night on a naval exercise, or the more general pursuit of the good life, Joaquin was no stiff.

As with almost all of his generation, the formative years of his life were to be defined by the horrors of the Spanish Civil War. Like his brothers, Joaquin served with the Nationalists, though he very nearly did not take part at all, escaping death in the chaos of those opening few months. Assigned to fix the guns on the battleship the Baleares, on which his youngest brother Paco, still only 18, was serving, Joaquin was called over to help on another ship. Using the very primitive technology of a 'bosun's chair', Joaquin was slung over on this precarious device, just in time to escape the enormous explosion behind him.

The Baleares had turned into a fireball, his brother Paco sliding down the hull with all those other unfortunates killed that day for there was not a single survivor. In all likelihood the crew of a submarine must have mutinied and gone over to the Republicans, torpedoing the ship. To have hovered around attempting to pick up bodies would have been tantamount to suicide, hence the sad fate of those who survived the explosion. The only ones who came to help in any way were the British navy, who had destroyers in the area. Sadly they arrived too late, and only were able to pick up the dead.

Wishing to take advantage of his brain, the navy moved Joaquin to the town of Aranjuez not far from the Madrid front where he was commandeered by a factory testing out munitions and various other weaponry. In spite of being popular with his workers, whose sympathies were likely to have been with the Communists, Joaquin, unbeknownst to himself, had already been marked for death by the locals which were Republicans. As he shared a second name with the ship that had bought Franco over from North Africa, and smoked Lucky Strike cigarettes, an American brand and associated with the decadent trappings of capitalism, the local partisans decided that he must be a very senior fascist indeed. Waiting until he was descending from the steps of his church one Sunday morning, they opened fire on Joaquin and Maria Rosa, narrowly missing them both. Taking her by the hand, the two fled as their assassins gave pursuit, sure that their time had come.

Reaching the refuge of their house, they rushed into the garden to bury their wedding presents, before barricading themselves in, waiting for the Reds to storm the house. But instead of the pursuers a black London Hackney Carriage appeared, driven by a friendly cockney, who happened to be a foreign correspondent for a London paper. The area was being overrun by the Reds, so hailing them in, their saviour drove through the town, past the front line and into Madrid, which was in Republican hands, smuggling them into the Peruvian Embassy. This was literally a case of the frying pan into the fire, since although they had cheated death, their sanctuary was anything but safe or salubrious. The shadow of death hung over the place, packed as it was with those who feared the death squads of the Left.

Bishops, former captains of industry and generals were huddled together in cramped and necessarily squalid conditions, the men and women on alternate floors from top to bottom, meaning that for the next two years Joaquin was only able to see his wife when they met on the stairs. When Maria Rosa was given the opportunity of accepting an amnesty mediated by the Red Cross, she took it and left the country for Biarritz. For Joaquin, a senior naval specialist, there could be no such reprieve, and another year of boredom and desperation convinced him that a daring and bold plan would provide his only way out.

Turning his by now filthy naval uniform inside out, Joaquin was crammed into a truck and driven into the countryside. There was no way of knowing whether the bodies packed next to his were those of fellow escapees, other displaced persons, or Republican sympathisers. Knowing only that he was deep in hostile territory, Joaquin hoped, as the truck neared its destination of Valencia, capital of the Republic, that he wouldn't be recognised. It was in these circumstances that the remark, 'You're a naval man, aren't you?' from the girl next to him hit Joaquin with all the force of a denunciation. He was lucky – she was sympathetic, but so easily could not have been. In Valencia the full extent of the plan's audaciousness, venturing on the comic were not the stakes so high, became apparent.

Joaquin was required to play the part of a French sailor, drunk out of his mind. Coating him in a couple of bottles of cheap cognac, he was dumped onto a stretcher and taken on board a French destroyer and taught a few words of French, '*Oui, oui, Madame. Oui, oui, Monsieur*,' the lyrics to a song he had to sing to perfect his disguise. It was the ultimate con, to attempt to give an impression of not having a care in the world when actually fearing for one's life. It was just enough to convince the Civil Guards at the end of the gangplank, who bought the story that Joaquin was a boozed-up sailor who had wrecked the town and needed to sleep the whole sorry episode off.

Charging onto the ship, he was flung into a cabin before anyone could change their mind, landing on his best friend, an army officer who had been praying in front of an icon on all fours. The ship set off to Marseilles, and from there Joaquin had to make his way through Portugal to rejoin the war that was reaching its bloody and prolonged climax. As he was moving from one adventure to another, I had not even been born.

It is also ironic to note that Joaquin was not even a fighting man, far less a fascist, merely one who had no empathy with Communism, and who had been born into a family that valued tradition and service over anything else. By the time I met him he was head of his clan, albeit different from them in every way, a line of energy and not a dour traditionalist in the slightest. Not only did he love everyone but he was loved back, a rare gift. He loved his wife, Maria Rosa, who was a very intelligent and capable woman. I suppose, like me, she regarded herself as just lucky to be with him, something I still consider to be true to this very day.

# *11. Marriage to Joaquin*

In the beginning of July 1975, dear Maria Rosa passed away in their apartment in Madrid. The whole family decamped and Joaquin wanted me to go. A very old friend, John Culverwell, who was staying in the house said, 'No, Vicky, don't move, he wants you and you want to go, but I advise you strongly, stay put. However much he wants to see you, the family will be against it.'

I waited until the next day and phoned him to give my condolences. Maria Luisa, his very pretty younger sister, answered the phone and said he was entertaining the family and put down the phone. I heard later he was furious with her.

He came south as fast as he could, but chaperoned by the family, who tried their level best to keep us separated. Another official funeral mass took place in his charity school, outside of Algeciras near the beach; I persuaded Elizabeth Luard, a loyal friend from Cuarton to accompany me. The church was packed not only with the friends and family, which is enormous anyway; but hundreds of the locals who adored Joaquin and had great respect for Maria Rosa. Elizabeth and I slipped discreetly into a middle pew, before Joaquin arrived with his brother-in-law, the Marques de Alos. Poor dear Joaquin was looking very pale and tired, but thank goodness had not cut his hair. Bang in front of me, I wanted to stretch out and curl up the back of his neck.

We waited for the mass to end, to see where the condolences and hand shaking would take place. I was very nervous, knowing that half the church knew I was his mistress, and very much in love. We left the queue of people and as I turned, gave him a huge wink and a smile of, 'Cheer up, this won't last for ever,' before disappearing into the crowd. Apparently he had Luis Antonio near him, one of his nephews, the champion of Spain in show jumping and Olympic rider.

When it was over, he turned to him, and said 'Where is Vicky? She has bound to have gone to Las Pilas,' his home farm on the edge of Los Barrios. Well, we hadn't, we had gone back to El Molino, knowing his house would be full of mourners and family; he knew I was at the service, that was enough.

Next day the garden was full of cork cutters, the cork has to be cut every nine years. In the space of one hectare I had 68-odd trees, so it was mayhem. Men climbing, loading strings of mules with plaques of cork. Amidst the flurry of activity, who should come down the drive dressed all in white, but Joaquin himself.

'Joaquin, what are you doing? You must stay with your family and should not be out driving on your own.'

'Rubbish!' he replied. 'I can do what I want, and I want to be with the woman I love.'

I told him in no uncertain terms, that he had to be patient, and wait at least two weeks, without us seeing each other in private.

'Anyway, come in, now you are here, and have a drink.'

Two days later, I was summoned to Las Pilas; he needed help with a translation. Feeling very awkward and embarrassed, I went. Six cars were parked behind the farm and exactly what I imagined, the house full of people. Typical Spaniards always turn up when the bar is open! I asked a sister-in-law what did he want and went into his office, she grinned and said, 'Just an excuse to get you here!' At that he came in and shoved her out and shut the door. Oh dear, he was seriously desperate.

'I can't leave the house, I am followed everywhere I go, they won't let me see you, to hell with the lot of them, lets go to the beach tomorrow?'

'No,' I replied. 'Two weeks minimum.'

*

The weeks passed and Joaquin and I resumed our relationship as we approached autumn. There was huge upheaval in Spain, the

Generalissimo Francisco Franco was fading away, though his family kept him alive on machines and drugs as long as they could, meanwhile sending trunks of possessions out of the country. Franco's daughter, Carmen, was married to Cristóbal Martínez-Bordiú, tenth Marquess of Villaverde, the Doctor; a very smooth operator. The future Prime Minister, Adolfo Suarez, had his huge trunk stopped by the customs, but he had HRH the Prince of Asturias's (Juan Carlos) permission not to have it opened.

The 22nd November 1975, Franco passed away and the on 27th November, HRH Prince Juan Carlos was crowned King of Spain, cutting out a whole generation of Bourbons. Joaquin and I were up in Madrid, as anyone with brains could see this was coming. We had to walk across town to the Palacio Real, to see them come out on the balcony. The city was alive with emotion. Juan Carlos and Sophia of Greece, his wife, wanted to keep the coronation very low key, while all the *aristos* dying to have a court reformed were very disappointed that he refused to have one.

Instead he drove his motorbike in and out of his private residence, The Moncloa, and when necessary hid in the boot of his friend's cars to escape the press. As a great skier, he used to don a disguise, to sail down the slopes unnoticed. A lovely young man, quite shy but he was born into his destiny, and carried it off with humour and great dignity throughout his career, as being king in our modern times is a career without doubt.

Don Juan de Bourbon, the young king's father, who in the line of succession, should have rightfully been crowned; as his elder brother, Don Jaime, was deaf and dumb and had years before resigned from the succession, including all his heirs. Franco hated Don Juan for political reasons, and the whole family was exiled to Portugal and Switzerland at the beginning of the civil war. Franco was buried with great ceremony in the Vallee de los Caidos. A huge memorial dedicated to the fallen on both sides was actually built by the prisoners from the Republican army.

Juan Carlos was a very popular monarch, and Franco had prepared him thoroughly, having been brought up as a cadet in the army, spent a year on the naval training schooner and obtained his wings in jet fighters. He and Sophia of Greece were married in Athens and

Joaquin and Maria Rosa were at their wedding. When Joaquin was a young midshipman, he had brought in a cutter with eight sailors to pick up Don Juan's father and mother, Alfonso XIII and Victoria Eugenia of Battenburg. He was standing on the stern at attention, and the queen turned to her husband, and asked, 'Who is that gorgeous young man?'

In Madrid, Joaquin started making noises, wanting me to reform his apartment. I was already quite upset at the idea of moving into Las Pilas, and replied, 'Please, darling man, look for a new one, I simply cannot live in Maria Rosa's country home and Madrid as well.'

He made every excuse, being so adamant that he would not find anything near his family or his office. Later I gave in, he kept on flattering me, telling me I had the best taste, that El Molino was fabulous and we could keep a third as a *pied-à-terre* for us and sell off the rest. The flat was huge and covered the whole of the top floor with a balcony around the edge. Which in the late '70s was so polluted, no one ever used them.

Whatever the physical location of our house, we were undeniably living in sin. In 1976, a year after Maria Rosa's death, one early summer evening at El Molino, farting around in the pantry, getting the drinks ready, suddenly Joaquin went down on bended knee.

'Vics, I love you, will you marry me?'

So sweet, though I knew it was coming so was not really surprised.

'Well,' I replied, 'if I don't marry you, I will have to move out of Spain, as we can't go on living like this. Anyway, now it is not possible as my divorce has not come through and under French law I have to wait nine months to be sure I am not pregnant.'

'Nonsense, I have been to the Archbishop in Cadiz with Padre Martin, and they've told me, as you were married to a Catholic only civilly, who did not obtain an annulment, you are considered by the church as an unmarried girl,' he replied and produced the most beautiful ruby ring.

I had a good laugh at that one, but it was true, while the law was still in *vigor*, the Spanish church's counted first and foremost, the civil marriage was simply an added bureaucratic requirement. Six months later the system was reversed, we just made it through the loophole.

At the time we did not know the law would be reversed, hence I told Joaquin that there was no rush. Hugh and Sheila and their kids were coming in August, and that would have been perfect timing.

Joaquin's urgency was because he wanted us to be married before we started our planned cruise to the Baleares, Ibiza and Mallorca, Espalmador and Formentera on Marigalante II in July. So he was determined and set the date for the 17th July. I was getting cold feet, another older husband, head of this huge clan; was I mad? But I loved him so much, adored the ground he walked on, I could not imagine living without him, and was sure he felt the same. He had discussed this with his brothers, who apparently told him, when you're 80 Vicky will be 55, and then she won't be running around looking for younger men. They were very happy for him, as they knew his marriage to Maria Rose had been a long compromise, and felt he would have great fun with me, sharing our common passions for boats, horses and travelling.

On the 17th July, Vanessa's yellow Rolls Royce was parked outside El Molino, ready to depart for the service in the Sanctuario de la Luz outside Tarifa, my village. Chris and Antonia Cole, the next door neighbours, Hector Sanchez the doctor from Marbella and another darling nephew, Santi Cordoba, were all getting ready. I was so nervous I opened a bottle of vodka, being the only drink that does not smell, and gave everyone a tot. Or two. Chris drove the car, Santi travelled with us as he was giving me away. I was in a flat panic and laughingly told Chris to keep driving straight towards Cadiz, because I could not go through with it. 'Rubbish,' they shouted, 'turn right to the Sanctuario!'

On arrival at this adorable little chapel, I was shocked to see Joaquin and his family and the Judge Notaire all standing outside, my future husband in his tailcoat, looking very shy! Nobody had told me that this is a Spanish custom, unlike northern Europe, where the groom and best man wait at the altar. I flapped my hands to make them move into the church. To my horror my old girlfriend from Paris, Jacqueline Colliere arrived in an off-white dress, while I was discreet and wore pale green. The only problem was it was vaguely transparent, and the photographs made it look like I was naked! The charming service was watched over by our black virgin, Virgin de la Luz; in Latin countries we have witnesses instead of a best man, so Santi stood on one side and Anna, Joaquin's sister, on the other.

Hugs, kisses and congratulations all round outside the chapel, and I realized that from a Frenchman to a Spaniard, I was very much married not only to Joaquin, but to all his family as well. Finally we climbed into the Rolls and drove to the port where the Marigalante II was already moored at the quay inside the naval base of Tarifa.

We were greeted by the sailor Emilio, a good rogue, who was crying as he was very emotional, and the son of my guardian at El Molino, who we had employed as second crew member. How we all fitted on board I don't know, but at least she did not sink! Champagne and a wedding cake and everyone in superb form. After quite some time, we took a photo of everyone there around the yellow Rolls Royce. One and all started saying, 'Come on, we must leave the loving couple alone,' prompting a big laugh from some, but not all of them.

'No, we are going on the cruise too!'

We had invited Juaca, Maria Luisa's husband, Jacqueline, Santi and Anichi to join us. We had to fill the boat, and as we had been together for four years it felt very normal. I wanted to spend our first night in Africa, so we sailed for Tangiers, just opposite Tarifa across the Straits of Gibraltar. Before we arrived, Joaquin, who was always the captain of his boats, turned to me up on the top deck saying, 'I cannot possibly arrive in Tangiers in a tail coat!'

'Why not? You look very handsome.'

'No way,' he replied and rushed down to our cabin to change into slacks and a shirt. Such a pity, but he was adamant.

Arriving in the port, we went straight to the yacht club, where they were expecting us, and our guests had already planned to go ashore and leave us alone. Totally unnecessary but they had it all organized between themselves.

I had redesigned our cabin, some time previously; redecorated and managed to install a very comfortable double bunk and blue wallpaper. Only problem it was bang next to the galley, and as Emilio was first sailor and cook, the noise and the smells were quite something. Charming fellow and a good cook, but the mess he made was unbelievable. In the bow beyond the galley was the sleeping quarters for the crew, with their own hatchway, so they had plenty of space. Next door a tiny cabin for one person and in the stern two double cabins and a shower room and loo. So we slept easily five guests and us.

The day after our wedding night the famous *levante* wind started to howl, and Joaquin was very worried, though he knew the straits and the winds backwards. The forecast was for a maximum-strength *levante*. Juaca and Jacqueline, already nervous sailors and me too, were very anxious. To steady the nerves Joaquin and I went ashore to buy further booze supplies in the duty free port, leaving Anichi on the stern deck doing her nails. Suddenly a bicycle turned up with a Spanish fellow carrying a big packet; Emilio rushed out to greet him, and then brought this parcel on board and hid it down in his quarters. Anichi said, 'Heh. Emilio! What's going on? Who is this?' but she never thought more about it, and never mentioned it to us, until we were in Marbella a month later.

# *12. Honeymoon, Baleares*

The *levante* was howling around the harbour and in the rigging of the sailing boats, as Joaquin phoned non-stop to the *meteo* people learning that gale force was predicted for the next three days.

'Darling, I cannot risk taking all you land landlubbers through the straits in this wind and have you seen the sea? It is boiling with huge waves just off the coast. We will have to wait it out.'

Large sigh of relief from Jacqueline and I. The others were pleased as well, though not admitting it.

In the meantime we had fun visiting the back streets of the Kasbah, and some old friends from Paris, Adolfo Velasco, the Spanish boyfriend of David Edge, a very famous old queer, who had just died and left his amazing house in the Kasbah to Adolfo. Just packed with antiques. He used to make the most glorious kaftans, then opened another boutique inside the Mamounia Hotel, in Marrakech.

On the second day, Joaquin got very nervous and said our time was running out and he was going to sail come what may, the following morning. We packed away all the furniture on deck and he told us at 6.00 am that we had to close all the portholes and batten down all the hatches; Jacqueline and I were to stay in bed, horizontal and not move. Once we were out of the harbour, Marigalante II started rolling like crazy, bumping through the waves heading up the Moroccan coast towards Ceuta, the Spanish enclave opposite Gibraltar. Feeling sicker and sicker, I staggered up the stairs to the bridge hanging on to every support. There was Joaquin in his swimming trunks, legs wide apart to keep his balance, not turning a hair, working on his charts. He and Emilio never felt sick. Green waves of water were smashing against the bow and pouring down the deck, whilst Juaca and Santi were sitting behind him, looking green themselves, but no sign of Jacqueline or Anichi! '*Buenos dias, que quiere desayuno?*' Anyone for breakfast?

Emilio looked appalled, imagining he had to go down to the galley and cook eggs and bacon. Negative reply from all, except Joaquin who wanted coffee and toast.

The boat was rolling so much, her gunwales were repeatedly under water; one minute you could see the mountains in Spain, the next Jebhl Moussa in Morocco. I crawled towards the stern and hung on to the stanchion with my legs either side of it and became drenched each time the deck rose behind me at the most terrifying angle. Joaquin came out with a glass of something; 'Vicky, drink this, don't take a pill, as once we have crossed the straits and passed Gib the sea will be calm.' A neat gin and some lemon Fanta! 'And stay where you are, don't move!' Great advice. The other two women eventually joined me, Jacqueline as sick as a dog and very pale. Poor thing, she was beginning to regret joining me on the honeymoon.

Joaquin was having a ball, and loving his new boat, but came to the stern now and then, feeling very sorry for us. '*Que mala suerte esta mierda de levante!*' What bad luck this shitty *levante*! More gin and Fanta for everyone!

Finally we had crossed to the Spanish coast and rounded Gib, heading north east, towards Sotogrande; the sea was less wild, but very rough. Now we had a beam sea, which meant instead of plunging into deep troughs of water, we wallowed into the waves. By this stage we all felt terrible, but kept pushing Joaquin to go faster. Anything to arrive quicker in Puerto Banus, Marbella.

Eventually we made it, and I was pissed on gin. Now I know why all naval officers drink gin, as Joaquin was totally right, once inside the harbour, the rolling stopped, and half an hour later walking on the quay I felt fine. But exhausted.

Puerto Banus in 1976 was just becoming the playground of Marbella, and attracted yachts from all over the world; the Arabs had arrived, Adnan Khashoggi and the 85-metre long Nabila took up a whole quayside, then one of the largest yachts in the world with a helicopter landing pad, four speed boats winched to the decks and two jet skis.

Apparently, there was a fully functioning operating theatre on board, as he was a surgeon. It was serviced by 48 crew. Not to mention three or four wives.

The whole harbour was packed, but as Joaquin was very well known he got us a berth without any problem. Don Juan, father to Juan Carlos our king, was there in his sailing boat, surrounded by police and security. Joaquin had to go and pay his respects, as they were old friends, and we were all royalists. I knew his son Juan Carlos a little, as we used to spend time together with the Spirito Santo brothers in Estoril, when I had made various trips there during Sable's fitting out. Small world as one of the Portuguese boys, Bernardo D'Aurey Pinheiro became HRH's sailing companion. Joaquin and Maria Rosa were also at his wedding to Sophia of Greece in Athens.

We had planned to stay there a few days, but as we were late leaving Tangiers, Joaquin wanted to get moving, having arranged to meet his old friends Enrique and Conchita Arrias in Ibiza. The wind had dropped considerably, so we left and sailed north. The coast from Gibraltar to the Costa Brava is all dark grey sand, very sad looking, passing Torremolinos, Malaga, Murcia and finally arriving in Mojacar.

The Arrias's arrived a few hours later, and we all spent the night dancing in the local *feria*, an annual event lasting a week. So noisy but fun, one night was enough! We all decided to sail on the next day to the Mar Menor, passing the naval port of Cartagena, where as a young lieutenant in the Spanish navy, Joaquin, being a Cervera, was invited on board a US cruiser. An old tradition dating back to when his great uncle, Admiral Don Pascual Cervera y Topete refused to surrender to the American fleet during the battle of Santiago de Cuba in the Spanish American War. On July 3rd 1898, he strapped on his sword and brought his war-torn ships out of harbour to attack the Americans. Naturally all were blown to pieces, but recognizing the heroic resistance, the Americans picked up Don Juan out of the drink and piped him on board with full honours for his bravery. A plaque in his memory is still today at Annapolis, the US Naval Academy, and since his death, an active vessel in the Spanish fleet has always borne the name Almirante Cervera.

Joaquin was offered a drink on the bridge, and replied, 'A gin and tonic, please, sir.'

'Sorry, Lieutenant Cervera, our ships are dry.'

Joaquin said to himself, 'Never again will I bother with the yanks and their damn traditions.'

Early evening we rounded the Cabo de Palos, and sailed into the Mar Menor, inland sea. It was just being developed, and the new harbour not yet finished, so we had to navigate the channel, police and customs. As we stopped for these along a temporary berth, I wondered at the time why Emilio was so nervous. He looked like he was about to start peeing in his pants.

As there was nowhere to tie up, we all had a swim inside what was going to be the harbour and continued across this most amazing waterway to the far side. The Murcia airport was very close and Jacqueline decided she had had enough and wanted to leave to get back to Paris, and Juaca too wished to get back to Maria Luisa, his wife. So Joaquin saw a pontoon in the distance and headed for it.

Suddenly I saw bathers in the water very close by, walking in the sea, but we were too late, Marigalante II hit the bottom and came to a halt. The sea-bed was a mass of weed, large fronds of it waving in the current. I offered to dive with my snorkel and check out the propellers. They were fine, so Joaquin relaxed. We all laughed and wondered how we were going to move. 'No problem, tomorrow is another day.' Out came the whisky, while Juaca went ashore and found out about flights.

Jacqueline was very naughty and had been flirting like mad with both Santi and Juaca, all fun and games; and Anichi with her great sense of humour, took it very well. I was pissed off though, as Jacqueline used to come and use our bathroom, slinking through our cabin in her sexy walk, just at siesta time. She had said earlier, 'Ha! Ha! You invite me on the boat, I will ruin your honeymoon!' She was a bitch but great fun. We were always having rows, I was very glad that she was leaving the next day.

We had the most fabulous fish dinner in the restaurant, and very early next morning, all the men got up to see Jacqueline off. Phew! *Au revoir*. What a relief. Emilio and I spent our morning slashing the seaweed, and pulled the hull off the bottom using the dinghy. Out to the sea proper and we sailed north heading for the fishing village Altea, stopping for lunch at Benidorm, a huge ugly tourist town, just full of cheap high-rises. As we sailed into the bay, we nearly got caught in a thick cable they were using for a kind of tourist attraction. Joaquin had not seen it and we all yelled, 'Stop! Stop! Go in reverse!' He was very cross, and as we sat down to lunch, he went below to have an early siesta. He never had set times, and just did what he wanted, when he felt like it. He was such an amazing character and had a wonderful physique and presence; everyone adored him, males and females, so he used to get away with murder.

Terribly boring coastline, grey beaches, and flower farms, acres of plastic, and built up in every direction, but now the sea was very calm, so out came the backgammon to while away the time. We arrived at Altea early evening; it used to be a very pretty fishing village, but now ruined by monstrosities and packed with Spanish tourists. At dinner at the yacht club, there was no sign of the Arrias's, we were getting worried by then. We found out later, he had been sick and had to go to hospital, with an infection of herpes!

Next day at dawn we sailed for Mallorca, leaving Ibiza to starboard. Joaquin wanted to leave this island until last. It was a glorious day with a flat sea, flying fish and dolphins galore playing in our wash, and racing us in the bow stream. Joaquin had radioed ahead to the harbour master in Palma asking for a berth, and told him our time of arrival. He was an incredible navigator, and always arrived at a point exactly when he said he would. Coming into the harbour was very exciting, masses of yachts and two new yacht clubs built since my early days in the '60s; the cathedral loomed high on the horizon over the town. We found our berth, very tight, so Joaquin had to reverse into the space. He was so calm, while Emilio panicked. He turned around with his back to the wheel and manoeuvred the gears, so Marigalante II just slipped between the two yachts on either side within inches. People on the quay stared with their mouths open. In later years, each time he did this, I used to say, 'Every time you reverse like this I fall in love with you again!'

Waiting for us on the quay were Josele and Clemencia, who had come to join the cruise. A nephew and niece of Joaquin's, he was his sister Anna's son and brother to Anichi, married to Clemencia, Maria Luisa's daughter. Not allowed in the Bible! In Spain no one cared. A delightful couple and both very intelligent.

We spent two days of shopping and loading fuel and chatting up old friends of Joaquin's in the yacht club. One night coming on board, I smelt something odd and went down to the engine room, which was accessed from the stern between the guest cabins; to my horror found a huge lamp that was lit and upside down on a mat. It was used by Emilio to catch calamares – squid. The engine room was filthy, engines covered with oil; I groaned and turned off the lamp quickly. If it had burnt all night, the mat would have caught fire.

I said nothing to Joaquin but ripped through Emilio the next day. Of course, he had been fishing over the side, seen us returning, and in a panic left the lamp in the engine room. He was a very charming fellow, but so disorganized and dirty; his galley was literally a horror of mess. How none of us got food poisoning was a miracle.

One particular morning Joaquin wanted to go to town, and Santi and I joined him. Buying fruit, Joaquin took over and decided to argue with the shop attendant if certain melons were ripe or not. Santi and I were being treated as basket holders when my Irish temper boiled over, I said. 'Joaquin! Stop it!' and swung the basket at the back of his head, shouting, 'Buying fruit is a female job, I won't accept being treated as a slave, having wined and dined the whole of Paris. Go back to Marigalante II and get Emilio to clean the engine room and his galley!' I walked out of the shop seething with rage and left the two men to finish.

Back on board nothing was said, but he never went shopping again with me in tow. I laughed to myself remembering advice from my mother years earlier: hit them once over the head, and you won't have anymore trouble!

Joaquin got away lightly with the shopping basket. Thinking back to my marriage with Jacques, I remember one evening when he was being particularly foul, I swiped him with a frying pan as he walked down the back corridor.

Enrique and Conchita finally arrived and we heard all the explanations of the herpes, we giggled as we knew it was a sexually transmitted infection; dear Conchita, very naïve, could not think why we were laughing.

They decided to stay in Palma while we were itching to move on; I was dying to see the far side of the island but Joaquin wanted to go first to Cabrera, a tiny island to the south east. No one was allowed there as it was a military base, but having served in the navy, Joaquin obtained a special pass. A rocky coastline, gorgeous sea but not much else, until we rounded a headland; there stretching in front of us was a narrow entrance into a fjord-like bay, literally huge, sheer cliffs on either side and a tiny military base at the very end. To our surprise there was another yacht anchored in the middle.

'Hmm!' said Joaquin. 'This is the king's boat, Fortuna.'

Sure enough the speedboat we had all gossiped about, The Cigarette, a present from the USA, was lying along side. We discreetly dropped anchor some distance away from them, and were all naturally curious to know who was on board, as there was a great deal of activity. The three *infantas*: Felipe, Elena, and Cristina, and other children, his friends and security.

We sent Emilio with the dinghy to get our fresh bread from the military. We were not allowed ashore, but there was nothing to see or do anyway. Swimming and snorkelling; not even any wind for the windsurfs. I had two on board and loved this new sport. Even Juan Carlos had sailed before dawn. This was the island, where any wild or exotic animals being imported into Spain, spent three months of quarantine.

We all decided to leave the next day for Ibiza, the centre of crazy happenings and home to many friends, both Joaquin's and mine from Paris. It took us four hours to cross between the islands, as we cruised down her east coast looking for a good anchorage to stop, swim and lunch. We found the most delightful bay, with a very narrow entrance; Joaquin was quite mad and took Marigalante II right into it. People swimming, a huge rock in the middle and he just twisted the wheel and his engines and dropped anchor in the middle of them. The swimmers were terrified when they looked up at the hull, he cut the engines and grinned down at them, saying, 'No problem, come and sit on the stern.' We had what you call 'an admiral's walk', a wooden platform where one could sit with a drop-down ladder to get into the sea, and offered great protection from the propellers.

After such an early start, it was heaven to dive off the deck, swim to the white sandy beach and chill out, despite the packed tourists staring at us. The pine trees were full of cicadas making so much noise in the heat, you could hardly hear yourself speak. After a good lunch, for which Emilio produced his calamares, and a long siesta, we upped anchor and left for Ibiza, the capital of this lovely island. Joaquin was very worried about getting a berth as the port was packed, but he was amazed to find the main quay empty, and the captain of the port signalling to him to tie up in the middle of it. As soon as we were moored, he went ashore to the office and asked why we had such an honour.

'Sir,' he replied. 'HM Don Juan Carlos is arriving any minute now, for security we had to empty the quay of other yachts but His Majesty asked especially if you, Don Joaquin, would agree to be alongside him. Apparently he has a great interest to see your new boat.'

Joaquin was delighted, of course, and curious to know why the young king wanted to know about the Marigalante II. The Fortuna tied up next to us an hour later, gangplank down, and the family milling around. Discreetly we were having a drink and watching the going's on. Emilio and I unloaded my Vespa "Pegasus" onto the quay and fixed on my donkey baskets, ready for the shopping next day. Juan Carlos came ashore and I just said, 'Hello.' What else can you do in shorts and a t-shirt?

'Could I come and see Don Joaquin tomorrow at midday, as now we have to go to dinner?' he asked very politely.

'We would be delighted,' I replied, grinning. He obviously knew I was Joaquin's wife and all the details.

'Where are you going with your Vespa?' he continued.

'I'm just warming her up, as she has not been used for sometime, tomorrow is the shopping day. Do you remember Estoril, some years ago, when we partied together with the Santo Spirito boys and Bernardo and Georgio D'Aurey Pinheiro?'

He was very surprised, and said yes, he did, that was why he recognised me. True or not, he was very charming and much better looking than when he was a young teenager.

Clemencia went ashore to check out the bars where everyone met in the evenings; the *Mono Desnudo* was the most famously debauched; we got to know the owner Michael Whaley and his two brothers years later when they came to Tarifa to build a hotel. Clemencia was chatting up friends from Madrid.

'Where have you come from?' asked one.

'Marbella and Sotogrande.'

'Oh! La! La! That is Lourdes in comparison with here!'

She came back to the boat, and laughing told us what this guy had said to her and said she was high on the smell of hashish walking down the quay where the bars were!

Santi in the meantime was below decks with the binoculars ogling the girls on other boats, who were naked washing down their decks, displaying all the red bums of their friends just arrived a few days earlier from Madrid, obviously not used to sunbathing in the nude. We protected the royal family and the *infantas* from seeing all this, and we had frogmen swimming under our two boats as added security.

We were all tired, so planned dinner on board. I went down to our bathroom, where, sitting on our loo, I had a direct view through the porthole to a cabin of the Fortuna as the two daughters were being put to bed. That was the worst of being on a boat, the moorings were so close, one was always cheek to jowl with one's neighbours. Why the king wanted to be next to us I don't know. It was lovely though not to have anyone on the other side.

The next morning I went off shopping, and found three or four harbour police on the quay very near Marigalante II on my return. No sign of Emilio, so I went on board to find him. There was Joaquin standing to attention, very shy, and the king talking to him about the technicalities of building a fibreglass hull. I'll never forget the green t-shirt I was wearing, emblazoned with 'I am a virgin!' across the front. I saw the atmosphere was tense, and said to them both, 'Why don't you have a drink? Sir, can I get you a gin and tonic?'

He grinned and replied, 'Thank you, Vicky, I would love one.'

Joaquin could not believe his ears and frowned at me, but relaxed immediately, while I winked at Emilio, and told him to get the ice, and then get the shopping on board.

Joaquin was very much the naval officer, had been brought up in the navy, and suffered the consequences. While I had known Juan Carlos when he was in exile as a teenager. If you cannot be natural in Ibiza, then there is no hope.

When he left, Joaquin said to me, 'You cannot ask the king if he'd like a drink!'

'Why not? Immediately you both relaxed. You don't have to stand on protocol when you are on holiday.'

The next day we slowly drew up the anchor and left the port of Ibiza for the island of Espalmador to the south, only an hour but we had to navigate between the reefs to find the famous beach, where all the naked hippies were hanging out.

The most beautiful white sandy cove, the water was so clear, one could see the bottom at four metres; sadly already full of beer bottles and other rubbish. Such a shame the human race is so sloppy, and back then there was no idea of protecting the environment.

During lunch, Santi again was glued to my binoculars, watching the goings-on aboard the next yachts; eventually Anichi grew cross, and told him to shut up and stop looking at the red tits and bums!

After a good siesta, we all climbed into the dinghy and went ashore, to walk on the beach. Joaquin and I went to the left, the others to the right; after five minutes Joaquin said, 'Come on, Vicky, let's strip off,' which we did and fooled around in the little bays on the most glorious sand and clear sea. What a change from the mainland and her grey, dirty beaches. After a while we walked on, both starkers and to our horror met the Minister of the Interior walking towards us.

Holy Moses! Joaquin, who knew him well, was horribly embarrassed, as I whispered to him, 'Pay no attention, because if you put on your trunks, it will look worse!' We passed him, smiling like idiots, then met him the next day in Ibiza, and pretended nothing had happened.

We slept in the bay of Espalmador, on a fabulous night, no wind and the sea totally translucent; come midnight we all swam naked in this glorious sea, and finally the nieces and nephews relaxed, laughing their heads off.

Next day we went and discovered the actual island of Formentera, nothing very special, but a charming little town and a good harbour. A very hippy bunch of tourists who seemed to spend their time bicycling or smoking hash. We spent a lovely few days there, between swimming and snorkelling and exploring the fish bistros on the island, until Joaquin decided it was time to move and make our way back to Marbella. This time he left very early, telling us all to stay in bed; we actually headed straight for Motril on the mainland, where we had a rendezvous with my darling cousins, Hugh and Sheila, and their two little girls Catherine and Louise.

Joaquin had arranged for his driver to pick them up and bring them north to Motril to meet us. Arriving very late in the port, there they were looking very worried that they had missed us. Great reunion, and they were thrilled to join us; Josele and Clemencia left to catch a flight back to Madrid, whilst Emilio and I changed the sheets in the guest cabin quickly.

In the two days in Motril, recharging our batteries, Sheila, a redhead, typically Irish with freckles, caught a nasty sunstroke. She was sweating hot and cold for two days with a high temperature; we all insisted she stayed in bed. Not very easy on a boat. Hugh, very much the British naval officer, was delightfully sympathetic, and yacked non-stop to Joaquin about the technicalities of the instruments that he had installed on the bridge.

The next stop was back to Puerto Banus. This time Joaquin brought the boat straight up to the quay in the middle, bang up to Pepe's fish restaurant. The mass of people on the quay were dumbstruck as he stopped her within inches of the tarmac, idling the engines; he leant over the upper bridge and talked to his friends nearby. We were given a berth, and planned to stay there a few days. After the decks were washed, we all changed and made the salon shipshape. I arranged for Emilio to cook the two little girls supper and plug in the television for them, telling them we were having dinner at Pepe's. We had just started our meal, when to our surprise, Catherine and Louise came running to our table, crying.

'Vicky! Emilio and Dominguin are drinking and dancing in the salon with the music full on, and not getting our supper!'

Joaquin was furious and stormed off to read the riot act. We sat the girls down and ordered a meal for them. When Joaquin came back he was very puzzled by the sailors' behaviour, and muttered that something was up.

Puerto Banus was then packed with tourists, locals and foreigners, boutiques, bars, restaurants all along the quay. Behind them, were apartments all built like an Andalucian village, higgledy-piggledy with iron balustrades and funny windows, painted white. It was delightful, despite the Ibizcencos saying it was Lourdes! The bars and nightclubs were pumping. Santi and Anichi took Hugh and Sheila to Menchu's, the hot spot of the moment, while Joaquin and I took the girls to bed, and saw no sign of the sailors.

Joaquin was woken up early by the harbour police, armed with a search warrant. Naturally he told them who he was, and that the yacht belonged to him. They were embarrassed, but told him that Emilio had 17 kilogrammes of marijuana on board during the whole cruise and he had passed it on to his contact the previous evening. We were all stupefied and Joaquin more so, shuddering at the thought of being caught in Ibiza or Motril, where he was less well known. Anichi then remembered the guy on a bicycle with a package in Tangiers, and obviously they were celebrating the evening before, when they handed over their goods! We found out that Emilio and Dominguin had chewed off a whole corner of the block. It was apparently the real McCoy, hard, pure marijuana, and obviously the police had caught the fellow who had picked it up.

Joaquin made it clear that Marbella was not his home port, and it was better that the police interrogated Emilio in Algeciras, promising not to allow him ashore until we got there.

To this day I think it was a put-up job by the police, as the fellow in Tangiers turned out to be an ex-policeman and the whole thing stank of suspicion, very weird. Back in Algeciras, all Joaquin's brothers pushed him to sack Emilio, an ideal opportunity as he was so sloppy and dirty, but he had been in Joaquin's employment since he was 18, and they adored fishing together.

Everyone decamped to their homes after a tearful farewell and hugs all round. I took Hugh and his family back to El Molino, as my other cousin David Craig and his wife, Jane, were arriving soon. Even if I had thought to go to Las Pinas, Joaquin's farm, we would not have fitted in, as it only had four bedrooms. I always said I would not give up my home, especially after the struggle with Jacques.

Three to four days later, I answered the phone at El Molino, to hear Emilio's wife, Luisa crying her head off. Emilio had been taken to Madrid by the police. Poor woman, I tried to calm her, but there was not much I could do knowing Joaquin had gone to a board meeting in Jerez de la Frontera for his bodega Real Tesoro, and would not be back until evening. I rang his brother Jose Maria and told him what had happened. With his contacts in Madrid he was able to talk to the chief inspector. They had Emilio for a few days but as there was no proof that he had bought the marijuana, he was released and he came home. I took one look at him and saw the bruises and cuts on his face.

'Joaquin, look at Emilio. He has been beaten up badly by the police.'

'Rubbish, our police don't beat up people,' he replied.

I was amazed. He was so naive and adorable, he just could not think badly of anyone.

# 13. El Rocio

Being married to Joaquin was as thrilling and fulfilling as marriage to Jacques had been disastrous. As our affair had intensified it was obvious we shared not only a sense of humour but many mutual interests and now we were married we had a ball.

We could not help but thrive in each other's company, but prior to our wedding the illicit times were tempered with guilt, as Joaquin loved Maria Rosa dearly.

We had discovered our mutual love of the Spanish Rocio and the *ferias* shortly after we met, and our fun times in these had given us ample opportunity to spend time with each other.

Whilst every Andalucian city, town and village has its own pilgrimages for its patron saint, virgin or other much-loved local figure, the El Rocío pilgrimage has cult status. It is the most famous, important and colourful in the region attracting huge numbers from across all Spain and beyond.

This tradition dates back to the 13th century, when a hunter from the village of Villamanrique discovered a statue of the Virgin Mary in a tree trunk in the Doñana park. A chapel was built where the tree stood, and it became a place of pilgrimage. Devotion to this particular version of the Virgin was initially a local affair but by the 17th century, *hermandades* (brotherhoods) were making the trip from nearby towns at Pentecost; by the 19th century, they came from Huelva, Cadiz and Seville, on a journey taking up to four days. Over the next century, the cult of the Virgen del Rocio became more and more widespread.

It always takes place over the weekend of Whitsun, the seventh weekend after Easter, and for many years it was an annual highlight for Joaquin and I. The village of El Rocio is tiny with sandy streets and the church, and rows of little white houses that were occupied only for this amazing unique weekend once a year.

Before we were married El Rocio provided the perfect opportunity for Joaquin and I to spend time together as Maria Rosa was not overly keen on the festivities; they were joyous, raucous times, with loved ones, friends and family alike. One of my favoured memories of our early Rocios was in 1973, the first year Joaquin dressed properly and looked extraordinary in his *traje corto* and *sombrero ancho*, either grey or brown, but as he was so tall, none of the Spanish *zajones* (chaps) were long enough.

The first night is always chaos, a mad mayhem of everyone looking for a bed and a place to dump their clothes and a typical scrabble for the loo. The courtyards behind the houses were especially for the horses, stacked high with alfalfa (lucern); and a way out for them to the back streets, which were all sand, and the little terrace in front was very quickly heaving with friends and neighbours.

In 1973, there were no, or at least very few, shops in the village. Everyone had to bring all their goods and chattels with them, and horses and wagons with bullocks, flamenco dancers and gypsies and gentlemen were streaming in from every direction. People bring mattresses and bed down anywhere they can. There are impromptu parties, open-air masses, horse races and competitions between the *hermandades*. And lots of singing and dancing, at all hours of the day and night, to the beat of the famous Rocio drums.

Next morning, those that were riding, had to hurry back to the Palacio Doñana and find their mounts where we had left them the day before, a good 25km from the village. Refreshed and clean, we started the final leg. My mare Fabiola was in fine fettle, and I was glad, in a way, that Joaquin had decided not to come. He would not admit it, but I could see the night before had been too much for him. He had not ridden that distance in all his life and just was not fit, plus he may have had a guilty conscience about leaving his wife alone all day, of course!

As we returned to the village on horseback, we could hear the music and the drums. Our horses pricked up their ears, and recharged their batteries with excitement, and good old Hortensia (our lovely cart horse, a roan Breton mare) snorted and pulled at her traces, rocking the carriage so her passengers yelled, and we arrived at the village with a great aplomb. We stopped outside the Hermita for those who wished to pay their first respects and prayers to the Virgen del Rocio; the crowds were so dense no one could get near the entrance, and this was only Friday evening.

Arriving in front of our little house, we were greeted by those who had come by car, or like Joaquin stayed the day to recuperate, and out came the containers of jerez and the party started again, until yours truly drew a line and insisted that we left our poor animals to rest. We rode the horses and led Hortensia to the back courtyard, where the grooms took over and led each one to their stables; never have I seen 12 animals so relieved of their saddles and tack, comfortable straw bed and buckets of oats. I love my animals so much, and those of my friends, they come first, but there are some ghastly horror stories about those that are abused at the Rocio.

All traffic in the village of El Rocio is on four legs. Prancing stallions with uncut manes and braided tails, four-in-hand harnessed mules and the teams of mighty oxen, which the Rocieros use to haul their Madonnas past the scalloped entrance of the church to receive the Virgin's blessing.

The procession of the Madonnas begins on Saturday morning and lasts until late at night. The wagons that carry the Madonnas are called *sin pecados* and are elaborately worked in silver and gold, mobile altar pieces brought from the churches of the brotherhoods. One by one these *hermandades* make their way to the church of El Rocio. The senior members of each brotherhood riding ahead in lines four abreast, followed by their town's *sin pecado*, attended by a surging throng of supporters, clapping, chanting and beating drums.

The traditions and superstitions that surround the legend of the discovery of the Virgin Mary statue are endless, and started well before Christopher Colombus. When he arrived at Cadiz, ready to make sail with his four schooners, he was told, 'Sir, we cannot sail now, it is El Rocio.'

'What difference does that make it?' he replied.

'Well, the crew only come back tomorrow, then they will need four days to recuperate.'

Now we know full well, what he meant.

Every seven years, they hold another pilgrimage, called the little Rocio, in mid-August. The heat is stifling, so they ride at night, and take the Virgin from her Ermita, and the men carry guns and shoot blanks (thank goodness) all around her, to leave her for a year in the main church in the local town of Almonte. I always wanted to do this, as it is very informal and relaxed, but as August was always time for the boat and the Tarifa beach, and our many house guests, one simply never got around to it.

Writing this gives me the buzz up my back, the passion and the memories are just so sentimental and so moving, a totally unique experience. And everyone who came, Catholic, Protestant, even Muslim were under the spell of the Virgin. I am not religious, I personally despise the dogmas of the church and set religions, but the colour and gaiety and the passion of the people for their Virgins, and especially the Virgen del Rocio and our black one in Tarifa, where Joaquin and I got married, have always held an enormous gut-wrenching sentiment. This is inevitably all tied up by my adoration of Joaquin and the love of being together.

For the first few years of our marriage we continued our trips to El Rocio, continuing to enjoy both the customs and traditions as well as the opportunities for revelry with our friends.

In 1978 I had managed to have a *traje corto* made for Joaquin and *zajones* that were the correct length. I had also bought him a very gentle grey gelding; big fellow and strong. This year Joaquin invited Paul and Leonora Saurel, he was a young but very clever American banker, and she was from a big El Salvadorean family, who had been great friends and relations to Juaca, Maria Luisa's husband. Leonora subsequently became the El Salvadorean ambassador to the United Nations.

On my side I invited Comte Michel de Ganay and his new, very pretty Danish wife, Birgitta. He was a French stock broker and lived between Paris and Buenos Aires, Argentina; the family owned land south of Sevilla on the Guadalquivir; simple for them, a groom rode their horses to Sanlucar, and met up with us once we crossed to the Coto Doñana. This is a huge area of land that runs between the Guadalquivir, the beach and the province of Huelva. Sand dunes, marshes, pine trees and wild game. The Palacio Doñana, our halfway stop-off, used to belong to the Gonzalez Byass family, but had since been sold to the World Wildlife Fund and is now a sanctuary and a national park. Only because the pilgrimage of El Rocio had for hundreds of years passed through the Coto Doñana, the way was opened up for the *hermandades*.

I had arranged this year, to rent for all of us a newly built house away from the village centre, as our old house had been booked since the previous year at a phenomenal price and the village had doubled in size. I could smell this was the beginning of the end.

Sandra van Heel was a friend of all of us, who lived in Portugal and travelled non-stop, designing clothes and holding dress shows; all the young nieces were roped into modelling them. She brought a charming Portuguese with her, and an old friend from Sotogrande, Kim Cabrita Vinas, mad as a fruit cake, but great fun!

As we were mounting our horses on the beach, Hortensia with the carriage had gone on ahead, as the first sand dunes were very heavy going, I heard a couple of locals, who were watching me gently kick Fabiola's legs forwards, in order for me to mount her easily. When you are wearing *zajones*, a 17-hand mare and a Spanish saddle, it is not an easy feat. They were saying, watch this woman, she is the only one who knows how to ride properly. I felt very chuffed, but as I was still riding in the Rocio in a *traje corto*, I needed more teasing to get me into a flamenco dress. It felt so stupid to ride astride in a dress. Realizing though, now I was Joaquin's wife and a Spaniard, I would have to change and follow in their traditions.

Michel and Birgitta were having a ball, and both rode beautifully, while Paul and Leonora somehow looked out of place. They had no sense of the ridiculous, so could not relax, and took the whole thing too seriously. One really has to be mad, fun, wild and a bit of a boozer to enjoy the Rocio, leaving behind board meetings and accounts for another day.

Once in the pine trees, each brotherhood had a time at the little house in the centre, we unharnessed Hortensia and gave her a bowl of oats, while Joaquin, now slightly pissed, set up the baptism ceremony. All those who had never been before were baptised with whatever muck we could find, horses' pee, jerez, slugs of gin, you name it. Crossing the equator was nothing compared to your first Rocio baptism. Everyone drank more jerez and laughed at the various reactions.

On our way through the pines, when the men all went off hunting wild boar and an occasional red deer, one of the fellows from Madrid rode straight into a pine tree. Was he a mess? He came out bleeding and shocked. I jumped off and helped clean him up with whatever we had. As usual, exhausted we arrived at the Palacio, and were ferried on to our new house in the village, leaving the horses and grooms to camp. It was a little house but with much better plumbing and a kitchen fitted out. In previous years everyone washed in the well and cooked over a wood stove!

Poor old Sandra got sick and stayed in bed. We all had breakfast at different times, depending on our hangovers but laughed our heads off when we heard young Mariano, a nephew of Joaquin, buttered his arms instead of his toast, staring at Birgitta, admiring her blonde model looks, with his mouth open.

We rode around the village, looking for the Gonzalez's, the eldest brother a great friend of Joaquin's, Sir Manuel Gonzalez Gordon, the only Spaniard knighted by the Queen. Their Tio Pepe was the most popular sherry in England for years. The family was originally Scottish. He was the person, who adorably leant Dorine and I his room, on our first pilgrimage, where we slept head to toe, and woke to the Rocio drums under the window, with terrible hangovers. No one had advised us not to mix jerez with whisky and red wine. We weren't quite sure which side of hell we were on!

The jerez in Spain came straight from the bodegas untreated, no additives, and if one drank it, without mixing it with other alcohol, one could drink it all day without a headache. Friends wanted to import it to their home countries, but without the additives, it did not travel well.

1979 really was the beginning of the end; we could not find a house, it was becoming impossible. We got very fed up and told dear Fernando, our lorry driver, that we would rent his lorry and pay him for his time; adding to it three tents and all the paraphernalia. We sent him on ahead to find a quiet place on the outskirts of the village, no mobiles in those days, so communication was impossible. Hugh and Sheila were on holiday in Portugal, and had planned it so they could join us. She was dying to ride Furia, a lovely spirited mare; like myself she adored horses and everything that went with them. I dressed her up in my spare *zajones* and jacket, and poured jerez down her throat. The only thing that did not suit her at all was the *sombrero ancho*. 'Bad luck, leave it, look at me in a flamenco dress. Once one is used to it, it is no problem.'

She changed into a skirt laughing, saying, 'Never would I imagine riding in a skirt!'

We left Joaquin reading his newspaper, and with Anichi and Santi we took Sheila from one *caseta* to another; having a ball, pissed as a newt with the jerez. They had left their car outside the village and had booked a room at Matalascañas, which in the '70s was easily accessible. A beach resort just 25km south of the El Rocio, beginning to develop; now a horror of German tourists and high risers.

1980 was my last trip to El Rocio. A catastrophe, it pissed with rain from day one, but at least the rain provided some humour. Carlos Peman, a great friend from Seville, arrived already halfway gone, and passed out on a bale of hay in the stables. It was raining so hard the whole yard was deep in water, and Andy Lacey, a mad American friend with a special sense of humour, gave the bale a kick and sent poor Carlos floating slowly down the stables to the horses' entrance and onto the street. Surprisingly, he survived the night, and reappeared for breakfast looking very white and sour.

Later, sitting quietly on our horses outside a friend's house, a local woman came pushing past, grabbed my mare by the bridle and jerked her head roughly to the side, muttering something like, 'Get out of my way.' And this was the third day!

Horrified, I replied, 'Señora, you come here to see the pageantry, the horses, bullocks and wagons, beautiful people dressed in your local costumes; why do you want to be rude and hurt the faithful horse, that has brought us here?' I vowed from that day on, I would not return. So be it.

The village had doubled in size, roads were built, supermarkets opened, tarmac road to the beach and buses galore brought in the tourists. *Basta*, it was over. When we think, our friends before us slept on the ground and washed with buckets of water from the wells. Our little house was knocked down and a three-storey was built with flats in its place. I have heard from friends that the crowds now are so tremendous, one cannot ride out on the streets, and Sunday one cannot accompany the Virgin anymore on horseback. So sad that the lovely traditions of Andalucia, and the world, are getting ruined by the masses, the hype, advertising, and the creation of easy access. No fete has ever been so special and so deeply moving as the Rocio. Anyone who has done the pilgrimage, from wherever, Sevilla with Triana, Huelva, Jerez de la Frontera, Sanlucar de Barrameda, or even Madrid, will have unforgettable memories. Such is life and so it goes on. We were very lucky to have seen it, as it was.

# 14. Ferias of Jerez and Seville

Aside from the traditions, colour, customs and emotions, the horses played an enormous role in my love of El Rocio, and inevitably horses became a big part of my life in Spain with Joaquin, breeding and competing.

In early May, annually sandwiched between the Feria de Sevilla and El Rocio, we attended the Feria de Jerez de la Frontera, also known as Feria del Caballo (Horse Fair). I always took my best horses, most memorably in 1978. El Mansour was superb, a young Arab yearling who was a flighty, naughty youngster and spent his time on his back legs. Our lovely chief groom, Ignacio, had a hard job controlling him. He had banged his leg against the door in our new stables and formed a *sobre hueso*, a splintered bone.

For this reason he did not win a prize, but did he show off. He walked on his hind legs non-stop, waving his forelegs and beautiful head at the crowds. He was sold that night to an Egyptian Arab breeder from Cairo. We met in the bar of the Hotel Jerez and shook hands on the deal.

The following morning, she came up to me and said, 'Sorry, Vicky, I cannot buy El Mansour, the cost of transport to Egypt is outrageous.' I was dumbstruck.

'You said once Arab breeders shook hands, that was a gentleman's agreement; and now you want to renege on our deal? I insist you must pay our price.'

Joaquin later on said, 'Vicky you cannot do this with the Arab dealers in Jerez.'

'Joaquin, if we don't do it now, they will walk over us. They think they own the world, and as we are new Arab breeders, they are totally taking the mickey out of us.'

I stuck to my guns and sent El Mansour back to his stable; two weeks later they were back with the cheque, and my baby boy left for the north of Spain, and then Cairo. A small victory but a couple of years later worse was to follow.

My young Anglo-Arab, Almirante, won first prize in Jerez, bred from his sire, Destroyer, with whom we had crossed one of our mares, Pamplenosa. The judge came up to me very privately, and said, 'Vicky, you certainly don't come to Jerez with medium bloodstock; you do not come at all, or you bring superb animals.' I felt very chuffed, but he continued seriously.

'We cannot give you the top prize, *Campeon de Campeon*, as your neighbours who are Spanish will be so jealous, as they have been breeding Anglo-Arabs for years. You and Joaquin are very new breeders, and they just won't accept it, so you know you have won, but officially I have to give you the Reserve Champion.'

He was so charming, I had no other choice but to accept his decision.

I told Joaquin all what he had said, but he was delighted, and next day brought all his friends to see the colt, very proud of what I had achieved. To my horror, Almirante lifted his tail and shot them all with a deluge of liquid diarrhoea. The *feria* ground does not allow owners to treat their own animals, but Ignacio and I went back to the horse box, and found what was necessary. I had learnt a lot in veterinary work in the previous five years. I found out that the neighbours in the stalls next to us were so jealous, they had crunched up broken glass and fed it to the colt when no one was watching. To make matters worse, we were not allowed to move him before the *feria* ended. A horror story. We smuggled him out of the *feria* grounds at night and took the poor fellow back to his stables. I turned him out to grass and told Antonito, Ignacio's nephew, to look after him round the clock. I injected him twice a day with antibiotics.

Three to four days later, I noticed lumps of manure all over his field, 'Heh, Antonito! Don't tell me Almirante still has the diarrhoea?' I had been running around helping the politicians in the local elections that were taking place. Terrified, knowing how difficult it is to cure diarrhoea, we brought in new vets, but he went downhill very rapidly. Antonito and his girlfriend slept in the stable with him, crying his eyes out. I rushed to the big hospital and asked my doctor friends to come up with a cure, we tried everything. He was in such pain, he used to bang his head against the wall. Three days later he was dead. Can you believe it, a young healthy colt of just three years old?

We had an autopsy done in Madrid, and glass was found in his intestines. I begged Joaquin to take the bastards to court, but he replied, 'Vicky, you don't know what the local horse breeders are like and we'll never win.'

Very sadly we took his body the next day to our farm at La Zorilla, and buried him amongst the bracken, not far from the lake; reading the psalm that dedicates the love to animals, and painted a memorial on a big stone: 'Almirante. Never to be forgotten.'

Joaquin thought I was quite mad, but that wee fellow as a baby used to follow me around the stables, even leaving his mother to do so. Damn it, there is nothing worse than losing a baby that you have brought up. Antonito and I, plus the lorry driver and Antonio Lopez, our tractor driver, stopped off at our local bar, El Frenazo, and seriously had a drink, we were all so upset.

At least some good came of the sorry episode. A few months later, Antonito's girlfriend announced she was pregnant and they were going to get married; the result of three nights in the stables! We did what we could, and had the wedding in the garage, hung bracken on to the beams and ferns in the windows. It poured with rain and we were soaked. They absolutely wanted their wedding photos taken in the house, so Joaquin and I went through deluging rain to satisfy the young couple's wishes.

La Feria de Sevilla took place every April and in 1979 I had decided to take Rociera, filly of Fabiola, who had been trained to the Spanish dressage. A dark grey and a beautiful animal, typical Anglo-Arab as her sire was pure Arab and Fabiola had three-quarters thoroughbred. We stabled them that year at the military stables, but Ignacio and his nephew Antonio had to ride them quite a distance in the mornings to meet us at the yacht club, and we were in the saddle until nearly dark. This was the new *feria* ground, it was a square of eight parallel streets criss-crossed with *casetas*, little tents for each family or club. The actual streets were paved but full of horse shit and pee, very slippery, and to get from one *caseta* to another to find one's friends was a nightmare, negotiating traffic jams of horse carriages, some six in hand. I watched the coachman of the Domecq's with an eight-in-hand manoeuvre his horses with such dexterity between other carriages coming in the opposite direction. I felt quite sick watching him with awe.

The main big *caseta* was the Aeroclub, where everyone met; it was the oldest club and had had a place in the *feria* for hundreds of years. The women were all dancing flamenco and bottles of jerez were consumed in their thousands. In theory we were not allowed with our horses on the sandy pavement between the actual roads and the *casetas*. Of course we paid no attention and rode right up to the fence where our friends, delighted to see us, brought out little glasses of jerez in a bronze container. It was amazing the amount one could drink without falling off. Rociera was very highly spirited and to control her in these crowds was not easy. Joaquin's horse, Platero, the one I bought for him, another grey, was very solid and tranquil. Ignacio, who had followed us on foot with his nephew, immediately sussed out the situation and asked Joaquin if he would like to go into the Aeroclub. Relieved without losing face, he dismounted and went to join his friends, while Ignacio and I had some fun showing off our dressage skills and dancing our horses on the sandy pavement.

I had great fun and went from one *caseta* to another as I knew all the Spaniards, and was invited to other clubs, Domecq's and Gonzalez's, Terry's and Sandeman's. There are no public *casetas*, except miles to the north of the *feria* ground next to the swings and roundabouts, where none of us went. I felt so very sorry for the foreigners who did not understand this, and watched them wandering around looking lost, as at each *caseta* they were turned away by the guards at the entrance.

Come 5.00 pm the streets began to empty as the carriages made their way to the bullring on the other side of the river in the old town. A huge traffic jam, intermingled with horses, blocking off the bridges. Gone were the days when the carriages dominated the road and the entrance to the ring, when the coachmen had all the space to show off their magnificent horses. Today to turn a six in hand with packed traffic on either side was no joke.

Joaquin and I were not passionate about the bullfights, and stayed on at the *feria* until fairly late. Coming back to Marigalante II, moored by the riverside, for a quick siesta, it was not long before we heard, 'Vicky, we're here. Where are the *copitas*? Open up the bar.' Exhausted we struggled to get ready and start again.

Everyone loved to come to the boat as a first meeting place, how Emilio and I coped, I don't know. We passed dirty glasses back through the windows of the salon, and clean ones full of whisky or whatever, out the other side, as slowly Marigalante II sank deeper and deeper into the Guadalquivir. Around midnight, if we were lucky, we had dinner somewhere or in the yacht club and then made our way to the *caseta* that was hosting a flamenco that night; or straight back to the Aeroclub, where gypsies played flamenco every night; *sevillanas*, *rocieras* or *bullerias*.

The flamenco was known to be the music of the dawn, and the real *cante jondo*, deep song, started at around 5.00 am and lasted until it was light. Joaquin was a great aficionado, and knew many of the singers, especially Lola Flores. He had contracted her out to various big dinners he had given in Madrid, before my time. He told me once she had a fight with her mother, scratching each others' eyes out, and he had to throw them out of the apartment. Maria Rosa was very upset apparently, but as Joaquin said, 'They're gypsies through and through, and you cannot expect them to behave like ladies!' Lola Flores was a real character and entertainer who became very famous.

To our horror next morning, we had a phone call via the yacht club from Ignacio, saying that Rociera was very sick. He thought it was equine flu, as many of the military horses were streaming at the nostrils. Together with a friend who was a vet, we rushed to the stables, and there she was looking very much the worse for wear; temperature very high, breathing with difficulty, and not eating. Our friend said it was the flu, and an epidemic had broken out in Pineda, the equestrian centre. 'Don't move her, but send your other horses home immediately, before they are all in quarantine.' Which we did; the *feria* was ruined for us there and then.

Ignacio was marvellous, he sent his nephew back in the lorry to Las Pilas with the other horses, and he stayed to nurse Rociera through the worst. Poor bugger, he did not sleep for days, and when he did, it was beside her in the stable. The antibiotics worked, thank goodness, and a week later she was home.

For the Feria de Sevilla in 1980 we invited S.A. Moulay Ali of Morocco to come on the Marigalante II, to cruise up the Guadalquivir and spend the *feria* on board. Joaquin said, 'This is great, but how will I take him around the *feria*?' I smiled and told him not to worry. I had secretly bought a *milord*, a lovely traditional horse carriage, and trained his horse Platero to harness and a young man to drive it. I had it redone in dark blue and cream cushions and arranged transport to Sevilla.

As Moulay Ali was renowned not to be a good sailor, I picked him up in Cadiz and drove to Sanlucar de Barrameda where we boarded the boat, and navigated up the river; he was very happy and relaxed to see the Coto Doñana from the riverbanks, and to arrive in Sevilla at the Yacht Club. Joaquin was very nervous, as he knew that the next day I would be off riding Rociera and he would be with the prince on his own, despite the company of Anichi and Santi, the Marqueses of Cordoba and Anichi his wife, Joaquin's niece, and Maria Luisa.

We were all in on the secret, so the next morning, he was thrilled to see waiting at the gang plank, the *milord* with Platero and the young driver, very well dressed in a classical uniform. 'Oh! Vicky, what have you done? I don't believe it.'

I replied, 'Now you can relax and take Moulay Ali where you want, and I will accompany you.'

Platero behaved himself, and they went round the *feria* in great style, drinking jerez, which I had provided in a cool box under the seat. To Joaquin's horror, Moulay Ali was recognised not only by the press but by the Moroccans in the crowd, who stopped the carriage and started by kissing his feet and hands, and whatever else they could grab from street level; shouting and singing his praise. Joaquin was so embarrassed in front of his Spanish friends and family. He turned to Moulay Ali, and politely said you cannot allow this in the *feria* and we cannot stop and cause a traffic jam. Very quickly he took him to the Aeroclub, arranged a table discretely at the back away from the street, and organized the flamenco to come and dance for him, introducing him to all his friends.

I went on riding, visiting other *casetas* but soon went back to join them, as no one spoke French and I knew Joaquin would struggle with his English. As we were having lunch, a great chamozzle was taking place outside, and there were two Arabs on superb Arabian horses, dressed in the robes of the royal household, carrying long spears and old-fashioned muskets. Moulay Ali jumped up and told us that his youngest sister-in-law, his wife's baby sister, was also at the *feria*, and these were her horses. Why, we laughed, is she not riding them?

Lalla Amina was the only one born in exile, when her father Mohammed VI was ousted by the French. She was walking along the sandy pavement beside her horses, surrounded by ladies in waiting and a whole crowd of onlookers. She was dressed in pants and a jacket, and looked very out of place amongst the Spaniards in their beautiful flamenco dresses. We sent someone from the club to tell her that Moulay Ali was with us and to come and join us, which she did, though reluctantly leaving her horses in the parade on the street.

We learnt that she was only interested in her horses, having a husband who was either drunk or very rude, and had put her off men completely. She lived on the outskirts of Rabat, and trained her horses for all the equestrian events, including an international three-day event. We asked her back to the boat in the evening, where I can remember her behaving like a school girl, trying to push her entourage into the river; she was young and had been brought up very freely, unlike her brothers. Later, when I knew her much better, I saw the serious side to her and the capacity she had for organizing big events and shows. We became good friends during the three-day event in Rabat, and despite her rather rough exterior, she was very kind and even sent her horse box to Las Pilas, to pick up our horses that were competing.

I had a team of young riders and we were all practising in my arena, when our driver Paco came running down, saying the princess's lorry was in the port and we had to go and show their driver the way, and to translate his French. On my three-day event horse, Banana, I rushed off to help them. I jumped him over a big tree trunk on my way. Shit, he stopped dead and not taking the jump seriously, I went flying over his head, landing once more on my right shoulder and dislocated it, yet again. I had done this previously in Sotogrande, practising for a jumping competition on a double fence, which he had done perfectly and like an idiot with my adrenalin high, did it once more. He did his famous stop. I went over his head and under him; he fell on me and the fence on him. Our driver took me back to Las Pilas, in agonising pain, where the foreman made me drink two cognacs. Then the hospital said I needed an anaesthetic and could not give it to me until midnight because of the alcohol. What a bore, all my young years with dislocating my left knee and now the right shoulder.

I told the doctor he had to put it back in there and then, that I had six kids to look after and had to leave the next morning for Rabat. They produced a horrible looking contraption, and said, 'This is going to hurt.'

'Get on with it, there is no other solution.' It had happened twice before, so I knew what I was in for. They pulled my arm like mad, and snapped it back in place, one holy scream and trembling, I grinned at them, 'See, it is the only way.' I was bandaged all around my chest, and told not to move.

Somehow I managed to help load all eight horses the next morning and catch the ferry to Tangers, feeling like a right arse with all the young riders very sympathetic.

Four hours to Rabat and another one to find the Centre Hipica and their stables. Lalla Amina was there to welcome us, after a few drinks and a delicious meal in their club, straight to bed, but I felt hot and dirty wrapped up in these ridiculous bandages. Desperate to take them off, and miserable that Banana was not with me, despite his faults. I found out months later he had navicular in his forelegs, and as the pain was very bad on landing after a jump, he just stopped dead when he could. I kept him on, as I loved him dearly, as a dressage horse, and together we made the grade of kur four to music. No more jumping with him, just not worth it, either for the horse or myself. I have dislocated that shoulder at least half a dozen times since. Now in my old age can hardly move it.

The kids did very well, and came home with some prizes, and the excitement of competing in Morocco and crossing the straits with the horses on the ferry, left them with an indelible memory.

## 15. Our Stables, and the 'Peste Equina'

Away from the crowds of the Feria de Jerez and the glamour of Sevilla, our local *feria* took place in Algeciras, just when the real heat started, at the end of June. Everybody rode through the streets and there were dressage competitions in the middle of town; the daytime was a miserable disaster, but the night was heaving. The *casetas* were packed, flamenco on every street corner and they went on till dawn. I even had friends from Sevilla and Jerez, who asked to come, as they had heard it was such fun.

Year after year, Fabiola and I won the dressage, and Rociera was second. This was the Spanish high school, piaffes, flying changes, and *Passaje Español*; beautiful if your horse is trained, and you become a pair. Later I more or less gave up the Spanish high school dressage, and reverted to the classical international one. Trying an extended trot on a Spanish-trained horse and saddle is not easy, though today they have brought in classical dressage on Spanish horses.

September was always the annual *feria* of Tarifa. On the first Sunday in the month, the *cabalgata*, the calvacade, of the Virgin came out of the Ermita where we got married, and was carried on the backs of young men to the main church in Tarifa. The locals were dressed properly in their *traje cortos*, and four by four the horses followed the Virgin to the village. Spectacular and very moving.

We watched it every year, riding our horses up and down the grass verges, but were never able to join the *cabalgata*, as women were not allowed. Today apparently the custom has changed.

This back country towards the mountains was absolutely gorgeous, huge areas of fields for the cattle, and higher up all the mountains were covered with cork trees. We used to ride over them from Cuarton through the valleys and streams, and rocky paths, winding our way down the mountain. One day with a group of nieces and Sheila, we crossed a stream, and suddenly we were attacked by a nest of wasps. I yelled at the kids, to get off their ponies and strip off their t-shirts, as they were all bucking and rearing. The wasps were inside there shirts and under the bellies of the ponies. We were very lucky, and got away lightly.

Also on this mountain, I can remember coming home to El Molino, on my own, when the thick fog of the *levante* came down, and I could not see an inch in front of me. I just had to leave the reins free, and let Fabiola make her way. We were miles from the main road and had no compass. Somehow we found one of the tracks of Cuarton, and crossing the main road, somehow managed to find El Molino. Domingo, my guardian, was out of his mind, saying Don Joaquin had been there three times, desperately worried and had gone to fetch the Guardia Civil. Was he relieved when he saw Fabiola's droppings on the drive.

We moved between El Molino and Las Pilas often during the summer, depending on how many guests we had. It was lovely being back in my home, but, of course, the stables were at Las Pilas. One evening, Joaquin was in Madrid, and I was having dinner at Alambique with the Luards, Milet Delme Radcliffe and George, her latest beau, and two others. We made a bet: who would arrive first at the Ermita on horse back to get there at dawn. Typical me, I said I would beat them all. They all looked stunned, as they knew I did not have the horses at Cuarton then. I left and drove to Las Pilas, waking up Ignacio by rattling on his window. Quietly I explained the bet and asked him to get Fabiola for me.

'Señora, she is in the lower field, as you know, now mid-summer they are all out at grass during the night and in the cool of the stables during the heat.'

'Never mind, be an angel and go and catch her.'

Well past midnight we set off, through the back *canada*, which was tarmac, the noise of her shod hoofs sounded very loud, a few odd lights to show me the track between two houses and we were out in open country. Now it was pitch dark, no moon, somehow she knew the way and I remembered each path. The odd feeling of not knowing, however, if one was going down a slope or up a hill was very weird. We rode around the back of the town and up over the hills, watching the lights of Gibraltar twinkling in the distance, but total blackness around us, I could not even see her ears.

Cutting across an industrial estate, I realized the deep black was changing ever so slowly to dark grey. It was so quiet, I could only imagine where we were. Talking and patting her, I felt such love for this animal, and the confidence she had in her mad mistress. Not wanting to go behind the Serafin, Hugh Millais's lovely house, where Vanessa and I stayed years earlier, as the ground was very rough, and steep, I headed for the main road. No traffic, no noise, we slowly made our way up towards Pelayo, a little village mid-way to Cuarton. The dark grey turned into a strange light and I realized suddenly I was looking at the road.

Dawn had arrived, it was mystical. As I rounded the corner, before the village, the bushes on each side became dark silhouettes and the little houses took shape. Turning into the old road, I saw with joy that the bar was open and lights on. Wow! For a coffee and a pee, I dismounted feeling a bit sore, and slung the reins over a pole, giving my noble mare a big hug. Pepe the owner came out, 'Señora Vicky, what are you doing? Are you mad, it is only 5.00 am?'

Laughing, I answered, 'Only trying to win a bet. I have to be at the Hermita in Tarifa before 8.00 am.' This was our final timescale.

'*Hay, udes la señora para aqui la mas loca! Darme un café con leche y rapido, tengo cinco minutos.*'

On we went, and took a shortcut behind La Miranda, the home of Maria Luisa, and headed into the mountains, now bathed in sunshine and the Straits of Gibraltar was full of clouds, that often covered the sea in the very early morning. Now we are on a sandy track, that winds into the hills, and thanks to the coffee, energy levels were up again, so we trotted at a long Spanish pace and made up time. Once over the crest and parallel to the military land, we cut off down the valley along tiny paths that joined up with the track that eventually led to the Ermita. At 7.45 on the dot we were standing at her main gate, feeling very smug but slightly woozy after a *nuit blanche*.

We waited and waited, but nothing. Making my way to a café outside the Ermita grounds, looking for another coffee, I heard in the distance, clip clop, and there they came up the track. 'We don't believe it, Vicky, how did you get here so early?' In Spain, no one gets up in the summer before 10.00 am at the earliest, even the teenagers and kids only appear ready to go to the beach.

I admitted that the only way to have done it, was not to go to bed at all, that I had left Las Pilas after midnight, Pelayo at 5.00am and arrived at the Ermita at 8.00am. 'Anyway, whoopee, I've won the bet, now let's go and have a swim.' We all rode to the estuary of the Tarifa river, and let the horses play in the shallow water. Fabiola would try and catch the fish by stamping on them with her hooves. We tied the horses to a tamarisk bush and lay in the water. The actual beach was too far, and with nowhere to tie the horses.

I took Fabiola back to Palmoncilla, the farm of Anna, Joaquin's older sister; their groom had been on a Rocio with us, so no problem. All her children loved the *ferias* and horses and the naughty fun Joaquin and I were always organizing.

As we gradually attended less of the *ferias*, turned away by the crowds and traffic, we made up for it at home, not just taking advantage of the surrounding countryside for riding out but organizing serious competitions. In 1981 at Las Pilas, we held our first big cross-country event, just before Christmas, which was a huge success.

The judges were all old friends of mine from the Federation, and we put them up. The riders were all housed with family. Adorable friends from Sotogrande were jump judges, other professional dressage riders sat for hours at the dressage arena. Colmenar, the bottom cottage, was the well-used bar. I don't know why, but everyone loved the atmosphere. I drove the judges around the arena in Hortensia's cart from the Rocio, the weather was lovely and the course was difficult but challenging. Everyone had a ball, and persuaded me to go on running them. Which I did, only bigger and better, as our neighbour, Quentin Agnew Larios, joined in, and we had the course enlarged to include roads and tracks. Then he built his own course at Monte la Torre, the next door *finca*, which gave the riders a much larger and longer cross-country course, with some huge jumps and fun water ones.

The dressage and show jumping, was still held at Las Pilas; our cross-country was not for beginners, but riders who did not want to break their necks, and those with young horses in training. It was very exciting having Quentin as an enthusiastic course builder, though we had our shouting matches, over details, and when he disappeared with my list of riders. I was competing as well as organizing, so my nerves were well strung-out.

Belinda Braithwaite and Michael Whaley met at one of our shows, and ended up in a love affair. She persuaded Mariano, our nephew, to find her a horse that she could ride from Sotogrande to Paris. She bought Dragon and rode this fellow the 1,700 miles to Paris with a Doberman for company. Belinda was an amazing character, very gutsy, ready for anything, jumping out of planes with parachutes, hang gliding, and riding through the Rockies. She eventually married Michael, lived in Tarifa and had four gorgeous children. Her ride through Spain was well catalogued, and her book, *A Girl and a Horse and a Dog*, was a great success. Sadly they are now divorcing, though I don't know why.

During the life of *concursos* and shows, we were well mixed-up with an American couple, Olivia and Peter Scully, who had a big *finca* outside Puerto Santa Maria, breeding horses. Peter was a charming upmarket American involved with the *bodegas* in Jerez. I knew I wanted to buy a new horse that was well up to high school dressage and cross-country, one who had a big heart and was brave. Olivia said she had the ideal animal for me, a French thoroughbred called Meridzta, a five-year-old light bay. So I drove over there, and was allowed to try her on their cross-country course; absolute heaven, she was light on the hands with a beautiful gait and a lovely character. We had clicked from the first moment, and flew with a laugh into their cross-country. Big natural fences, until one moment we turned a corner and faced a fence that had been hidden; it was broken and falling on the ground. She did not hesitate a second, and cleared the whole thing in one enormous leap. My heart went out to her, and I knew she was ideal for me, but damn it, the Scullys knew it too. I was in love with her right away, and tried to argue the price, but with Olivia one never could win.

Once back in Las Pilas, and she was settled in, I turned her out to grass in the evenings, the little grass we had. I spent every late afternoon riding her in the arena, dressage and jumping, plus twice a week riding her out into the mountains. Since Fabiola, who had sadly passed on, I never had a mare so loving, so trusting, and so brave. The only thing she missed out on was the Spanish dressage and going to the Rocio or the Feria of Seville.

We made it up by winning dressage tests, jumping and cross-country, and having lovely rides in the mountains. In her dressage actually, she was very difficult to keep quiet, being very highly strung and the slightest movement of one's muscles, set her off. Not the good steady Banana, but fascinating for me to try and control her. Her paces were superb, so soon she was learning the extended trot, which was to die for, and her pirouettes were very controlled. Changing leg at a canter she loved and once understood, she did her flying changes in mid-air.

# *16. Las Pilas/La Zorilla/Selling the Cortijo*

Of course, our life with horses would not have been possible without being lucky to enjoy the different properties in Spain, particularly Las Pilas, but not only was I fortunate enough to share these houses with my husband, he also shared and encouraged my enthusiasm for the renovation and restoration of old buildings. Where Jacques had taken little or no interest in this aspect of my life, beyond a patronizing sneer, Joaquin was the complete opposite.

No doubt it helped that his father, Don Pascual, a very clever man, had bought up a lot of property as well, that seemed valueless at the time; the locals laughed and said that particular land was only fit for goats.

'No, that will be a fortune for my grandchildren,' he answered.

True, as today it is one huge mass of apartment blocks.

Joaquin's farm, Huerta de las Pilas, was on the old road to Los Barrios; when his father advised him to buy the property, it was miles outside the town and only accessible by a dirt track with a huge boulder in the middle. Huerta is an orchard, and the ground was rough, except where the oranges were growing. When I first knew it, Joaquin had cattle, the local *retinto*, big red animals, then Friesians as a dairy herd, sheep and chickens in a battery. In other words, a mixture of farming products, not to mention a huge swimming pool and a lovely garden. The house itself was very old, 17th century, but as Joaquin had added on to it in every direction, it was a real hotch-potch of a place. Very attractive though, with a covered terrace, old tiles on the roof and a gorgeous back patio. Ideal to hide away from the *levante*. Sadly the rooms were too small and bleak, with dark doors and terrible 19th century furniture. I scratched my head and thought how can I live here, it's so depressing.

Outside was filthy with cigarette butts just thrown on the ground, old warehouses full of junk and God knows what. Putting everything I had into yet again another project, I widened the terrace, ripped down the climbing vines, added seats along the wall, totally renewed the staff kitchen, rebuilt the chimneys, tripled the size of the stables, demolished half of the outhouses, and built a stallion paddock and a dressage arena with a show jumping circuit.

My horses were installed in his new stables, his fields and paddocks were fenced off to allow the brood mares and foals peace and quiet, while my competition ones and Fabiola plus her foal, the then three-year-old Rociera, were separated.

The house was very old and damp, and dark. I knew in my guts that I had to get on with it and make it as cheerful as I could, and bring up to date all the installations; for example the boiler behind what was our main bedroom, had rusty pipes and was covered in asbestos. I used to go to bed terrified it would blow up at any minute. I redid the bathroom, with lovely green and white tiles, rebuilt the cupboards, changed the curtains and bedspreads. I remade all the sofas in the main room in a lovely beige and white material. And I put in German windows, widened the terrace and cut back the foliage. At last, some light entered the house bringing an atmosphere of the 1970s into a Spanish farmhouse of the 17$^{th}$ century.

Time was marching on, and the town was running towards us at full speed. The orchards were being massacred, donkeys were shot, and chickens stolen. I was miserable at having to leave El Molino when I got married to Joaquin, with its wilderness of cork trees in exchange for this suburban farm. He always promised me he would spend the week at Las Pilas and the weekends at El Molino. It never happened. I had a couple to look after it, and went there every week to keep their moral up. It is very depressing for staff to live on their own with no boss to complain about! I had realized by then that Joaquin was never going to live there, between his family, the Marigalante II, plus his business in Madrid, it was a fait accompli. There was no way to argue with him; I loved him so much, I naturally gave in and concentrated on building up the stables.

Having caved in over moving into Las Pilas it was inevitable the same would happen with the apartment in Madrid, where Joaquin was spending a lot of time for his various board meetings. He begged me to divide his apartment in two; flattery supposedly gets one nowhere, but he put it on flat out, repeatedly telling me what fabulous taste I had! Eventually I did give in, but warning him, 'I know no workmen in Madrid and this is going to be a big job. We have to remove the roof to be able to cover in the huge terrace, and maybe put in supporting beams to hold up the new roof.'

He asked me to work with his nephew-in-law, Rudolfo Baldrich, an Argentinian architect. I wasn't pleased, 'Don't muck me around with Rudolfo,' I replied.

He started off by replacing the front door back to front, so coming in, you would hit someone inside, who was getting coats from the cupboard; then he insisted there was not enough space to make a guest loo. I said to Rudolfo, 'Go and look at the original plans, if there is a loo on one side, then there has to be another on our side?' Joaquin, with his father, had built the whole block years earlier, and the one next door, so all the apartments were lived in by his brothers and sisters and their families, of course. A rabbit warren of Cerveras!

We started by pulling down the inside walls and putting in supporting beams, dividing the front rooms and covering in the terrace. Rudolfo, a charming young man, but not practical in his designs. Finally, I took over the *chantier*, and very diplomatically moved him aside. The whole top floor that was Joaquin and Maria Rosa's home, I cut in one third for us as a base in Madrid and the other two thirds we sold to a Madrileno.

Their side was a very nice apartment, with a big salon, dining room, brand new kitchen, and two bedrooms with ensuite bathrooms. Joaquin sold it immediately that I was ready, plus the two parking spaces underground. Madrid had become a nightmare of traffic, and parking was worth a fortune. To think in my time on planet earth, I could remember Madrid with *serenos*. They looked after the street in front of the residences, banging their heavy sticks, thump thump, '*Don Joaquin he llegado, sitio para aqui por usted.*' 'Don Joaquin has arrived, here is a place for you.' They opened the car doors, helped the ladies up the steps and saluted them goodnight. The charm of the old Madrid: empty streets, cafés on the sidewalk, huge open spaces down the C/Serano to the Park Alfonso XIII.

When I was still married to Jacques, most summers I drove, needing a car in Spain, arriving in Madrid I stayed at a hotel that no longer exists, in the middle of fields and grass. Now you can imagine, high rises and double-lane traffic in every direction. Not to mention the pollution.

Our third was finished, decorated and made as funky as I dared, the drawing rooms were divided in half, with Joaquin's desk, chimney, television, in one half, with a sliding door to the rest. I had to make a quick change in the construction, and move the door to one side. As we were building, the roof started collapsing with an awful crunching noise! We rushed to jack it up with beams and cement pillars; quite something. The famous loo was in red and blue, with a plastic wash basin. The corridor to the back was with a bamboo wallpaper, white and pale green and shiny to give more light, and easy for Carmen, the *gallega*, to clean. Our double bedroom, and bathroom all with a lovely blue and white material on the walls, and blue carpet in the bathroom and champagne-coloured bath and basins. Joaquin's dressing room just fitted the two beds I still have today in Africa, very Napoleon III.

Carmen was so overwhelmed when I had finished, she was lost. She was the most unpleasant female that you can imagine; she adored Joaquin, worshipped the ground he walked on, but loathed me. The *gallegos* are renowned for their bad character, and Galicia renowned for its filthy weather. She was awful and used to bang the plates on the table, when in a bad mood. We gave the staff a month off in the summer in Las Pilas, and Joaquin would bring Carmen to replace them. A disaster, she hated the countryside, had no one to chit-chat to. The life of a concierge is what she missed. We were always either at horse shows, out on the boat or travelling. No one could say she was overworked.

Whatever I thought of her skills as a housekeeper, Carmen was valuable company during one of the most momentous events during my life in Spain.

I was in Madrid with Joaquin, and had gone shopping in a taxi driving down C/Alcala, round the Cibeles and up the Gran Via. The driver had his radio on, and we heard shouts and gun shots from inside the *Cortes*, the parliament. He got into a flap and stopped the taxi alongside the pavement, and I said, 'Don't be a fool, turn up the volume and listen.' As I said this, we watched in horror at tanks coming towards us.

The driver was obviously a communist, and begged me to get out of the taxi, saying, 'I am off to the frontier as fast as I can. This is the military taking over Spain and I'm out.'

I replied, 'Don't be so silly, stick to your guts and watch what is happening.'

We heard on the radio the takeover of the *Cortes*, the colonel of the Guardia Civil, Tejero, holding up the ministers with his gun, shoving them all on the floor. His guards with rifles surrounded the benches, with Suarez, the Prime Minister, crawling behind them, trying to hide.

I gave the taxi driver a rude sign and walked away, up the huge pavement towards the tanks, and the Plaza Mayor, thinking to myself, how is it that I am always in the middle of the most extraordinary events? Looking back on my life, between the black out in New York, being shot at in Paris and now the *coup d'etat* in Madrid. *Basta*, that was enough.

People were out on the streets, whispering and gesticulating; the Spanish are great gossipers, nothing like the old saying, *Il n'y as rien comme la salicite de la vieille femme Espagnol*. In a group of curious spectators, we watched as the tanks rolled to the right and lined up around the *Cortes*. Young tank commanders, looking very bewildered, were sticking their necks out of the turrets, making sure where they were. Probably none of them had ever been in the centre of Madrid before. Now without a radio, I had only one solution; to go back to the flat, as fast as possible, wondering where Joaquin had caught this incredible happening. I had no idea where he was or what he was doing? Impossible to find a taxi, the streets were deserted; I kept walking and finally came up the C/Lagasca and turned into C/don Ramon de la Cruz, our street. I was saluted by all the concierges and they were all talking and chattering.

'What is going on?' they all asked.

'Turn on your TVs and watch, the king will have to make an announcement very soon.'

Back in the flat, good old Carmen true to her post, was hanging out beside our concierge; as usual she did not greet me but said that

I had come back much earlier than she expected. I told her to come up to the flat and put on the television and for once not to argue. I telephoned Joaquin at his office, but he was out in meetings. Carmen and I watched, enthralled, as one government minister after another was interviewed by the press. Slowly we learnt that Suarez had escaped from the *Cortes*, and was heading for the airport but all other members of parliament were locked into the building.

We heard the general of the northern division was going to make a statement very soon. Joaquin's friend, General Jaime del Bosch, had already taken his troops to the streets in Valencia and literally captured the town. News came on that the king, Juan Carlos, would appear on the television later. We found out that, in the meantime, he had already talked to Thatcher in England, Kohl in Germany, and other heads of state. They all said, 'Don't let the army take over, you have done so well to keep the democracy going, it would be a criminality to return to fascism.'

Nearing 10.00 pm, Joaquin came home, 'What is going on? I have walked for hours and seen no taxis!' Carmen and I laughed.

'Don't you know there has been a *coup d'etat*?'

'What? Give me a whisky, quick!' and he glued himself to the box, asking me non-stop questions, as slowly a different faction of the army turned up at the *Cortes*, and arrested those with Tejero. Tanks were turned 90 degrees and moved off to their barracks. All army barracks were closed immediately.

At midnight, King Juan Carlos appeared on television, looking very smart in his full dress uniform, but also looking very serious. He gave an excellent speech, which treated Colonel Tejero and his colleagues as traitors to his reformed democracy. He was not going to stand down and he would arrest the army officers who had mutinied against his authority. Strong words from a young man in his early 40s. Following a civil war and Franco, he was taking a big risk. During the whole speech, he had his young son, Felipe sitting beside him, obviously pulled out of his bed, stifling yawns; Juan Carlos wanted to show his country, that it was not only him but a monarchy with an inheritance and an heir as well.

We crept into bed in the early hours of the morning, exhausted but fascinated with what was happening. Joaquin was very worried for his friend, Jaime; he found out later that he had been arrested, and his troops sent back to their barracks. We subsequently spent many a moment with this charming man in a prison up near Pelayo, close to El Cuarton, trying to cheer him up, as he could not talk, he was surrounded by guards, I proposed that Hortensia and her cart would pick him up with a pile of flamenco singers, and we would disguise him and whip him out through the gates. Naturally, it was not possible.

Obviously everyone had an opinion in the aftermath. Two days later Joaquin and I were at his club, Puerto de Hierro, having lunch with his friends, all of whom were very fond of Jaime de Bosch. The crowd around the bar were all horrified, all of them implying what a shame the *coup d'etat* had failed. Most of them right wing, retired army officers or navy, like Joaquin, were arguing for and against the king's position. I kept my mouth shut and moved away, thinking what idiots, imagining the country run by these military, pompous, narrow-minded colonels. For Joaquin's sake I did not partake in their discussions, and kept a very low key.

Later we talked alone between ourselves, he was very broad minded and open to all new ideas. When I argued against the attitude of the military, he agreed thoroughly. A lot of back stabbing went on for some time and it took the country quite a while to eliminate the generals and colonels who were in power, retiring them and replacing them with a much younger set. The younger officers had had a far better education, and all had been to university. They were not influenced by the civil war, so they all believed in democracy, however hard it was to achieve it and to hang on to it. It was fascinating for me to have been in Madrid, and live the drama at close quarters, and to continue in the south, watching the first elections take place. On my Vespa I used to drive between polling booths, handing out leaflets and explaining to the locals how to vote and for whom. I did not like Suarez, a greasy individual, but he was centre. As our foreman, Marcelino, asked me, 'Who do I vote for? I have never voted before, so I am lost.'

I replied, 'If you are not sure, go for the centre, there you cannot go wrong and watch how he manages the country, so you will know better next time.'

They were terrified of Joaquin, so always came to me for advice.

*

Between Las Pilas and Madrid I was obviously spending less time at El Molino. On top of all this, El Cuarton was slowly falling apart, no one came, the company was going bankrupt, roads were never taken care of, and all the fun of the previous years had gone. Although I could rent it out in summer, the sensible decision was to sell; I could not cut myself in half. So I started advertising her with the glossy magazines and big agencies in London, New York and Frankfurt. In the meantime, I sold Alambique; now I was married, there seemed no point in keeping her on, plus the crash in real estate in the Tarifa area meant there were no antique buyers beyond Sotogrande.

It had been on the market for a couple of years, when in 1980, I was holding a clinic at Las Pilas, the phone went and it was the manager of El Cuarton, who said, 'Vicky, come up here quickly, we have an American couple, who want to buy your house.' I could not believe my ears, despite lots of interest, the market was not good. I told him, that I was busy and could this couple meet me later in town, at the Hotel Reina Cristina, in two hours. As I understood, they had already seen the property, and could not imagine a couple out of the blue would want to buy El Molino.

So I finished with my riders, showered, changed and told Joaquin I would be back later and drove into town. At the Reina Cristina, one of our watering holes, I bumped into Pepito Larios, the Duque de Lerma and the judge, Manolo Ruiz Gomez. Laughing I told them I had come to sell El Molino. Looking round the bar, all I saw, was an old couple sitting on their own, but could not believe that this was them. I knew the name was De Wolf, so wandered up to them, and asked them politely if they were the people who had visited a house up in El Cuarton.

He jumped out of his chair and asked in a broad American accent, 'I say, you must be Vicky?' He was huge man of 6ft 4in, with a big grin, and he introduced me to his wife, Marianne. Real Bostonians, out of a picture book. I called over Pepito and Manolo and introduced them; the Americans were thrilled to meet Spaniards who spoke English. I would have rung Joaquin to come and join us, but knew he was busy and far from keen to socialize with Americans who he didn't know.

Later we became great friends. They were quite delightful and said my house was fantastic and beautifully built, and they wanted to buy it there and then. How much was I asking? It was all too quick, very American; but once the others had left, I told them, 'One does not rush into talking business in Europe, especially in front of others, now we can start.'

I explained that the property was registered with a Swiss company with bearer shares. Doc, his nickname, was absolutely thrilled, especially when he heard how he could take it over without signing anything in Spain. We agreed on a price and wrote out the sale contract on a piece of loo paper! He wanted the house as it was with all my antique furniture included. Very sad but it was a weight off my shoulders. We agreed to meet at a fixed date in May at a very chichi restaurant on Lake Geneva. From the border he phoned me, slightly worried, saying, 'Vicky, you will stick to your word?'

'Doc, I have never yet done a dirty deal, and not likely to do one now, and as it's so simple, you take over my bearer shares of the company and put them in your safe.'

'How will I know that I own the property?'

'You will have the bearer shares, those are the proof of ownership.'

Finally he understood.

He was a retired officer in the American navy, and when he heard that my husband was the great nephew of Almirante Don Pascual Cervera y Topete, he had turned to his wife and said meeting me and finding the house was made in heaven.

Back at Las Pilas, Joaquin was very chuffed and opened a bottle of champagne, congratulating me. 'Hold on until May, you never know?' I had only the loo paper signed by us both as proof!

Come May I flew up to Geneva and met Doc and Marianne at the lakeside restaurant we had chosen. I handed over the papers of the company and the famous bearer shares and in return he paid me one million dollars. Then we drank champagne seriously. It was actually a rotten deal, as his daughter sold El Molino five years later for triple the amount to some Germans, having emptied the house of all my lovely antiques and selling them in the US for a fortune. Sadly, her mother had died in the house, and Doc a few years later. They had been very happy, it was so sad to watch them getting older and finally passing away.

As well as Las Pilas, Joaquin had bought out his brother, Jose, and his sister Milageos's share in La Zorilla, a huge cork forest of 300 hectares, up on the mountain range above Los Barrios. In 1978 Joaquin bought La Zorilla, a very challenging project; wild open spaces of bracken, grass and streams. We planned a lake, catching all the water we could from the mountains, and to rebuild the guardian's cottage, bullrings, paddocks and eventually build a large *cortijo* for us and guests. Antonio Moreno, the guardian, and Lou, and their four children, all lived on the property in a shack. I could not even call it a cottage. So the first thing we did was to build a decent living area for them and pipe water to their new cottage. I can remember Maria, their last child, was born in the shack, a tiny little baby who spent her time scratching her face. I was worried but Lou just laughed and said no problem. She was a sweet woman, with a heart as big as the sun; I became very fond of her and her children.

Some years later we had a big shock when Lou was found head down in the river; luckily she was discovered just in time, and hauled out. She had had a very nasty heart attack. Immediately Joaquin and I took her to a specialist in Madrid where they did all the tests; an excellent social security wing attached to the private sector in the hospital La Paz. I had to accompany her all the way, as she had never been in Madrid in her life. Antonio came too, but was useless. She was operated on by the top cardiologist, and stayed two weeks in hospital. Then she stayed in our staff rooms above our apartment, while recuperating.

Always in a good humour and laughing, she said, 'If this had happened a few years earlier, before Don Joaquin bought La Zorilla and married to you, no one would have taken care of me, like you do Señora?'

They had such bad luck; the following year he developed cancer of the lungs, one of their kids had an accident and was paralysed from the waist down, then another son was killed by a rogue driver, while he was working on the new road.

# 17. Shooting

Joaquin's dream for La Zorilla, as was mine, was to open it up for shooting; we were already breeding pheasants at Las Pilas; and at the end of 1977, we had the first shoot, and invited Hubert Pantz and François de Riocourt amongst many more, serving a big paella in the bracken, jerez all round and pheasants hurtling off the mountain.

Great fun but it was not up to the standard of an international shoot. Sadly, this was when I realized Tarzan, my cocker spaniel, was so blind he could not see the pheasants in front of him. Since then I have had only Labradors. Kim of Palgrave I bought for Joaquin's birthday present the next year. I had arranged his birthday celebrations a day later, 25th September, to coincide with the flight. He asked me non-stop, 'Why do you want to change the date?'

'Ha, ha! I have a surprise for you.' He was always longing for a good gun dog.

I had previously asked all his brothers and sisters to dinner, and his niece, Milagros, to be hostess while I was at Malaga airport picking up Kim. The plane was delayed and it took ages to collect the dog container. At last I finished the paperwork and put my arm in the container, talking doggy talk, 'Come on, Kim, you've arrived,' trying to pat his nose. I was treated to two very yellow eyes just staring at me.

The vibes worked and slowly he came towards me and putting on a collar and lead, eventually staggered out of his box, and walked a few steps. Poor bugger had been in there since 6.00 am that morning. He looked at me with those huge eyes asking, 'Who are you and where am I?' Being in a hurry I got him into the front passenger seat, and left flat out for Algeciras, knowing the dinner had started and imagining Joaquin in a tizz. At Estepona I stopped for petrol and let him out onto grass – wow, relief! He finally peed. No time to feed him, so I kept going, cuddling his head as much as I could.

We arrived at Las Pilas at last, a good hour late. I put him on the lead and slowly came to the corner of the terrace, where we dined every night; I patted Kim and told him, there at the end of the table is your new master, and let him off the lead. You cannot believe it, he walked down the whole table, 14 of them, and went straight to Joaquin and laid his head on his knees.

I think we were all crying, it was incredible. From that day on, Kim never left his side. Except, of course, when he was in his office or in Madrid, then he was with me as a constant companion, and loved coming out with the horses. He was a superb animal, and when they were shooting together, he was the pride and joy of Joaquin.

In the summer, he would swim in the pool, diving for whatever spending two or three minutes under water. On the Marigalante II he was not so happy, but would lie under Joaquin's feet at the wheel, just watching him.

I had bought Kim from Michael Clarke's sister-in-law. Michael, with his brother John, owned Plessey, and was also a very keen shot. Shortly after we married, Michael Clarke invited us shooting at his home in Essex, Braxted Park. I love shooting, but knowing the English attitude to women, had to keep very quiet. Pheasants are such stupid birds and so big, you can't fail to miss, but it happens surprisingly often. Being very fast, I much preferred quail or partridge or, even better, turtle doves in Morocco where I could get two with one shot.

Braxted was great fun and finally Michael, who knew my frustration, allowed me to shoot in place of Joaquin. Nervous, with all these pompous Brits watching me, thank goodness I did not make an arse of myself and brought down every bird that flew my way. The Englishmen put down their guns at the end of the drive and clapped, Joaquin was very chuffed, whilst Michael grinned saying, 'Well, now I know you can shoot, maybe I will have to allow you a place on the line, but Vicky, you do know in England women just don't shoot, it's very bad form?'

I just looked at him, thinking what a narrow-minded bunch of twits!

After Braxted we flew to Austria where we had been invited to shoot by Baron Hubert Pantz, our host with the pink pig, at his schloss in Austria.

Excited, as I had never been to Vienna, despite skiing many times in Austria. Prince Heinrich Rosenberg-Orsini, half brother to Alfie Auersberg. My old friend from Kitzbuhel and New York, who taught me to ski properly, met us at the airport. Alfie was one of Kenya's first white hunters. A delightful family, but one who sadly came to grief. Alfie is now dead from a cerebral haemorrhage.

Heinrich and Joaquin looked very similar, and got on majestically, sharing the same sense of humour. He took us to the hotel and then out to dinner, as he was staying at his club. A real Austrian, he owned all the mountains south of the Tyrol, on the border with Italy and only came north east to Vienna once in a while.

'I do hope you did not come up to the city especially for us?' I asked him, suddenly feeling embarrassed.

'There was no way I would not have come, when you, Vicky, and your Spanish husband come for the first time to Vienna.'

I felt awful, with no autoroutes, it must have taken him hours. The next day he had business meetings, which made me feel better.

I was dying to go to the Spanish riding school in Vienna, and the opera. Compared to the Spanish school of Alvaro Domecq in Jerez de la Frontera, the one in Vienna was out of this world. The Lipizzaners were a breed apart, very Spanish in their form but with incredible agility in their movements. The opera was as I imagined it to be, fabulous. We had a box, and within five minutes Joaquin was snoring quietly behind me.

Next day we hired a car and drove south west to Hubert and Terry Pantz's most lovely schloss. He was Austrian, but married to Terry, one of the wealthiest Americans in Europe. She had married various husbands, but lived a long part of the year in Marbella, and I had known them from my Paris days. She was thrilled I had remarried with Joaquin, and laughing on arrival, said 'Ha! Vicky, what a difference from that damn Frenchman?'

The weekend was way over the top, a crazy crowd of mixed Europeans and a spattering of Americans; the whole organization was based on the fact that we were all going on Monday to another huge shoot in Czechoslovakia. Behind the Iron Curtain. It was so expensive, we all shared the costs, and we were both fascinated to see what the communist countries looked like. We left in a cavalcade of BMWs and Mercedes, driving parallel to the Danube straight towards the border just south of Vienna, full of cartridges and guns. Very flat land and mile upon mile of agriculture, but not a soul in sight; very weird. As we approached the Iron Curtain, we began to notice the fence with its barbed wire, interspersed with towers every kilometre, supposedly for the border guards.

Nearing the crossing we were all on high alert, and fascinated to see the atmosphere of the border. Double fences, machine guns, Alsatians, guards in every direction who ordered us out of the cars and ushered us into quite a good-looking café, with surprisingly fine coffee, rolls and chocolate.

Our chief guide took all our passports, and Hubert accompanied him to the border police; he had obviously arranged the whole thing in advance. Waiting for them, we all asked for the loo and were escorted by a machine gun.

With the passports retrieved we took off again, across no-man's-land and into Czechoslovakia; further miles and miles of flat boring land, but as evening approached we passed through various villages, where the houses were small, and with very few people on the streets. It all looked so cold and dirty, sad and barren; the villagers who were walking near the road wore threadbare coats and all looked miserable. Seemingly no electricity, as the houses all had paraffin lamps and cottages were only lit by lanterns. Finally the countryside became thick with trees and big forests, with streams and small rivers breaking the monotony.

We arrived finally at the castle of the Hohenzollerns, a magnificent estate, which the communist government rented out to high-flying Europeans from the west, who wanted to shoot pheasants in their thousands. It was the most amazing operation. We were shown our room, with a large double bed covered in damask, stinking of dust and mould. The bathroom was huge with an enormous bath but the taps all broke and came off in our hands and water tepid.

Later in the bar, Joaquin met some Spaniards from Madrid, what a small world. They had been shooting and found it fantastic and knew Joaquin from other shoots in Spain. During dinner, I was very naughty and teased the red-coated butler, asking him if he liked living in the communist world, and what kind of life did he have? Joaquin was very cross with me and told me to shut up, 'Why?' I replied. 'We have to learn all we can about life here, while we have the chance.'

Already with our cavalcade of rich cars, I felt awful for these desperately poor people, who had no hope of ever becoming solid citizens; the whole country was pathetic. We had a lovely old man who was dedicated to be Joaquin's loader, and being so incredibly cold, we offered him slugs of slivovitch, plum brandy, which he drank with a big grin on his face. He was so poor, the coat he was wearing, was full of holes. I told Joaquin I was going to bring him a bottle of vodka the next day, and he replied, 'Vicky, take care, this whole thing is organized by the commies and every move we make is watched and counted for.' Right up to the point where the commissaire has a machine which added up every pheasant we had shot. We found out later, that hundreds of them were beaten into the hedge dividing the guns from the beaters. Taking off, they flew into our line of fire to be massacred. Not very nice, but the pheasant is a very stupid bird. It was a huge experience but we both decided never to do it again.

# *18. Our Travels, Senegal, Morocco*

Throughout our marriage Joaquin and I loved to travel together; we kept up a tradition of every year going to a hot country to get out of the filthy, wet, damp in the south of Spain. Of course, there were Januarys that were gorgeous, but not many. La Calma de Enero was renowned for flat sea, no wind, a total calm in the straits, and a full moon over Africa.

We started this annual getaway in 1978 with a simple desire to head due south. Paying due respect to his working commitments, Joaquin pretended he had business in Senegal, so no problem, off we went to Dakar. Doing what he thought he had to do, Joaquin met up with the Spanish ambassador; then we visited the slave market and their departure point, hired a boat and went fishing; and I became horribly seasick. Next day we hired a car and headed off south to the Casamance, in southern Senegal.

Then the adventures started; quite late, getting dark, I saw in the rear window a car miles away in the distance, and said to Joaquin, 'Watch out, we have the last room in the lodge and if this bugger is going to overtake us, then we are screwed.'

So I pushed my foot flat out on the accelerator, and shot through the forest as fast as I dared. Joaquin, always a good sport, did not murmur. We swung into the lodge's entrance and as I jumped out, the other car caught up with us. I yelled at Joaquin.

'Stay there! I am running to the front desk.'

I booked in and relaxed, as an argument took off between the manager and these newly arrived Belgians. We had made it with minutes to spare. I was panicked, as I knew from the map there was nothing between this lodge and the estuary that divided Senegal and the Gambia.

We were shown our room, Holy Moses, two bunks on a cement floor crawling with little creatures. Joaquin threw a fit and refused to sleep there. 'No panic, we will find somewhere else in the bush.'

Anything to keep him in a good humour, I got him a drink. Two whiskies later he had calmed down, and I explained if we had lost the room to the others behind us, then we would have had to sleep in the car. It was pure jungle; there was nowhere else to go. They gave us an omelette and chips and explained their country, and organised a hovercraft for us to discover the inland waterways the next morning.

By then we had all the information about the border crossing and the ferries to the Gambia, an English enclave surrounded by Senegal. Despite the bed bugs we had slept well, and after exploring their creeks in the hovercraft, left for the border crossing and the ferry.

Once in the Gambia we were gob-smacked to see English policemen, the Union Jack, high-rise apartments and smart hotels. Very odd in the middle of Africa. Joaquin said, 'Come on, Vicky, we must stay here one night at least and get a good dinner and a decent hotel!' Which we did, despite the fact that I found in our room some fellow trying to steal from us.

I closed the door behind me, and said, 'Hey, you! What are you doing?'

Looking terrified, he started blabbing about something. 'Get out before I ring the reception,' I hissed. Which he did very quickly. Back at the beach Joaquin was worried stiff, and insisted he wanted to report it. This was the only time we were nearly robbed in the two weeks we were in Africa.

Left this weird country the next day and very happily re-entered Senegal, which was a French colony. They had educated their people, built roads and hospitals for the people, so the atmosphere was very different to the British colony behind us.

Arriving in the Casamance was not only fun, as we had to cross six to eight rivers, all on floating pontoons, huge mangrove swamps and darling little kids so black you could hardly see their eyes. It's funny, once one is in the south of a country, they are relaxed and happy, fun loving and naughty. Sad today, as they are all fighting again with the country to their south, Guinea Bissau.

We had a delightful hotel right on the beach, south of the famous Club Med, but much quieter, with good fishing and very nice staff. Joaquin adored getting brown all over, and one day was naked on the beach. Wow, did he suffer for two days with his private parts in agony. Soaking in vinegar was the only solution.

Once relaxed, we made many excursions in dug-out canoes with fast outboard engines, weaving in and out of the inland waterways between the mangroves. I simply loved this beautiful area, it was an idyllic place for a holiday away from everyone and everything. I would love to go back, but am sure it has changed like the rest of the world, and as far as I know the fighting still continues.

*

In a later foul, cold and damp January, Joaquin asked me would I take him to Morocco, that he wanted to see it properly and look up S.A. Moulay Ali and perhaps try to do business with him. I replied, 'I'm delighted, my darling man, to take you anywhere, but don't have illusions, you will never do business with the Moroccans.'

'Why not? You know them all, and you speak French fluently?'

I shrugged and replied, 'You'll see.'

I booked the ferry to Ceuta, with our four-by-four, and a hotel in Rabat and telephoned our friends in Casablanca. Leaving Las Pilas, Kimmy looked crestfallen, he had smelt the turtle doves and snipe, that we loved shooting in the mountains behind Tetuan. On one of our shooting escapades, we had arrived in Ceuta, and Joaquin, horrified, looked at me and said, 'Oh! Vicky, I am so sorry, I have forgotten my passport.' I swore every rude word, but nothing to do, he had to ring the driver at Las Pilas, explain where he could find it, and to give it to the captain of the next ferry. Very cross with himself, he slunk off to the big hotel in the port, while I walked the dogs, Kim and Polo, a young yellow female, highly intelligent, around the moats of this fortress town, a Spanish enclave.

With traffic in every direction, two Labradors on leads is not funny. Finally I found an open space, alongside the moats. I let them run free and watched Polo like a hawk, not trusting her totally. Suddenly I heard an enormous bang, sounding like a car or a plane landing in the moat. I looked over the edge and saw circles of water, getting bigger and bigger; there in the middle a black head appeared, I felt quite sick; it was Kim coming to the surface. He had jumped up on the parapet, the crusty yellow sand stone had given way, and he fell 200 metres at least.

Thank goodness it was blowing a light *poniente*, and the current of the sea was running from west to east. The poor animal was obviously alive, and scrambling on the edges of the moat, looking up at me with such a forlorn expression. It was a vertical wall, so not a hope of getting him out. I turned and yelled at someone near me, grabbed Polo and put her back on the lead, and asked this poor person to follow me. By this time, a big crowd had gathered, all muttering that no animal could withstand a fall of such height. I rushed along the top, shouting to Kim to follow me, which he did, bless his heart, looking pathetically up at me every few metres. I stopped the traffic and tore down the slope to the yacht club, followed by this stranger, dragging Polo behind them.

Once at the club, I stood on the edge, and called him non-stop, slowly he understood, and swam towards me. He was still shaking with fright. One of the stewards brought me a rough towel and helped me to get his circulation working again. I was crying, and Kimmy just looked at me with such love, in those big yellow eyes, I nearly died of relief, while Polo rushed around him, licking him non-stop. Not a bone broken, or a torn ligament, let alone a muscle pulled, incredible. Back at the hotel, the whole town had heard the story, and Kim was then a famous fellow.

This time, as we were not going shooting, we had left the dogs behind, and drove to Rabat south on the main road, where we stayed at the Hilton, and then on to Casablanca, which is the industrial capital. Rabat is the real capital, where the king has his palace, and surrounded by all the embassies. We had already contacted our Moroccan friends, Najat and Assiz El Belghiti, who had the most lovely home on the outskirts. Naturally we got lost and turned in circles; finally Assiz came to meet us. He and Joaquin had a lot in common, as he was the Minister of Fisheries, and we had made friends in Al Hoceima the previous summer, taking them fishing and inviting them to Las Pilas with their three gorgeous children.

Najat was a very elegant person, and looked and behaved totally French. She had decorated her house with all the latest French materials. We had a lovely bedroom, but laughing together, because there was no furniture, no cupboards or drawers, nowhere to put anything. So we left our cases on the floor. I found out later, that this was typically Arab, they just don't hang up their clothes.

We sat down on very low sofas to a round table, with six or eight other guests, as well as Hajdi, their elder son, Hicham, younger son, and their daughter, Kenza. All highly intelligent and very good looking. Never have I seen such a meal, it went on for hours, three main dishes followed by a couscous. Najat knew I adore couscous, and hers was very special. I asked her afterwards, 'What do you do with all the dishes? The amount that was left over?'

'Oh!' she said. 'It all goes to feed the staff. Don't worry.' I thought, *what a pity and such a waste, the couscous alone would have been sufficient*.

After a superb dessert, the other guests got up and left. I learnt after many dinners in Morocco, that this is the reason one eats so late, even worse than Spain! The longer the hostess keeps her guests waiting, it means she is delighted to have them, because they know they are expected to leave once the meal has finished. Amazing, but that's their tradition.

Assiz and Joaquin talked business, and the next day I phoned Moulay Ali, and he made an appointment for Joaquin to meet his business manager, and the director of the national railways. Desperately boring, but I had to accompany him to translate, as Joaquin spoke no French. One of his company's great successful inventions were the electric automatic switches between train stations, also all the equipment used in airports for the flight controllers, and the telephone boxes used at the entrance to cities, dividing one main line into thousands. What a brain, to think he designed and invented all this as a young man.

However many meetings Moulay Ali had arranged for him, nothing much came out of them, hours of being polite, but one could see they were not going to invest in a Spanish company. They were too unsure of themselves and wanted handouts under the table non-stop. He was very disappointed, as he had already done good business in Algeria; but I had warned him Morocco was very different. He was too much a gentleman to stoop to their level of *bakshish* and honestly did not understand it.

'Darling heart, forget it and enjoy visiting the country, have fun with the royal family and my friends in Marrakech; business in this country is impossible. Look at our lovely friend, Andre Dubonnet, who sold his fabulous *hotel particulier* in Neuilly, the smartest area between the Bois de Boulogne and Paris, to the king, who offered Andre a huge piece of land near the Palmeraie in Marrakech in exchange. He waited four to five years, and still did not obtain a building permit. He landed up broke!'

We said goodbye to our friends, and with lots of ideas and contacts left for Marrakech; excellent roads, flat agricultural land and very green. It had been raining there too. For the hell of it, we had booked into the famous Hotel Mamounia, good thing we did so then, as it changed owners very soon after, and out-priced itself, becoming one of the most expensive hotels in all Africa. In those days it was fun, the town was still clean and the traffic minor, and the views up over the Atlas Mountains staggering. Snow-capped peaks and huge ravines.

The hotel itself was very elegant, lovely young boys bowing and scraping, horse-drawn carriages at the door, huge swimming pool and orange groves surrounded by massive walls. In the hall, I bumped into Adolfo Velasco, a Spanish queer selling antiques from his boutique in the hotel lobby.

Joaquin just stood there with his mouth open as Adolfo was dressed in one of his robes, with his flowing hair.

'Adolfo, meet my Spanish husband, Joaquin Cervera.'

'Oh! I know your family, delighted to meet you, come, come, we must celebrate this with some champagne on the terrace,' where he swung with a flourish, kissing hands and showing off to all his admirers.

What a character. Immediately, he invited us to a dinner that night, in the kasbah, and lunch at his house the next day. Joaquin was most amused; He forgot his business deals, relaxed and from then on had a ball.

The next day, we did the kasbah, starting off as any tourist in the main square, packed with locals, snake charmers, water carriers, dentists pulling out teeth, hawkers of every colour, selling everything they could, smelling of fresh mint and herbs mixed with donkey shit and other delicacies. Wandering to the far end, we made friends with a charming guide, who took us into the real *souks*, down tiny alleys, archways, dark with the shade of over-hanging carpets, black-eyed girls staring at us out of their doorways. If we had been alone, within five minutes we would have been lost. Mohammed, as they are all called, our guide, then showed us that each street was dedicated to a speciality; one to making carpets, another to leather goods, another to dying materials and, of course, wanted to know what we were looking for. 'Kaftans,' I replied. 'Pretty ones, and a *djellaba* for my husband.'

Joaquin looked horrified, and said, 'No way.' In later years we persuaded him to get one, and he looked fantastic in it.

We were led down a tiny sloping street and there were hundreds of kaftans hanging in the sun, men galore shouting at us, 'Madame, madame, come and see!' First in French, then English. We were invited to drink the classical mint tea, sitting on a carpet, while the fellow's wares were spread before us. After arguing like mad over the price, eventually I bought four. Useful presents and very cheap, but they don't last long, as once washed, they fall apart.

Round a few corners we came upon the tannery and the stink was disgusting. Here in huge pits, they dumped the skins of all the recently killed animals, and poured in some product to cure them and then a dye to give each one the colour they wanted. I did ask and it was fascinating to learn, but I cannot remember now for the life of me what it was. The smell though is unforgettable.

Off in a trotting half-Arab pony carriage to lunch with Adolfo, we asked him if we could wash our hands, as the smell was still with us. His house was very Spanish with a lovely garden. Joaquin met a group of Spaniards and I was thrown into a whole mish-mash of people from Paris, including, to my surprise, Hetty von Auersberg who was living in Marrakech at the time. I had known her from skiing days in Kitzbuhel, and she was sister to Alfie, the Austrian playboy I met as he charmed New York in the mid '60s.

Talk about catching up, we had a good old gossip, she had a great wit and was very sarcastic. Hetty described the horror story of Alfie's first wife, Sonny. She was a desperately rich American, who had divorced Alfie as he was so naughty, and remarried again to a German. According to the speculation at the time, he had killed her with an overdose; except it didn't work and she ended up in coma. Of course, this was big news at the time, but now it is a famous story. Claus von Bulow was tried twice in the 1980s for her attempted murder, but was found not guilty. Sonny von Bulow spent nearly 30 years living in a vegetative state, before finally dying in 2008, with her family remaining convinced of Claus's guilt.

Socializing in Marrakech was fun when you knew half the people and had lots in common, but we were there for Joaquin to get to know the country, so we left for the Atlas Mountains and Ouarzazate, heading to Zagora and the valley of the Draa. The climb up the Moyen Atlas was out of this world. The women changed and became darker skinned, and wore lovely silk shawls and pretty dresses, with shiny metal jewellery in their hair. We had left behind the heavy skirts and old towels and turbans of the north. The hairpin bends were horrific, but the views were well worth it, and on each turn little boys were selling asparagus and great lumps of amethyst. Snow on either side with signs to the skiing slopes. Stopping at Ouarzazate for a coffee, we realized that we were already halfway to the Sahara. I always drove, as loved it, and Joaquin was either asleep or just not interested. While he was a brilliant navigator, and sailed the Marigalante II to an exact point on the map, and manoeuvred her in the tightest of ports, he was quite a dangerous driver, as he smoked with one arm out of the window, and didn't really concentrate on the road.

We arrived at the bottom of the valley and headed out towards Zagora and we were at last in the Sahara. Very exciting looking for miles into the distance, across never ending sand dunes. Zagora was the end of the line, and I ventured as far as I could, until the car decided enough was enough, and the sand was getting very deep. With Joaquin, I did not dare take any unnecessary risks, but vowed I would come back one day with a good Arab, and ride her straight across the open space to Erfoud, naturally with a four-by-four as company, carrying spare tyres and extra water.

The next day, we had to turn round and head back to where the road to the north branched off at Ouarzazate along the Route des Chateaux. We saw masses of camels and their young, after 30-odd kilometres, on our left there was the most extraordinary ravine with troglodytes dug into the cliff edge. These were what they called the chateau; as we looked carefully, there were Berber women dressed in lovely colours and children coming and going, goats galore and donkeys, and some old men sitting in the sun watching them. These were the old strongholds, fortresses against invasions from the desert, which stretched out to our right, in an endless expanse of sand.

Every 40–50km there was another one; no wonder the old Berber kingdom was impregnable. We drove all day between these fortresses, crossing dried up riverbeds, where today they had made concrete culverts. Joaquin stopped and studied how they were made; he was fascinated and wanted to copy them for La Zorilla. The idea was that the rivers, when in flood, flowed over the top of them, and normal rainwater went underneath through huge pipes.

At Errachidia we turned right and headed out into the desert; stubborn old me was determined to see how far we could go, and we landed up at Erfoud, surrounded by an oasis with date palms before continuing to Rissani, which was seriously the end of the road.

Looking at the map, there was a yellow track to our right, but only fit for camels or fully equipped four-by-fours, and I was right, it ended at Zagora where we had spent the previous night. Joaquin was thrilled to be in the Sahara and kept looking for the blue men, nomadic Tuareg people who have roamed the sands of the eastern and central Sahara Desert for centuries. They were a tribe apart, very tall and thin, with a greyish coloured skin, always dressed in blue with blue turbans, but we would have had to go hundreds of kilometres from where we were to find them.

So back we went to Errachidia and headed north west to the second pass over the Atlas Mountains in the direction of Fez. As we climbed up towards the pass it got colder and colder, and at 2,080 metres the snow was seriously deep. We stopped in a local café, as there were other cars on the side of the road we learnt that the pass had been closed and they were now waiting for a snow plough. Joaquin got angry with me.

'I told you so, it was too risky to come here without knowing if the pass was open?'

'Come on, look at what you have seen, we can always turn round,' said I.

'Hrrrgh! The only other road is miles to the east via Algeria!' he replied.

Thank goodness at that moment the snow plough arrived and started cleaning the road. Ha! When he got angry, everyone was terrified, especially his nephews and nieces, while I just laughed.

Once on the other side, the snow now cleared, we thanked the driver and gave him a good tip, for which he was very grateful and wished us a good journey. Back in the green fields and rolling hills, we descended until we found a decent-looking café and stopped for lunch. Was I relieved? No alcohol but excellent shish-kebab; we had our gin and Fantas at the back of the car, so feeling much better, we headed off for Fez.

We had heard it was a beautiful city, the old capital long before Rabat, thousands of years ago. We booked into the Palais Jamaii and had the best couscous that we had ever tasted in the Arab restaurant. It had been raining, and the *souks* were enormous but all on slippery cobbles, and as we discovered, full of donkey shit as the stables were on the sloping alleyways where the farmers left their beasts while they went looking for their goods. The hotel had already warned us that tourists had been lost in the *souks* and never found, and as the weather was against us, we returned to the hotel. Enough adventures for the time being, so we settled for looking at the old palace and other historical buildings.

Then on to Tetuan via Chechouan and the Rif Mountains; fabulous country, where in later years, Assiz and Najat invited us to a wild boar hunt. Tetuan was the main city of the north, very close to the beach, from there a short distance to M'diq, and Kabila. Our summer playground. We stopped and looked up Luis Llodra, who had a good laugh as we explained our trip.

'Vicky, you are mad, the second pass is often closed at this time of year.'

'Well, we've made it, and now Joaquin can say truthfully he knows the Atlas Mountains and the Sahara, and Marrakech.'

Whereas his family, and next door neighbours across the straits had never been to Morocco, they were unbelievably insular.

# *19. Safari Tanzania*

In 1984 Joaquin had to have an operation, and he was booked into the naval hospital in Madrid, with the most charming surgeon. The operation was to remove gallstones and the surgeon suggested he removed the prostate at the same time. I said, 'Wait a minute we are only recently married, what if there is a chance to have a baby?' One of the things Joaquin had always hoped for, as he never had any children with Maria Rosa.

He always said, 'Imagine a child between us, it would be gorgeous.'

The surgeon looked at Joaquin and simply said, 'Hmm, perhaps she's right.'

On the morning of the operation the Cervera family arrived in his room en masse. Oh Lord, I learned what they were like later on. I had guessed that this might happen and got myself to the hospital very early and told the hospital staff to keep them at bay. They were horrified, and asked me what did they think they were doing? There was at least 30 of them.

I replied, 'A family from Andalucia has a very different mentality from Madrilenos. As soon as someone is sick, they arrive in their thousands! Instead of leaving you alone and quiet, they all crowd into the room and never stop talking.' The nurses then threw them out.

It was a minor operation and he was home in our now new apartment very quickly. A strong fellow, he was as fit as a tiger in three minutes, so much so, he asked me, 'Where are we going this winter?'

'Heavens,' I replied. 'I have no idea, I did not think you would want to travel so quickly.'

'Why not? I feel fine and love travelling with you. Let's contact Fernando!'

Fernando Castillo, was a nephew-in-law of Maria Rosa who was by then Spain's ambassador to Tanzania. Joaquin and Maria Rosa had been on safari with him while he was First Secretary to the Spanish embassy in Nairobi, when Joaquin shot a large number of animals, including his first elephant. I, as an animal lover, said, 'OK, contact him, and then I will make the plans, but darling man, you are not going to shoot any more, you have shot quite enough. If we go on safari, a photographic one will be fine, there will be no shooting.' He acquiesced without a murmur.

Fernando was delighted as he loved Joaquin, and invited us to the embassy in Dar es Salaam. I contacted the doctor in charge of all vaccinations and jabs in the port of Algeciras: yellow fever, cholera, rabies, you name it. On arriving in Dar, the plane doors were flung open, and the hot air hit us all like a blast from a furnace, but it was pissing with rain so hard, that the water bounced back off the tarmac. Welcome to Tanzania.

Fernando was waiting at the bottom of the steps with two huge umbrellas and he ushered us through the VIP arrivals, with neither police, nor customs, just his official car with a grinning black driver, who said, 'Sit in the car, while I collect your luggage.'

What an easy way to arrive in this country, I cannot remember even needing a visa. The country was under the Socialist/Communist President Julius Nyerere, and its borders were closed and very poor. Nyerere stopped the tribal disputes and made the Tanzanians very proud nationalists, unlike Kenya, where there are masses of tribes all fighting each other.

The embassy was a modern cream building with a lovely garden of tropical plants, along the beach to the north, surrounded by other embassies. Every nation had a representative here. The men were thrilled to see each other and talked shooting non-stop, comparing their trophies. I think Fernando thought I was a bitch not allowing Joaquin to shoot, as in Tanzania hunting was and is today permitted, while in Kenya totally prohibited.

At breakfast, he turned to me and asked, 'Vicky, what prophylactic are you using?' I looked at Joaquin and started laughing, thinking what a cheeky fellow he was to ask such a question. Fernando immediately saw that I had not understood him, and most embarrassed, he explained himself. 'Come on what anti-malaria pills are you taking?'

Looking vague, I scratched my head.

'Nothing, the doctors in Algeciras said there is no malaria here; cholera does not exist but yellow fever, yes.'

He went berserk, shouting for his driver and secretary, and we were sent immediately to the hospital to be given anti-malaria drugs, and a vaccine against cholera, amongst others.

'Wow!' said Fernando on our return. 'The doctors in Algeciras are totally idiotic.'

'Yes,' agreed I, 'they did not even know where Tanzania was, and had to look it up in an atlas!'

He was horrified, that even Swiss Air, who we had flown with, had not explained to us how and when to take the malaria pills. He explained to me that we should have taken them two weeks earlier, and to be careful in the bush. Never thought more about it, until it was too late.

Fernando was a charming host, and showed us the yacht club, picnics on the beach, full of Poles, Yugoslavs and Russians, this was their holiday playground. He arranged a big dinner party with all the diplomats and ministers, when one particular ebony black Nigerian told me the most fascinating stories of his own country. The next day there was a *coup d'etat* there, and he was flown back very quickly. Fernando told us this man was the cause of it and he was imprisoned on arrival. Very sad to hear as he was a charming fellow and very interesting. That is Africa for you, in one minute and out the next.

To start our safari, we flew up to Arusha, where we were met by a lovely local driver called David, and a white Land Rover, all organised by the embassy. We drove through the town on sandy streets, with a lot of little men working away on sewing machines beside the road. I learnt later this was the local industry.

Our first night was spent at Ngare Sero Mountain Lodge with Mike and Gisela Leach, very much in the forest with hundreds of huge colobus monkeys chattering away in the trees. These are very special, with huge big tails and black and white fur. The Masai kill them to make headdresses for their spiritual dances.

There are a great number of Masai around Arusha and Mount Meru and south into the Masai Steppes. A totally separate race to the Tanzanians; different language, different clothes, and totally different culture. Nomadic, they live with their cattle and goats and live in *rondavels*, traditional African round houses, and travel for miles on foot.

Gisela regaled us with stories of how they, the whites, were all called up by the local politicians many years earlier and told, 'When you get home, you will find our guys sitting in your kitchens eating your food and their legs on your tables. You must not object, as the coffee plantations are ours now, you will be left alone as long as you don't put up resistance.'

It was one mass of coffee plantations for miles in every direction, they left Mike and Gisela alone as they were running a tourist business, but the farmers on West Kilimanjaro and the coffee estates were nearly all confiscated. Years later, as the country became a democratic republic, some of the land was returned to the original owners.

Very excited, we took off from this idyllic spot and headed back through the town bearing west, dead straight towards the Serengeti and the Ngorongoro Crater, one of the world's natural wonders and today a national heritage site. After an early start we travelled seven hours on rough roads, arriving at Lake Manyara, around 1.00 pm. Today, thanks to the new Japanese road, it takes two hours.

The park was full of monkeys, scurrying out of the bushes with their babies hanging upside down on their bellies, sitting on our windscreen making faces at us. Lake Manyara Park is at the foot of the Great Rift Valley, which cuts Africa in two. Running from the Nile Valley down through Kenya until it peters out in the Zambezi. We had spectacular viewing of huge hippos, literally hundreds of them in the lake, very exciting, as today hardly any. We were charged by a tiny elephant suddenly coming at us with his trunk folded over his head, pretending to be the big male, squealing in rage; we saw another big herd, all matriarchs with lots of babies, so adorable watching them meandering between their mother's legs and their aunts helping to push them forwards. Masses of giraffes, wart hogs haring around with their tiny tails stuck in the air, impalas racing in circles and thousands of water birds. It was a stunning afternoon, and despite it being ruined by El Niño ten years ago, flooded, with trees ripped out, I will always have a soft spot for Manyara.

Our next stop was Gibbs' Farm up above the Rift Escarpment, set in deep red soil; again coffee plantations and a very rich, cultivated valley. At Karatu, a small village, we turned right and as it was getting dark we hurried to find it before the sun set. A lovely old farmhouse, with small bungalows for their clients. A garden to die for, with every plant imaginable. Mrs Gibbs was an old resident, who sadly lost her husband and then all her coffee plantations, as Nyerere swept his reforms across the country.

She was a charming lady, and it broke my heart to see her slaving away in the kitchen, working her butt off, to keep the place running. We loved our first night out in the bush, the air was so clean and cool at night. The next day we drove into the Ngorongoro reservation, and arrived on the lip of the crater; what a view. The crater was formed when a giant volcano exploded and collapsed on itself some two to three million years ago, is 2,000 feet deep and its floor covers some 100 square miles, home to two huge alkaline lakes and a forest, with streams flowing in every direction. In 1985, there were two lodges on the rim and only three Land Rovers, compared to today, where every square metre has a lodge on it. Still, it's much wilder than Kenya. The sides of the crater are so steep, the animals, once down at the bottom, very rarely came up again; if they do, they are vulnerable to be hunted by the Masai, who are allowed to herd cattle through the crater. A 1,000-year-old tradition.

We were lucky not to have rain or fog, and an excellent sighting of a pride of lions, females and cubs with one young, very strong male watching over them. Each time a new male takes over a pride, the original male slinks off to join a bachelor group. The new younger male kills off all the old chap's male progeny, leaving the coast clear for his descendents. I have actually seen this in the crater last year. The original fight, the older male disappearing, and two weeks later the four male cubs just gone. Horrible, but it is nature in action, just like the impalas.

We had our picnic under a tree next to the hippo lake and wondered why David and a crater guide sat in the car. Oops! We found out pretty quickly, the birds swept down and nearly decapitated us, snatching our sandwiches from our fingers.

Coming back via the swamp, a whole herd of elephants, lifting up the swamp grass and covering their backs, and a tiny baby between mum's legs, squealing with fun and just covered with it, you could only make out his trunk. So sad, there are only two or three today left in the crater. We saw big rhinos out on the plain, and bingo! A baby was born. We watched with our binoculars, and within three minutes, this fat round bundle was up and trotting after his mother. The more you know about animal life, the more amazing it is.

The alkaline lakes were full of pink and white flamingos, in their thousands. The pleasure of seeing life in the crater with only two other Land Rovers for company, was naturally out of this world. Today it is packed, and with driving rules and regulations, one could imagine to be in Whipsnade Zoo. On our way up the escarpment, we watched two rhinos fighting and when one came very close, it was the only time I saw Joaquin a little nervous. Crossing an enormous puddle, I shouted to David to stop, all were very curious. I told him to back up slowly, and in the water two eyes opened. It was an enormous hippo, submerged, so muddy he was totally camouflaged. He just did not move. David said he would simply wait until night time to find deeper water.

Our first experience of the Ngorongoro Crater; the best I ever had.

We drove on, as we were booked into the first Seronera lodge right in the middle of the Serengeti, the largest national wild game park in Africa, passing various Masai villages and then the Olduvai Gorge on our right, a steep-sided ravine, where Louis and Mary Leakey had famously spent years excavating, discovering the first imprint of an upright man.

David our driver, filled us in on all the details, and asked us if we were happy to drive off piste. Joaquin was thrilled, as we came back up a valley and there immediately before us was the migration, literally millions of animals in every direction. The mooing of the wildebeest, screeching of jackals, low coughing noise from the zebras, all sent shivers down my spine. I have never seen a mass of animals in comparison to that day.

We had our sandwiches, sitting on the bonnet of the Land Rover, before a huge panorama of rolling grass as far as the eye could see, surrounded by ostriches, Grant's gazelles and Tommies (Thomson's gazelles), thousands of wildebeest and their babies. Amongst the herds, there were creeping forms of lions, hyenas and other predators, jackals, and at the kills, masses of vultures. Each one had their priority. Going on towards the Seronera Lodge, where there was water for the wildlife, and valleys, the wildebeest used to gallop up the slopes at frenetic speed, snorting in anger at our approach, and chucking their hind legs into the air. They seemed completely mad, snorting angry noises; I don't think I have seen mammals quite so crazy.

Arriving at the lodge, we realized it was a grandiose name; a tented camp was more correct. A long line of tents with showers behind them, and a laid out fireplace in front, fires burning to keep the lions at bay. Well, it was great to get there, but what an amazing experience; here we were in the middle of nowhere. Joaquin was ecstatic and after having his first whisky, wandered off to the bush, when a guard came running after him. 'Sir, please don't go off into the bush, you never know what is hiding in the grass?' Mortified, he came back towards our tent.

After a very good dinner, exhausted, we went to bed, the mosquito nets were hung around the cots, you could not call them anything approaching beds! Joaquin looked at the nets, and swore in Spanish, as they had huge holes in them, mine too.

'What the **** do we need these for?' and flung them up onto the iron support. Neither of us knew it at the time, but we both caught malaria that night.

The following morning, David took us out into the northern part of the Serengeti, amidst a glorious sunrise, with huge spaces of animals in every direction. Bumbling along a track, I spotted in the distance, a cheetah and three cubs, and whispered in David's ear, as I was standing in the back. 'Wow! Mama Vicky you are a great game spotter!' We approached very carefully, came within 100 metres, and just sat there watching them play with each other, while mum was beginning to get anxious. She eventually hissed at us and slunk off into the bush, calling her cubs to follow; we had had an hour at least of uninterrupted sighting, heaven.

Out on the plains, both men wanted to pee, stopped and got out, each to one side, whilst I stayed standing in the jeep. Suddenly with a mighty roar, a huge male lion came out of the grass, literally ten feet from Joaquin, and took off in the opposite direction, hunting down a zebra. Was he lucky!

Further on, we encountered sleeping female lions, driving up to them within one metre, and they never moved a muscle. We saw secretary birds striding around looking very pompous, crested cranes strutting to attract the opposite sex, silver-backed jackals, and masses of wart hogs, tails in the air, and running backwards into their holes. In this huge open space, there were many outcrops of seriously big rocks called *kopjes*. Lions were renowned to sleep on the top, so they could gaze into the far distance, and protect their cubs. We drove round one of these, and I had a gut feeling that something was going on; instinct, intuition, call it what you like. I asked David would he mind, going round again, as I was taking a video film, and there in a culvert, I saw a female lioness with a cub in her mouth, slowly slinking through the bushes. She was on her way, from the bottom of the rocks, where she had given birth, to the top, to keep her babies away from harm. Fascinated we stayed quiet, and she repeated her performance four times; and each time she passed the little opening in the bush, that I had found, she turned her gaze and just looked at us.

I just adored the bush and the Serengeti, the wildlife and space, and the migration was out of this world, something clicked and I vowed to come back and live here one day.

# 20. Kenya

We left Tanzania from Arusha, catching a monoplane to Nairobi. We had to stop on the border and the pilot carried our luggage across, the only border crossing open. We then caught a taxi to the capital of Kenya to the old famous hotel, The Norfolk; Toby Block, the owner, was a good friend of Fernando's. We had an interesting couple of days finding Kenya much more sophisticated than Tanzania, though she did not have the mountains, volcanoes, or the Serengeti. It was very English as it had been a former British colony, and there remained a large farming community of Brits living amongst many Kenyan tribes.

There are over 40 distinct tribes in Kenya, and which tribe you belong to is still the most important factor in social life. Political parties are mainly based on tribal allegiances rather than ideology. The largest of the tribes, the Kikuyu, the Luo, and the Akamb have adopted aspects of western lifestyles, whereas the Masai, Turkana and Samburu peoples live largely according to their traditions. Of course, the existence of so many tribes causes conflict; the massacre of last year was purely tribal, and we who live in East Africa know it is not over by a long way.

We had dinner at the Carnivore, a huge, and aptly named restaurant, with gardens and terraces, especially for eating 'bush meat'. Shooting in Kenya was not then prohibited, so bush meat was not only available but legal to sell. Today there is no more, the white hunters and all the romantic ideas around them have disappeared. Hemingway and his kudu are long gone, while in Tanzania, the hunting continues, in protected areas; shooting blocks, as they are called, are rented out to Arabs, various Eurotrash and nouveau Americans, who fly in, and then out again with the carcasses.

We flew down to Mombassa, where Joaquin had happy memories of fishing with Maria Rosa and Fernando, from the Pemba Yacht Club, where he earned the nickname, Mr Wahoo. The wahoo is a prized game fish and Joaquin had caught the biggest one in living memory. We had booked ourselves into a simple hotel located right on the coast, where we could relax on the beach for a week, recovering from the safari, and where Joaquin could get some fishing, and I some windsurfing. Despite a howling wind, and rough seas, Joaquin made for the fishing boats and tried to book one for the next day, but was told, 'Sir, *pole sana*, the last boat has just been reserved.' He was very miffed. Spaniards like Joaquin don't take 'no' lightly, and I thought to myself, *how am I going to keep him amused?*

Wandering along the beach, we went in and out of the hotels just to see what they were like, passing windsurfs all lying on the sand, but there was far too much wind to even contemplate hiring one. On a notice board I suddenly noticed a large poster, saying, the Royal Irish Fusiliers were beating the retreat that evening. I was gob-smacked as this was cousin David's regiment, and wondered what they were doing in Kenya.

We went to watch it, and introduced ourselves to the commanding officer, a charming blond colonel. He laughed his head off, when he heard I was David Craig's cousin, and showed us into the VIP seats, where we spent a lovely evening, watching the parade. Military music is always emotional for me, so desperately moving. We were dragged off to the bar, when it was finished and introduced to all the other officers. Finally, we learnt that the regiment was on manoeuvres in the bush, as every year a different regiment was sent to Kenya, in a post-colonial agreement between the two countries. It supposedly gave the British lads experience in the bush, but I thought afterwards, they were more likely to be helping to cut down trees, and clear the bush for the Kenyans than engaging in military exercises.

To our horror we learnt next day that the fishing boat Joaquin wanted to hire for the day, had turned turtle on its way back through the reef, as the waves and current were so strong. The wife of the guy who had rented it was seasick and went to lie in the cabin, and she went overboard, never to be found again.

I said to Joaquin, 'There you go, pure destiny, you were never meant to hire that boat; imagine, it could have been me in the cabin.'

'Don't say it, Vics, it makes me sick to think of it,' he replied.

Our lazy relaxation on the beach did not last long; typical male, Joaquin got restless and suddenly said, 'Hey! We cannot stay here any longer, you are so good at planning, why don't we go on another safari in Kenya? We have another week!'

I tried various agencies and found one, offering a trip for a week to Tsavo West, Amboseli Park and Kilimanjaro. Staying within the Kenyan border, we would have a very different perspective. Joaquin was thrilled and so off we went, in a minibus full of Germans and blaring music. I tried to make the best of it by chatting them up. Each time Joaquin complained, I quietly said, 'You asked for it, just try and get the best out of it.'

Arriving in Tsavo West, very near the Tanzanian border, we stopped at Salt Lick Lodge, a very odd building, with a lake underneath it, and walk-aways along the top to the rooms. Each room had a bell to push in the night, if wild animals came to drink. During dinner, herds of zebra and antelopes arrived; the Germans were thrilled. Much later in the night, a solitary male lion crept up for a sip. We just left him in peace.

On the following day, Amboseli National Park was glorious, weather divine, and the first sign of a massive herd of buffalos. Magnificent animals, staring at one with small piggy eyes while munching their cud. If one kept very quiet, they just stared back at us with curiosity, but no way would you want to annoy them. They can charge very quickly and have a huge massive head of solid bone, that could wipe out a human in a second. I have known two friends killed by buffalo charges, you do not muck about with them.

Amboseli Lodge was delightful and rustic, with the most stunning views of Kilimanjaro topped with snow, totally different from the western side. The next stop was, to my surprise, Kinondoni Lodge, the old property of Michael Cunningham-Reed, whose elderly father I had met years earlier in the South of France. It was a beautiful place with a huge water hole in front, miles of bush in every direction, and hundreds of little furry hyraxes jumping in and out of our terrace. To me, heaven on earth.

Studying the map I realized we had gone in a full circle, and would now be heading back towards the coast. The border with Tanzania was in a straight line about 50 kilometres away. How crazy to have to return to the coast, fly back to Nairobi, then take a double flight to return to Dar es Salaam. I could not see the sense in it.

I went down to the manager's office, and asked him if there was an easier solution? Could we not get a lift in their milk lorry? Of course, they thought I was quite crazy, but when I told them that Joaquin had been ill, and our international flight to Europe left from Dar, they acquiesced gracefully, telling me to go to the bar at 7.00 and meet up with the sergeant of an English regiment and ask him would he drive us across the bush to the border. The manager was sure he would do it, as the soldiers were very bored. I met this fellow and told him of our predicament, after a few questions, he seemed more or less in agreement. Then I added my relationship to David, and he roared.

'What? You are a cousin of Major Craig? I don't believe it!'

From then on, plain sailing. Talk about destiny, it happens to me non-stop. Two days later, we said our goodbyes to the Germans, who were all stupefied to hear we were leaving direct for the border, more so the Kenyan driver and guide who insisted we signed papers, saying we had left their tour of our own accord.

At 6.00 the following morning, we were picked up by a military jeep, with the sergeant, two other soldiers and even a medical orderly; he was worried that Joaquin was really sick. We crossed the bush in a straight line for the border, today the town Namanga; then it was a huge sisal estate. On arrival, the Kenyan police asked the military for their papers. It turned into an argy bargy until I suggested that if they had confidence, to leave their papers with the border police, and pick them up in half an hour on their return. The Brits were quite worried, but it was the only solution. The no-man's-land went on for kilometres, and I knew Joaquin was not up to walking across, and carrying our luggage in the roasting heat. If we had turned back, it would have meant two and half days of travelling.

Sweating inside, we got to the Tanzanian border, to face another problem; one huge mass of people, trying to cross into Kenya, in the other direction. Poor things were desperately trying to buy a bar of soap, cooking oil, packet of rice, anything. I just could not see Joaquin carrying his luggage through this human river. I leapt out of the jeep, and told the sergeant to hang on a second, as I pushed and shoved my way through the crowds until I arrived at the police. Asked them in clear, slow English, could they help me, as my husband had been sick, and I had to get him back to Dar es Salaam, producing two 20-dollar bills, shoved between the passports. They disappeared very quickly. The police asked for our luggage, and I just pointed back the way I had come. He immediately sent four fellows scurrying after me, as porters. When we arrived at the jeep, the army lads and Joaquin just opened their mouths.

'Come on, don't waste any more time, and make sure you look sick when you pass the police!'

Saying my thanks and gratitude to the sergeant, I asked him, 'Do you want me to thank your commanding officer for this adorable service your regiment has offered us?'

'Christ no, Vicky, I will be demoted immediately, I have told no one!'

I thought to myself, *what if the poor bugger was found out, that he left their papers with the Kenyan police? Oh! La! La!*

Anyway we made it, and Joaquin was thrilled, a quick taxi ride to Arusha and a short hop flight to Dar. We were back in the embassy for dinner two days ahead of schedule.

Once back in Europe, in Zurich, Joaquin said, 'Come on Vics, I am taking you out to the best meal we can find. After all those horrible sandwiches and gunk we ate in Tanzania, we deserve a good meal.'

I looked at him, and said, 'I am so sorry, but I feel very sick and tired, I want nothing to eat, just to go to bed.' He was very disappointed in me. I think it was beginning then.

Back in Spain the next day, all his family thrilled to see him, and off he went rushing round to see them, telling them all the adventures we had and the things we had seen; the lions and their cubs, the cheetahs, and all the rest of the wildlife. Poor Joaquin then had to go straight up to Madrid, to sort out problems in his company. Three or four days later, I went to the station to pick him up. To my great surprise, I saw on the platform all his brothers.

'What on earth are you all doing here?'

'Vicky! Don't you know? Joaquin has been very sick in Madrid, and fell in your bathroom and cracked open his head on the bidet.'

*Shit*, I thought, this is the malaria. Fernando warned us about getting it a few days after we arrived back in Europe. His brothers all said 'No, Vicky, it's his prostate, we told you, he should have had it out while in hospital before.'

Nonsense. As soon as he was off the train, I left the brothers standing and took him to the hospital, where one of the doctors was a good friend of mine. He took him into the laboratory, did a malaria test and contacted the chief intern, who was very against it, saying malaria did not exist in Europe anymore. The test came back positive; it was malaria and one of the worst strains. All the fault of the doctors in the health centre on the port, who never prescribed a prophylactic. The hospital had no medicine for it, except quinine, which was so out of date. I took him home, and told him to go to bed. In the meantime, telephoned friends in Marbella and learnt that a doctor in Ronda, also the local mayor, had won the Silver Cross in Jordan, for having eliminated malaria in the whole country. I drove back to the hospital, and told the intern my news. He did not believe me. We had a horrible row. I told him in no uncertain terms, that he was an imbecile and if he did not immediately come to Las Pilas and make a blood slide and send it on the bus that night to Ronda. I would sue him. He could not believe his ears, that a mayor in a mountain village was a world-renowned malaria expert.

When they all confirmed that it was true, and had spoken to him various times, they were finally convinced. The results came back confirmed, and Joaquin was put on the latest drug and told to stay in bed until his temperature dropped. The whole hospital came down to the lab to apologise to me. I think the medical officer in the port was sacked for inefficiency.

Next day I got it, nothing like so badly, but hot and cold for three days. I don't dare breathe, as I have never had a sign of it again. Now I live in Africa, but near Arusha where it is often very cold. Perhaps now I am immune?

*My first time riding in a flamenco skirt at the Rocio, 1975*

*Joaquin at his bodega 'Real Tesoro' in Jerez, 1975*

*Paris, my first renovated attic in the Marais*

*Our wedding in the Ermita of the Luz Tarifa, 17 July 1976*

*Wedding, 1976*

*Wedding group, 1976*

*Fortuna, the King's yacht, Island of Cabrera, 1976*

*Dehesa de la Zorilla, 1977*

*Almirante, 1979*

*Marigalante II and Fortuna, the King's yacht, Ibiza, 1979*

*Vicky and Caroline with Polo on the lake at La Zorilla, 1979*

*David and family, breakfast at Las Pilas, 1980*

*Miles and Polo in the lake at La Zorilla, 1980*

*On the Sanlucar beach 'Rocio', 1980*

*Vicky and Joaquin, 1980*

*Rocio, outside our first house, 1981*

*Vicky and Michael Clark, Morocco, 1981*

*Joaquin on the beach at Mombasa, Kenya, 1984*

*Puerta Vallarta, Mexico, 1985*

*Polo and her puppies, 1986*

*News Year's Eve party at the house of Terry and Hubert Pantz, Marbella. Bringing the pink pig as the mascot, 1988*

*Luis Antonio receiving his prize from his Uncle Joaquin, 1989*

*Vicky driving Hortensia in Sotogrande arena with the Colonel, 1989*

*Lady Sarah Spencer Churchill in Lyme Connecticut USA, 1992*

*Miles, Sotogrande, 1992*

*Packing up the stables, Las Pilas, 1992*

# *21. Craigs and Balfours*

Of course, in Spain I was surrounded by Cerveras, but throughout the years of our marriage close members of my family were also regular visitors to Joaquin and I, most notably the Craigs and the Balfours.

David and his wife Jane, had stayed a couple of times with Jacques and I at El Molino, but the first time they met Joaquin was in 1979 when they came to Las Pilas with their two young children, Caroline and Miles, then aged five and three. When they arrived, I had to explain to Joaquin, that they were not very sophisticated, as they dumped their baggage on the terrace and leapt into the pool!

'Hey, Jane, don't you want to show them their rooms first?' I asked.

'Vics, please, they are on holiday and have talked of your pool for the last eight hours.'

Poor little fellows. I winked at Joaquin, and said leave them be. He disappeared to behind the farm, and came back with an enormous inner tyre tube, and threw it in the pool. The wee kids were thrilled, and came out of the water very shyly to shake his hand and thank him. I don't know who was more moved.

We could only get them out of the water once it was dark, around 9.30, while David and Jane had their *copitas*.

'Surely your children are hungry? What time do you want their supper?'

Jane giggled and said, 'Vicky, we know your hours. We gave them sandwiches somewhere near Malaga, so no panic.'

Great! One problem less, they fit into our crazy hours. I have always been able to adapt to different countries and different time zones, but now being older, I find the Spanish hours quite crazy. I go back to the Tarifa area, to Algeciras and Sotogrande, and when my sisters-in-law ask me, mid-winter, to come to dinner at 10.00 pm, I answer, 'And what does one do between 6.00 and 10.00, it's dark?' They never seem to understand. I remember waiting for hours for Joaquin at lunchtime; in Madrid I would go and buy the Herald Tribune and go to Mallorca, to have some white wine and their delicious tapas. Going back to the flat, at 2.45 pm and still no sign of him. In Madrid too, everything closes between 13:00hrs and 17:00hrs. It's quite bonkers.

I tried in Las Pilas to keep fairly normal hours, but it was impossible. Joaquin would come home at 3.00pm, sometimes later; in the winter with shorter days, and three horses to train in the afternoons, I would go wild. Now in Africa, where times are so English, and everyone so proud, that they get up at 6.00 am and to bed at 10.00 pm. It's just nuts. They come to lunch and stay until it's dark!

I tried to give the kids the best holiday they ever had, with plans to go to the beach with Joaquin's great nephews; I dressed them up in Spanish clothes and took them to the *feria*, putting jasmine royale into Caroline's hair. In her flamenco dress, she looked adorable. I could not get them to move from the pool, and Jane simply said, 'No, Vicky, leave them in the pool, they are much happier together.'

It took me some years before I found out that they were like this back at home in Northern Ireland. Mummy never pushed them to play with other kids. Consequently they were very shy and very unsure of themselves. Mixed with the Spanish kids, who were the absolute opposite: naughty, loud and spoilt, total extroverts, it was not a marriage of convenience.

They came back the next summer, and simply loved to swim in the lake and play with the dogs. They were still very shy, but I pushed them off with other kids and arranged mad picnics on the Tarifa coast, and Joaquin took them to see the Spanish breeders and their pure-bred Spanish horses.

On one of the family's visits, it was early evening, and something struck me as I looked out of my bathroom window to see David swaying on his feet on the terrace below. I called out to him.

'Hi, fellow! Are you pissed again already?'

'Good Lord, Vicky, not at all, this is my first gin and tonic.'

'Yes, but apparently yesterday, you were hanging on to the banisters of that old *cortijo*, and Joaquin's nieces thought you were plastered?'

He insisted he was not then, or this evening. I had a funny feeling in my stomach and said, 'I think you need a medical check up, when you get back to Ireland.'

Which he did, as he knew, but was terrified to face up to it. He was diagnosed with multiple sclerosis, the same as his father. Brian Craig, who spent his last years in a military hospital outside Dublin, after spending the war years in Burma and a Japanese prisoner of war camp. He had been tortured horribly, so the army took care of him, but he had the same dreadful disease. David of course was panicked he had inherited it. Tragic.

Hugh and Sheila Balfour joined us on our honeymoon and were regulars from then on. Both were super fun, and, of course, Hugh being a naval officer had a lot in common with Joaquin, and loved our trips on Marigalante II.

In his illustrious career Hugh had been the commander of the Royal Yacht Britannia from 1972 to 1974, taking Princess Anne and Captain Mark Phillips to the West Indies and the Galapagos Islands on their honeymoon, and his connections ensured Joaquin and I got a very close view of the next royal honeymoon to take place on Britannia, that of Prince Charles and Lady Di in 1981.

To my mind Prince Philip seemed to have pushed Charles into a marriage of necessity, telling him he had to settle down and produce heirs to the throne and stop fiddling around with married women. Poor Diana was the unlucky victim and come her wedding day was still under the illusion that Charles loved her. The Foreign Office planned the honeymoon and arranged that the Royal Yacht picked them up at Gibraltar. Our Spanish king, Juan Carlos, begged them please not to use Gib, offering them the full services of any other port in Spain: Cadiz, Cartegena, San Sebastian, Malaga, wherever they wished. The talks over the sovereignty of Gibraltar were in full swing at the time and vibes between the two countries were not good.

The Foreign Office absolutely refused to compromise, but the inside political hiccup was never explained in the press. Admiral

John Mackenzie, married to Ursula Balfour, Hugh's sister, was the Admiral of Gibraltar at the time. He invited us to the big dinner he gave at The Mount, his official residence, in their honour the night before they arrived. Furious that the Brits had refused the offers of Juan Carlos, I went dressed in my flamenco dress.

I was seated next to a government dignitary, and turned to him and said, 'Well, you lot have put your foot in it once again, you have really made a diplomatic gaffe!' He was so cross he stamped my foot with his stick, and did not talk to me again. What a pompous arsehole.

The next day we knew there was going to be trouble with the Spaniards, and sure enough they blockaded the port with hundreds of little boats, and it took ages for Britannia to be able to leave the port. Joaquin, far from stupid, brought the Marigalante II up to port and kept her idling until the Royal Yacht slowly made her way around the rock.

Lieutenant Commander Rick Cosby, married to my cousin Catherine Balfour, was then officer in charge of the stern deck. We all waved to him and cruised closer to the Britannia. Charles and Diana had by then disappeared below decks and Rick told us later that the admiral in charge of royalty on board, had phoned him, asking why he had waved to a Spanish yacht. He had replied simply enough.

'Sir, don't worry about them, she is an English admiral's daughter, and cousin to my wife; her husband a Spanish naval officer, retired. Very pro-England.'

At this, Charles and Diana came back on deck and waved like mad at us. We sailed alongside them, until they turned to the east and headed out to sea. It was very rough, and the small boats that had blockaded them, were left far behind. We learned later, that Diana had picked up the phone in her cabin, and overheard Charles whispering sweet nothings to Camilla Parker-Bowles. Diana must have felt as I did back in 1966, just sick in your stomach. Poor kid, no one in Buckingham Palace taught her what she was in for, and how to prepare herself to be the wife of the Prince of Wales.

Of course, the majority of our trips on Marigalante II with family and friends were a hoot, but inevitably over many years, some cruises stand out for all the wrong reasons. Our summer sail to Ibiza in 1982, particularly so.

We had invited Joaquin's two nieces, the youngest ones on Maria Rosa's side, and a great friend of mine, Christie Leebs, half Austrian and half English. Her father, the Austrian, was given a huge piece of land up near El Molino and Alambique, just before El Cuarton; he had obviously worked with Franco on some scheme or other. When I knew her, she was getting a divorce from her English husband, and was a very keen ornithologist. She knew every bird in the Cuarton valley and the mountains. Now ruined by windmills.

Christie and I drove with the windsurfers strapped to the roof, leaving the car with Joaquin who was already on the boat, fishing with his brothers. He would then drive to Madrid, go to a board meeting, pick up the two nieces and drive back. That was the plan. At the last minute he invited the younger son of his brother, Jose Maria, Mariano.

We were thrilled to drive, as it meant cutting out all the boring coast, between Marbella and Alicante, and we had the same sense of humour, so giggled non-stop en route as we stopped in the little villages and re-met some refreshing youngsters. The new Spain was changing so much, and more so as we went north. Andalucia was still very much the south, with families still very old fashioned.

We had promised Joaquin to meet him on a certain day at a certain time, knowing he wanted the car, at the new yacht club of Mar Menor. I drive fast and we arrived a day early and not a sign of them; we rang up Motril, the port south of where we were, and they were still fishing! Typical Joaquin, no hurry. 'So sorry, darling, we will be there tomorrow.'

Christie and I went back to the countryside and made camp under some olive trees, waking up in the morning surrounded by goats. Next evening we went to the quay to have dinner in a bistro, and to her surprise I sat down and with some relief let out the most enormous fart! Obviously we both burst into fits of laughter. Some old twit behind her, called the waiter, talking haughtily in Spanish, of course, thinking I would not be able to understand.

'What pigs, they are completely disgusting! Throw them out.'

This made us laugh even more, the poor waiter did not know where to look.

Come midnight, the Marigalante II rounded the headland, we were happy to see her at long last. Joaquin was overjoyed, telling us the fishing was lousy after all. Somehow we all managed to cram in, poor Christie slept on deck. The men still had the cabins and young Mariano the captain's berth in the bow! We got rid of them and heaved the windsurfers on board as well as Pegasus, my Vespa, and Joaquin took over the car and left for Madrid. We were alone for three days, with Marianito, as we called him. There were two in the family.

When Joaquin returned, I had never seen him so cross, and the two nieces were very glum. It was difficult to ask him what had happened, for on a boat, there is little or no privacy. Eventually I discovered that the girls had offered to drive, but did so badly, it was dangerous. He had taken over, but he hated to drive and was miserable with the summer traffic to Valencia.

Fuming, he said, 'Those spoilt teenagers sucked gum all the way with their feet up on the dashboard.' I thought to myself, *oh dear, this cruise is not going to be funny*. It certainly wasn't too easy, they were too young at the time to share in our jokes, and I remember getting into an argument about the Catholic Church with Kikilina.

Then Joaquin got into a temper for no reason, and I stomped off the boat and took Pegasus for a good ride. Of course, I came back, but no one was laughing at breakfast. You cannot mix up three generations on a boat with success: Joaquin's, Christie and I, then Marianito and the girls. When we went ashore, poor Joaquin always had to foot the bill, no one else had a bean on them; except for the nightclubs, of course.

One day in the main port of Ibiza, we had all decided to spend a day at the beach, for a change. Christie though was not feeling well and stayed on board. On our return, we saw she was not alone, and we all thought she had picked up a beau. As we approached, we saw it was a young boy and she had wrapped him in a blanket.

He was a German kid of about 15. The horror of his story came out slowly, none of us spoke German. He and his father had been snorkelling off Espalmador, when a speed boat came roaring past them and sliced his father nearly in two. He had died in the water beside his son. It makes me sick to write and remember that evening.

The boy had been brought back by the Guardia Civil, but no one had bothered to look for his mother. We managed to understand she was still on Formentor, where they were staying. Emilio made some hot tea, as the child was shaking with shock, and someone rang the mother's hotel and told her to get the next ferry to Ibiza. Never get sick in August and never in Ibiza. The ordinary Spaniard behaved appallingly, no sense of kindness or respect. Christie and I had to take the lad by taxi to the ferry landing. Marianito had lent him some clothes, as he was just in his swimming trunks, the Guardia Civil had dumped him onto the quay beside our boat, and just left him. None of the Spaniards on the other boats moved a finger to help.

The next ferry arrived, and I saw her, a little blond woman in her late thirties. I told the taxi to let the boy reunite with his mother in his back seat. He was rude and grumbled, until I told him just to shut up and to try and be decent, the boy's father had just died. A horrible moment; Christie and I waited for them, as we had found that the body had gone to the morgue and if we did not hurry it would close for the night.

We accompanied them to the morgue, explained the papers she had to sign and then took them shaking and crying to the German consulate. She was extremely polite and grateful for our help. She spoke a little English, so we understood she had no money on her or cards, as she had run to catch the ferry straight from the beach.

The consulate was odious, and told me to get out of his office, that I had no right to help them. Extraordinary. He just said to her to come back in the morning. We took her to a small hotel, and let the manager know the whole story. He was the only decent bloke we found, he got us drinks and told the Germans they could stay the night for free and dinner was on him. We exchanged addresses and with hugs all round, left them to their fate. I did get a letter of thanks a few months later, but today cannot remember their names. I could cry easily now thinking of them on their holiday, and the shame of the Ibizencos, who treat the tourists like dirt, and the spoilt boat driver, who, of course, never came back to find the body.

*

In 1985 Hugh had been promoted to admiral and was posted to command the navy of the Sultan of Oman. The posting represented an unusual exercise of British sea power. In 1853, local sheikhs, pirates by nature, were coerced into signing a General Maritime Truce, guaranteeing a naval presence in the troubled waters of the Gulf, in parallel to one in the field exerted by the Trucial Scouts, traditionally commanded by a British officer.

After Hugh and Sheila had been in Oman for a couple of years, and settled, they invited us to stay. We needed little encouragement, so I immediately arranged the flights, visas, and booked an extra week in the United Arab Emirates.

It was a fabulous holiday, and as always with Sheila, we never stopped laughing.

Arriving at Muscat, the capital, we were met by Hugh and his staff. Practising my Arabic, I was shouted down. 'Vicky, shut up, everyone speaks English, they are all Tamil Tigers from Sri Lanka.'.

Great, good old Hugh, he put me in my place. Headed to his official residence, it was by now 2.00 am, and very hot. I stripped off and jumped into the pool.

'Vicky! Are you mad? The Air Vice Marshall lives just over the wall!'

'So what? Isn't he human?'

Hugh, when on a job, took life too seriously; on holiday it was a different story. Sheila was great and took us around the *souks* and the harbour, and the horse show with all the Sultan's family; simply charming people. So clean, rubbish bins on every corner, a huge fine if one was caught throwing rubbish out onto the streets.

Back then in 1987 no foreigners were allowed in Oman, and certainly no women. Unless one was, as we were, related to an official, and had already obtained a special permit. Today the country is wide open to tourists.

One day Hugh took us on a camping trip into the mountains; he called it 'wadi bashing', as we had to use a four-by-four, and go up river beds into the very mountainous terrain. Then he laid on a trip up to the Straits of Hormuz, overlooking Iran. We went by a naval bi-plane, crossing the land of the UAE, which divided Oman in two, flying over the famous Musandam Peninsula. Here the first world telegraph, and under-sea cable to India, was connected via a tiny island in the middle of this peninsular, during the reign of Queen Victoria. British troops had to defend it against pirates and thugs, shooting at them from the mainland.

Arriving at the Omani naval base, we landed on the airstrip, and Sheila took us to the mess, where we met the two officers in charge. During dinner, Hugh asked Joaquin what he would like to do the next day.

'Would you like to be my VIP guest, and come onboard a destroyer, that is arriving from Basra, Iraq and officially inspect the crew? Or would you like to go fishing? My staff here will take you.'

Joaquin, very rude, answered immediately. 'Oh, Hugh, fishing, of course! I have inspected enough naval vessels and crew for a lifetime.' Poor Hugh was seriously miffed.

On our way to bed, I giggled with Sheila. 'Oops. Poor Hugh has laid on all the VIP things for Joaquin, and all he wants to do is fish!'

They all got up at 5.00 am, as Joaquin had insisted they had to be out in the straits before dawn. We went back to bed, waking for breakfast, and there was the fishing boat coming ashore. Great excitement, he had caught two barracudas and a shark. The whole base was thrilled. Never had they got up at 5.00 am to go fishing.

Sheila and I went later to the beach, but we could not swim, the area has the biggest number of sharks in the Middle East. They collected in the straits, catching all the dirt and rubbish that comes down the gulf.

Leaving Hugh and Sheila, we went on to the UAE. It took ages to get through the police and customs, though fascinating to pass the time watching the Arabs from Saudi Arabia and the other Gulf states, rushing to the men's toilets, leaving their *jellabahs* in exchange for smart London suits.

Dubai was beginning to take off, but nothing like today. There was one main road leading to the port on the gulf, and all the land north west was beginning to develop. We found our hotel, and went straight to the restaurant, that moved in circles on top of a Tower. The view of the gulf and the shore in front of Iran was breathtaking.

I had various contacts, one a young pilot, who flew the private flights for the royal family; and another, an Irishman, who was the manager of Sheik Mohammed's stables. The pilot took us out to the fish restaurant, in another revolving tower. Telling us the most amazing stories of how he ferried the family's racing camels, tied to the deck, from Africa to the Middle East. How he piloted the planes to London, when they closed Harrods, and nearly emptied the store. My other contact, the Irishman asked us to visit the royal stables the following day; superb is not the word. Huge boxes, five-by-five metres, air conditioning and fans everywhere, deep litter of sawdust; we were both staggered. The most lovely collection of young stallions, the mares and foals were in another enclosure. Joaquin was determined to go back to Las Pilas, and improve the stables!

In another privilege, we were invited to the race track on Sunday to watch our first camel race. Huge paddocks of groaning camels, child jockeys were milling around the racecourse. The little boys were tied onto the back of the camels and had a piece of string to a halter. Today they are strapped onto *belchrome*, on a form of saddle. The camels were totally uncontrolled, and used to race out of the track completely, leaving the wee boys crying, I don't know in anger or frustration. Presumably they were beaten by the owners if they did not win.

We sat in the grandstand, surrounded by sheiks, all exchanging bribes, tips and jokes but there was no point trying to begin to understand them. Leaving the UAE we laughed together, 'Well, now we have an idea what the Middle East is all about!'

We were glad to be home, but with memories of Oman, that were simply unique, and only possible thanks to Hugh. If he had not been appointed to the Sultan, we would never have had such a personal experience.

*

In 1987 having no building project, I was getting itchy feet, and decided to buy two apartments off-plan in the new port of Sotogrande.

Trying to fit in with Joaquin's hours, it was impossible to actually build myself. This was the next best thing, redesigning the two apartments into one, always with my mother in mind.

She was by now a widow for the second time, as the wing commander had died the previous year, and I was hoping she would come and live in Sotogrande, to be near us, so we could look after her. I decorated the apartment with a Moorish theme, and had all the furniture handmade in Tetuan, across the straits.

Little kids working for the artistic centre painted them, and when finished, Joaquin as a saint, took Marigalante II over to Morocco and picked them up, stacking it all on the flying bridge. Once in the new port, the sailors on the quay, winked at me and said, 'Señora, wait until it is dark and we will unload everything for you.'

By then, the whole port knew what I was doing, and thought it was very funny, just waiting for the Guardia Civil to disappear. Smuggling Moroccan furniture into Spain was very naughty. The finished apartments, looked great with an Arabic chimney, handmade beds, sofas, three bedrooms, a big open kitchen, terraces back and front, and a lovely view over the port, where there was action all the time.

We had a Moroccan dinner on the quay, sitting on the boat's cushions to celebrate the occasion. David Naylor-Leyland and his little son joined us, looking divine in his *jellabah* and fez. He had bought a house in Sotogrande, married to a new wife, but she never appeared. The port was booming, and berths being sold at two a minute, everyone wanted to invest in it, including the Spaniards. To think I knew the beach, totally deserted with huge sand dunes and one tiny beach bar, where previously I had lost my car keys at a late night barbecue. Now a thriving port with yachts of all sizes, boutiques and restaurants, offices and two hotels.

Mummy came on holiday to Las Pilas with a Danish nurse in tow. We showed her what I had, yet again, created for her in the port of Sotogrande. We slowly encouraged her to take up residence, explaining, she could live there and be close to us, have fun in the port and make friends with the other elderly residents. She was very difficult, and had hysterics at night, once moved in, saying there were men next door who wanted to rape her! Always complaining about something, hinting she would only stay if we had her back in Las Pilas. Joaquin was doing his nut, as he couldn't stand her. We had an awful time with her, not to mention the Dane who was a pain in the arse!

Come June 23rd, her birthday, I had arranged a dinner in the *feria* of Algeciras at the main club. Champagne and birthday cake, organized by Manolo Ruiz, the judge. Once sitting down, she threw hysterics again, screaming that she could not stand the noise. Joaquin was livid, and told her in no uncertain terms to get up and go back home.

'Isabel, you are a spoilt woman, your daughter has arranged this party especially for you, the judge laid on transport with outriders to get you here safely, all you do is complain. Get up, I am taking you back now to Las Pilas.'

He stalked off and told me to sit down and enjoy the dinner, while he had to walk a long way to find the car, followed by Mummy, actually mortified, I think, as she never said another word. The whole atmosphere was ruined, and Joaquin was embarrassed *vis-à-vis* Manolo, who had laid it all on. We moved her into the apartment in Sotogrande, against her will, of course, with the Danish nurse playing games, and Mummy imagining all sorts of weird happenings. It was dreadful. I invited various old friends, and their parents to meet her, but she was totally negative; I took her out to the restaurants in the port, but she was never happy. At the end of the summer, we arranged to send her back to Malta, to her old apartment, with her two maids. There was no other solution.

# *22. Joaquin Not Well*

The 24th September 1987. Joaquin's 80th birthday. Wow! I could not believe where the years had gone. I had to do something funny for him, and I realized that our darling Breton mare, Hortensia, was 20 more or less on the same date. I had her decorated with flowers and bushes, hid her in the staff kitchen, a bit of a squash as she was very big, and brought her out to the back patio, the same time as the birthday cake. All the guests were most amused. She was just adorable, and never blinked an eye.

The following month, Louise, Sheila's daughter, got married. We flew over to England, and Louise had booked us into some of the most lovely hotels in the country, for Joaquin to see the beauty of England's countryside. Up to then, he had known London but nothing beyond. He was most impressed, and found the chichi country hotels very upmarket.

The wedding was in Dorset, in the garden of Hugh and Sheila's country home, Donhead St Mary. An English atmosphere, but delightful. Louise looked very pretty and totally happy, so we all prayed it would work.

It was the middle of winter, a wet, miserable evening. Joaquin told me he had a meeting with his urologist in town, that he had been twice already and now had the results of his x-rays. I was shocked, as he had not told me anything before this. He had trouble in his throat and had seen a specialist in Madrid six months earlier, but again never admitted it was cancer of the larynx, despite being very mild. We were always playing secrets with each other, but I felt, this evening, it was something serious.

I accompanied him, and seeing the doctor on my own, begged him to tell me if it was serious, and not to tell Joaquin. He came back to the waiting room looking very glum.

'Vicky, Joaquin has a huge tumour attached to his bladder.'

'Shit. Can I see the x-ray, please?'

The doctor knew that I was fairly clued-up over medical problems. Looking at it together, he pointed out the tumour.

'You must take him to Cadiz now and see Dr Flores tomorrow morning. He was my professor in urology. I don't dare operate on Joaquin in Algeciras.'

'Holy Moses,' I replied. 'It is dark already.'

'Yes, I know but you must go, and I will phone the clinic, to prepare a room for him now.'

I simply cannot remember what I told Joaquin, something along the lines that he had cysts and they had to be removed asap to prevent him getting cancer. He believed every word I told him, and trusted my medical knowledge completely. We drove to Cadiz, bought toothbrushes etc at a pharmacy on the way, while I rang Carmen, the housekeeper, and told her the sad story. Later that night I rang his eldest sister, Anna, in tears, I asked her not to say a word to the brothers, as Joaquin did not know, and I did not want him to know either.

He was operated on by Dr Flores the following morning; the beastly thing was scratched out of him, via the penis, and then bled out via the urinary tract. Spanish custom, once again, I had to sleep in his room. Sleep is not the word, as the nurses kept laughing and smoking outside in the corridor. I had not experienced a situation so unpleasant for a long time. It was just hateful, the clinic was tiny, and despite the operating theatres being excellent, the place was ghastly.

Come midday, bang on the door, and in came the family en masse. I stared at Anna, knowing she had not kept her word, and had blabbed to all of them. I was furious, but could say nothing. Naturally, Joaquin was very surprised, and I heard him telling his brothers that it was a very minor operation, but had to be done quickly. Give me a break, there must have been eight of them at least.

On the quiet I paid the fees direct to Dr Flores, and never told Joaquin it was cancer. I kept the test results secret, and four days later he was discharged, and we drove home. He was up and about within days, and never thought more about it, just kept asking me where we were going that winter. He had the most amazing stamina, and was always so enthusiastic about any plans in the future.

Knowing what I knew, I planned a trip to the Far East for the winter of 1989, thinking this will be his last chance, but making sure to include long stopovers and time to rest. I intended to fly to the Maldives for ten days of total relaxation, before going to Hong Kong via Singapore. I always had a passion for islands, and the Maldives were top of the list. On arrival we took a speed boat from the actual airport to our French island, Vabbinfaru. Sadly it was raining, the sea dark green, and quite a hoo-ha to get ashore.

A great time to relax, but nothing to do, except walk round the island in the rain, drink, eat and play backgammon! Joaquin had a well-earned rest, and despite the clouds, left looking a healthy colour, for three days in Singapore. He visited business acquaintances, then we hired a car and drove up to Malaya across the famous peninsula, visiting the most extraordinary fishing village built on stilts; again in pouring rain.

On to Hong Kong, where it was hot and humid; our contacts were not there, so we followed the tourist trail, up to the peak on the tramway, over to Kowloon, and next day the ferry to Macau. There it was fascinating, the border with China was a bridge with masses of steel and iron on either side. We all had to queue in line, and pass the customs one by one. So sad to see spikes of iron coming out of the sea surrounding the border. Macau was then still a Portuguese colony, duty free, and full of casinos, where the rich people from Hong Kong came to gamble. We, as bona fide tourists, were allowed a day pass to visit China over the border, accompanied by a tourist guide.

We climbed into a bus, and a delightful young man, perfect in blue shirt and white trousers, introduced himself as David. Obviously not his real name. He showed us around the town on the border, and we were all amazed to see modern apartments, hotels, clean streets and the locals all dressed in modern clothes. No sign of communist grey/green overalls and slouched caps. He chatted away about the politics of the day, and how Mao Tse-tung had ruined the country with his 'Little Red Book'; Chairman Mao's thoughts explaining to the people of China the ideology of the Chinese Communist Party.

I called out to David, from the back of the bus.

'David, you are being very free with your speech, are you not worried, that someone here, near me, for example, is going to denounce you?'

'Not at all, China is now a free country, and we have democratic politicians, who accept us as guides to talk openly about our way of life.'

I shut up, Joaquin winked at me, and we said no more, thinking it was all a cover-up. We were taken to a peoples' farm, and showed how the locals lived, thrashing their corn, and tending to their cattle. Even a tiny Hindu temple, where they were allowed to pray to whatever gods they wished; it appeared genuine, but somehow we did not believe it; whatever the truth both of us were very satisfied to have had a peep at communist China, it will never be the same again.

Back in Hong Kong, Joaquin picked up the suits he had ordered, costing peanuts; we nearly missed the way to the tailor, as we wanted to walk. Leaving the hotel, we ran into a mass of humanity coming in the opposite direction, it was literally impossible to walk against them. We had to cross the road by a footbridge, and walk on the other side of the street. All very fascinating, millions of people, huge skyscrapers, a very swinging atmosphere, the New York of the East, but neither of us had any desire to return.

Next stop was a real holiday; Bali; an eastern jewel in Indonesia. I had studied the island via friends who knew it well, and had given me all the tips. Only thing they had forgotten to tell us about was the weather. Never go to Bali in our European winter, one should go in July/August. Every other day, it poured with rain, tropical storms soaking the country; it was so bad one night, that our hotel was awash, and we had metres of water in our room and patio. The staff came to get us and piggy-backed us to the dining room!

The island though is divine, and all the Hindu festivities so colourful; weddings, funerals, lotus gardens and huge dragons in papier-mâché wiggling their way through the villages. We had a car and driver, who had taken Sandra van Heel's father around the island various times. Sandra was passionate about the Far East, and had always encouraged me to go. She was very interested in the esoteric religions, and superstitions of the Hindus and their gods.

The beach was heaven for the days we were not visiting the island, and the little town near us, was within walking distance. It was charming, with fun bars and excellent restaurants, and the food was as good as the hotel's, which now, although I cannot remember the name, I can see it in my mind's eye; but it was probably pulled down and a skyscraper built in its place. We visited nearly all the island, full of Hindu statues, flowers, with monkeys in their temples and chanting monks.

Joaquin had a marvellous time, and a serious change from his life in Spain. No medical problems. No side effects. He had to have a check up every six months. After the first one, he was given a year. So back home, back to the animals, the horses, back to breeding pheasants, and preparing Marigalante II for the summer.

David and Jane visited with the children. Miles was 13, and Caroline 15; they were growing up fast, making friends with Quentin's young, they started going out to kids' parties and meetings on the beach. Though very shy, the Spanish atmosphere helped them to come out of themselves. Caroline loved the horses, and came with me to the mountains, to help exercise them. We took them out on the boat, and to Morocco as much as possible. Sadly, David's multiple sclerosis was worse each time he came, and he could not balance properly, and fell over continually.

Jane was very worried.

At the end of the summer we had what they call a 'clinic' with Mark Phillips, then Princess Anne's husband. It was held at Cathy Gaggero's farm up behind Sotogrande; he was a good instructor and gave Meridza and I some good tips for our cross-country jumping, though sadly he did not stay long enough to make a big difference.

Come Christmas, we had the big family party. The typical Spanish family planned their fete for 24th December, and midnight mass in the family chapel, La Ermita. I stuck to my Anglicized traditions and had a huge dinner on the 25th at Las Pilas. We invited all ones friends who were alone and naturally all the family. Little presents on each plate and a big tree, with carols sung in the background. This tradition I kept up only until the following year. After that Joaquin was so ill with his cancer, that I cancelled it.

For New Year, we were invited by Vanessa and Freck Vreeland to Marrakech, to their crazy but fabulous house in the Palmeraie. It was so cold, it was awful and darling Joaquin felt it badly. One tiny fire in our room, and we only got warm at midday. Moulay Ali was very sick too, and had cancelled his infamous New Year's party. We had already been to two if not three of these, they were most amusing, though so very dark, one could never recognise one's friends from Paris. The king had the official guests to dinner, all male, while the wives were sent off to the harem.

At this stage, Joaquin was beginning to look older and sick, seeming seriously out of place in this younger, funny crowd of house guests. We only stayed over the fiesta, then headed home.

We went to Ireland, to show Joaquin where Daddy was born, Luttrelstown, County Wexford. Helen Skrine, Daddy's cousin, had us to stay at Butlerstown Castle, her family home, which was next door. She took us out on a boat, up the River Barrow, knowing Joaquin's passion for boats and water. David, Jane, Miles and Caroline, came with us. David was very wobbly on his legs, but managed. Poor Helen did her best to entertain us, but Joaquin was very bad at chatting up old ladies. We did not stay long, and drove round some of the most wonderful castles of Ireland, and stopped at Doneraile Court, the St Leger home. The dowager Viscountess Doneraile had already died, the land had been taken over by the Land Commission, and the house was being renovated by the Hon Desmond Guinness, head of the Irish Georgian Society, with volunteers from America. During which the lawyers of the estate spent the last pennies travelling to America to find my cousin, son of Algernon, my great uncle.

Richard St Leger, his son, came over to Ireland to claim the title. A long complicated story, but he never succeeded. Irish lords were no longer allowed to keep their seats in the House of Lords, so it was not worth the effort and the paperwork to reclaim the title.

The contents of the house had been put up for sale at a huge auction, where antique dealers from London bid for all the most priceless silver and engraved crystal. The family had no hope of recuperating anything; the prices had been fixed beforehand. I bought and paid for two pieces from an antique dealer in Bond Street: a lovely ink stand and a tiny milk jug, both pure Georgian silver engraved with the family crest. Such a shame, the lawyers were crooked, and nothing was left, except a whole room in Dublin full to the brim with papers on the St Leger inheritance.

# *23. India and Sri Lanka*

At the beginning of that spring, 1990, the polo ponies in Sotogrande started dying of a strange disease. Vets were called in from Madrid, blood tests were done, and it was found that they had contracted 'the African horse disease', or as we called it, '*la Peste Equina*'. A swarm of locusts had been seen two weeks earlier, and we all thought they were the cause. Animals were put in quarantine and separated, no good, they died non-stop and in agony, in their stalls, spewing blood and gunk from their nostrils.

I was called up by the Federation in Madrid, and asked if I could contact Professor Erasmus in South Africa, the world expert on this disease. None of them had good enough English to understand him.

Of course, I did what was asked, and learnt that every ten years or so, the disease affected the equine race across the straits. Also the quarantine that was obligatory under Franco's regime, had been dropped by this new socialist government. It took us months of research to find the origin of this horror. Everybody was obliged to keep all horses in their stables; all shows and events cancelled. Breeding at the studs stopped. Any mules or donkeys let loose by the gypsies were shot on the spot, and buried immediately covered by very strong whitewash.

I spent my time on the phone to Erasmus, and the Federation. We found out that the owner of a zoological park near Madrid had imported a number of zebras from central Africa, bypassing the quarantine, transporting them direct to his property. Then a trekking group set off from nearby, and took their clients south to Andalucia, where one of their horses died. As they were close to the River Guadalquiton, they buried it in the sand bank, and three days later the horses in Sotogrande started dying. *Voila*! This is the conclusion we worked out, how the disease was spread. A theory to be believed or not, but logical to my mind.

It was a long miserable time for us horse lovers, and every time the ban was lifted, another horse died, so the restrictions were continued. The gypsies were impossible to control and broke the law continually, despite our best efforts. All the *ferias* were cancelled, as were all the shows, and all equine transport; special Guardia Civil set-up blockades at every crossroads, handing out not only huge fines but they also sent the animals being transported straight to the nearest knacker's yard. So naturally those of us with a bit of brain just did nothing, except ride in our properties. I even had to get the vets from the veterinary school in Cordoba, who were now excellent, to come to Las Pilas, to actually operate in the stables. One of my thoroughbreds had a growth on her leg, and our Arab mare a fistula wither.

I seem to have been plagued with this problem, as Paddy my pony in Devon had one, and Daddy cut it out, but it grew back, so he had to be let loose on Dartmoor. Then Santiago, a rough horse we kept in La Zorilla to round up the cattle, and now Iaba, the Arab. It is caught from goats, who are immune to it, but eating in the same field, pass it on to cattle and horses. It had attacked the shoulder bone so dramatically, that I was able to put my whole arm down into where the disease had eaten it away. As she was a brood mare, we just left her alone, and eventually sold her to the Domecqs. Riding horses cannot be thoroughly cured, as any pressure from a saddle and a rider, brings it on again.

Joaquin was in great form, sorry for me and all the equine woes, boring as it went on for a year and a half at least. He and I went to Cadiz to have his check-up, and he was given a year of not needing to return. He had some crazy idea of becoming a foreign resident, as a friend of his had advised him to take out a Santo Dominican passport. Maybe because the socialists were cracking down on taxes, and the large families were paying big time. The modern Spain was not what it used to be, when I can remember one of the Domecq's laughing in the past, saying, 'Taxes, what are they? I pay an accountant to be sure I don't pay any of them.' He would go into his *bodega*, order 200 cases of jerez to take to El Rocio, sign for it and then never pay.

No wonder half of the *bodegas* in jerez went bankrupt at the end of the '80s.

In the autumn, I phoned Jane, to see how David was and for the first time in my life, I heard her complain.

'Vics, he just does nothing!'

The tone in her voice was so depressing, I felt immediately that something was seriously wrong, so I said to Joaquin, 'I have to go to Ireland, I don't know what has happened, but Jane is very upset.'

He had adorable Carmen and an extra new Philippine woman, Jose, to look after him, and he told me, 'Go, Vicky, I am fine, your family must come first.'

I arrived in Belfast after three flights to get there, and very surprised to see another cousin waiting for me. She said nothing special, except the family was waiting for me. They lived in Antrim, in a lovely old house with a huge garden, as we drove up the drive, Fiona de Courcy-Wheeler, this other cousin, told me the ghastly news that Jane had died very suddenly two days previously. She knew I didn't know. No one had told me. Typical Irish, they did not think to reverse a phone call or send a telegram, and everyone was so shocked and crying their eyes out. Caroline was there, as was Miles, who had been brought home from Glenalmond, his public school, where he had just started in September.

I rushed into the house, where David was looking grey and miserable, and the two kids hugging each other, all fell into my arms. Very slowly they told me how it had happened. She had an enormous cerebral haemorrhage, while cooking and fell over the stove onto the floor. David, of course, was not very savvy, and it took him time to find an ambulance. Once in hospital, darling Jane died shortly afterwards.

She was cremated, and the funeral was held two days later. So I had missed it by a day, her friends and family, and my other cousins had just left. The children, seeing me arrive, broke into big smiles, I could see them thinking someone has come to save us. Miles had thought that his schooling was finished, and my first remark, was for him to get off his arse, and go back to school as soon as he could, knowing that hanging around his sick father was totally negative.

I was very disappointed in their lack of communication, just could not understand them, especially David. The children, I could see their lack of intuition, under the circumstances. The following day we picked up the ashes and spread them in a lovely field under the trees. So sad and worrying, as we had all followed David's illness, and never in our heads imagined that Jane, the force behind the family, would die before him.

After a couple of days, I booked Miles onto the flight for Edinburgh, rang the school, and asked them to take care of him, stressing I needed to be in contact with his house master and the financial director. It took me a year of discussions, but eventually won. Miles was allotted a special education, as his mother had died and his father had MS and he lived in the UK. Northern Ireland was in the UK.

Caroline was a different problem, she was about to start her A-levels, and I asked her straight out, what would she prefer? To go on at her school, and come home every evening to cope with her father; or join a private school and become a boarder? She chose to stay on at her school in Belfast as a day girl. She was and is highly intelligent, and passed all her exams with top marks. Mad on horses, as all of the family. She worked part-time for a breeder of thoroughbreds, and bought her own horse, and raced him. Never have I known someone so dedicated to what she wanted to do, and so stubborn. Her father drove her mad, with his sarcastic sense of humour, and with the MS, as he wandered around their house breaking things and leaving everything in a mess.

I met a very high-powered lawyer in Belfast, and set in motion a 'children's trust' based in Gibraltar, as I saw the National Health would clean out David financially, leaving Miles and Caroline penniless. For the time being, I hired a housekeeper, and between a neighbour and myself, arranged a way of life that was temporarily all right for both David and Caroline. I think she had a very tough time, with her exams, losing her mother, who she adored, so suddenly, and being left to look after her father, a very sick man.

*

The next winter Joaquin and I went back to the Maldives but to a different island; this time we had our own bungalow and an adorable private beach. It took longer for Joaquin to relax, and swim with confidence. One way to keep him happy on holiday, was to get him some juicy novels.

We had planned to go to India to discover the south and meet old friends of Sandra from Madras on the east coast, and cruise down the inner waterways of Kerala. We flew to Trivandrum, the southernmost airport, and waited to pass customs. I was very surprised to notice the other passengers getting their passports stamped, and moving on to collect their luggage, which I could see down below us on a carousel.

Joaquin, looking very brown and fit, was reading his book, paying no attention to what was going on, when a customs officer and a policeman came up to me.

'This man, your husband? Very bad man.'

I looked at them as if they were mad.

'What do you mean?'

They showed me his passport, where to my surprise, his visa was ending on that particular day. The policeman shoved us rudely out of the customs area. Quickly I saw a duty-free shop, and rushed over to buy a bottle of whisky, shaking at the knees. I saw the agent, who was meeting us, and quickly asked him what on earth was happening? Apparently Joaquin's visa was outdated on the day we arrived in India. No arguing with the police, who tried to push me out of the airport.

'Go, go, you can leave and go with your agent to your hotel.'

'How on earth can I leave my husband with you lot, who hardly speak English? He is a Spaniard, and a gentleman, look at him, he would not hurt a fly.'

A nightmare, we were accompanied by two policemen and guns, to a room on the third floor of the airport; one miserable fan, and a hole in the bathroom floor with a bucket of water. Joaquin just did not know what was happening. I asked the police, at least get us some of your curry, which they did after about an hour. Once he was relaxed with two or three whiskies, I left him to talk to the agent, who was a very nice man and so sorry for us.

It turned out, when Joaquin had got our visas in Madrid at the Indian embassy, just before Christmas, he was not told that his passport was about to run out, so automatically the visa, ended with the passport. Now I advise all my friends never travel with a passport that does not have a minimum of six months *en valor*.

The next day we were accompanied to breakfast by two machine guns, then I asked the director of the airport, what we should do. While I telephoned the Spanish embassy in Delhi, 3,000 kilometres away, could my husband sit in the VIP lounge? This he agreed to, while he explained, that the real problem was because of a Saudi prince, who had arrived at Trivandrum the week before with no visa. He gave *baksheesh* to the police, then once in the country, ran amok, smoked drugs, beat up some girls, causing mayhem. So now, poor darling Joaquin was paying the consequences.

I could not get through to Delhi, only to friends in Sri Lanka. We were able to fly out the next day, as we had to leave the country to obtain a visa. I was given a boarding card, while Joaquin, poor thing, was taken on the plane accompanied by the machine gun. Were we glad to leave. It was so embarrassing.

So our plan to visit the southern part of India was scrapped, such a shame, especially for Joaquin, who sadly never made it. In later years I went with Sheila and Kit Pinto Coelho to the north, and then alone I discovered Kerala and her waterways.

We did, however, visit Sri Lanka. Arriving in Colombo, the capital, this friend of mine had booked us into the big hotel on the sea, and kindly took us out to dinner, telling us all fighting was with the Tamil Tigers on the east coast, so not to adventure too far. Three days in this dull place was already too much, and a storm was crashing huge waves on the coast.

'Come on, Joaquin, let's hire a car and at least discover the southern part of the island, and find you some fishing.'

He perked up, and said, 'Well done, Vicky, you always have great ideas.'

That night at dinner, we met the most charming woman, who lived in Sri Lanka; she brought out a map, and insisted I took it, giving me lots of tips of best fishing areas, and how to drive up to Kandy, the old capital, where the British soldiers used to spend their summers to avoid the heat. We took off down the coast, and found the place she had suggested, a very nice hotel in the jungle but right on the beach. The manager said he would arrange a boat to take Joaquin fishing the next day. He was so keen, that he got up at dawn and disappeared. While I was having breakfast, he came back.

'Heh! What happened? You're back so soon?'

'Silly bloody fools, they took me out to a fishing boat that is lying off the coast, and told me to fish from it. They said it was too rough to trawl.'

He was livid and very disappointed. February is great to travel to get away from the wet Spanish winters, but totally the wrong season to fish, and he was only interested in barracuda, sail fish or blue marlin, all the big fighting chaps. Oh dear, I tried so hard to keep him happy. Knowing he was still fed up with the way they treated him in India, all I could suggest was to continue our exploring of the island, and to make our way over the mountains to Kandy. Which we did, and thank goodness he fell asleep in the car, as I had to navigate through at least three barriers on the way up to the tea plantations, keeping an eye out for terrorists.

We stopped at a plantation, and were showed around it; interesting, and beautiful rolling hills with tea as far as you could see. We kept going, a terribly tiring drive, and it went on for ever, each mountain was followed by another. Distances on the map were all wrong. When I could hardly keep my eyes open, we ran into thick fog and had to crawl the last 50 kilometres. Finally we arrived at the old hotel, where the British army had billeted their officers, but there was so much fog it was impossible to appreciate the surroundings.

Thank goodness, the next day was glorious, and we woke up to heavenly views over the mountains; the manager told us to relax and said clearly, without the famous map, where to visit in Kandy.

One day and we were renewed; Kandy is a lovely old town surrounding the stunning 17th century Temple of the Tooth, which is believed to house a tooth of the Lord Buddha himself. This precious relic attracts white-clad pilgrims, bearing lotus blossoms and frangipani, every day. I was dying to see it, but Joaquin was finishing his latest book, and sat under a tree; I found a guide, who was able to get me into the inner sanctuary, thanks to some *baksheesh*! He turned out to have been Mountbatten's driver, so we had a good laugh. Going back to join Joaquin, he asked him, 'Sir, why are you not a Buddhist?'

He was rather surprised and replied, 'My father was a Catholic, a Christian, I am sure your father was a Buddhist, so therefore you follow your parents' religion.'

He was silenced, but came with us to the fabulous gardens on the edge of the town, a memory to Mountbatten and his officers, with the most enormous umbrella tree. In part, there was nothing else but orchids. It was quite gorgeous. Wandering around the gardens, we had another sighting of the most disgusting bats, simply huge, hanging upside down, they looked quite revolting.

We had seen them again earlier, in a cave, near the road, smaller but just as filthy, the whole cave full of their shit. The stink was awful. Another temple was dedicated to them, I did not go and see them, thank you, they were hideous.

The Craig family came again the following Easter, Miles now 14, Caroline coming on 16. I had David to Las Pilas as much as possible, he now needed help to change flights either in Paris or Madrid. To have him and Joaquin together was not easy, they did not have much in common, as well as the language barrier. Joaquin's family was very sweet to him, as he did have a lovely Irish soft character, especially Maria Luisa, who had spent a lot of time in Ireland.

I got fed up, David was so negative, and desperately lazy, and laid back. Without Jane to be the strong dominant partner in the family, they were lost. Joaquin and I realized we had to take care of Miles, he was still a baby, and needed family loving care. Being at his public school in Scotland, we had to take him out of school at 'leave-outs' and half-term, which we did, the three of us visiting castles in Scotland and taking a tour of Ireland.

# *24. Joaquin's Death*

After another hateful summer of *la peste equina*, and literally hundreds and hundreds of dead horses, we escaped on another travel plan to the island of Santo Domingo, the other half of Haiti, but totally Spanish.

We had booked ourselves into La Romana, an urbanisation on the east coast, where Joaquin had been advised by his friends in Madrid, was the ideal place to buy a house and become a resident. I said nothing, but thought the idea was crazy, far too complicated at his age, and secretly knowing he had cancer.

It turned out to be a dreadful place, with a golf course, a very small beach and desperately boring people. Incredibly bourgeois. The village nearby was rustic and funky, with a lot of fishing boats, and a long peninsula with coconut palms, but that was it. I could no more imagine living there than butter in your hoo-ha! Joaquin did meet friends of friends and they discussed well into the night, the pros and cons of taking out a Dominican passport, which meant you had to buy or build a house and become a citizen. I was sweating that he would insist we did it so I suggested that we drove around the island, and looked at other places before any decision was made. Living in a Spanish community around a golf course, was not my idea of fun.

We did this, and had glorious drives through the jungle and mountains, and landed up on the north coast at Puerto Plata. A coastal village in full development, divine beach and palm trees, hippy atmosphere, with small hotels and bistros. My gut feeling, this was the area of the island where tourism would develop, and become a swinging, fun place to live.

Back in the capital we had a meeting with one of the top lawyers, and spent hours talking to him and his wife, and exchanged addresses and fax numbers. Thank goodness nothing came out of it, and we actually never heard from him again.

We flew on to the Cayman Islands, where the tax system was very similar, except it was impossible to become citizens, only residents; that also depended on owning real estate and taking up residence for a minimum of six months. I went to the judicial side of Barclays Bank, where I had an introduction; a very British lawyer, who gave me all the laws and regulations, which I passed on to Joaquin.

The island was very Americanised, flat, hotels and what they called condominiums in their thousands. Large areas of swamp and mangroves, it had a feeling of Florida on a small scale. The famous beach was out of this world, bleached sand for seven miles on end.

We met a lot of friends, and I was fascinated with the passion of diving, and took note of all the dive schools. As sea water, rivers, and lakes were a natural habitat to me, I was always lost when I was not close to them. The colour of the sea was exquisite, one could gaze at it for hours; a turquoise green, pale blue, darker as it reached the reefs, it was just heaven.

We did not stay long, as time was limited, but enough to visit one of the last condominiums being built actually on the beach. The plans were finished, and 80% of the apartments were sold off-plan, there were two left on the third floor, and one on the ground floor.

Jokingly I said to Joaquin, 'This would be a much more fun investment than a house in Santo Domingo, just look at the sea and the beach. The tax laws are the same, and one would be protected by the Union Jack.'

The next day I went to the office of the developer, and got all the details, price and percentage rates, ways of payment etc. It was, though, too much of a decision to make on my own, and I just felt it was too much of a hassle for Joaquin.

On to Jamaica, a quick hop from the Caymans. We had booked into a hotel at Ocho Rios for three days on the beach, but Joaquin was bored. I rang Sarah Spencer Churchill at Montego Bay; she was thrilled and asked us to her lovely home. She could not put us up, as the house was full, but she arranged for us to stay at the yacht club. Wow! The island had changed since my last visit. Not only high rises on all the skylines, but the attitude of the people was very negative. Sarah was in great form though, and loved meeting Joaquin. As usual, her house was full of queers. Sat down to a long table for dinner, and very sweetly put me next to Joaquin, to be able to translate, if he got lost. Halfway through, the conversation came round to the Caymans; I learnt that Sarah had just bought the last ground floor apartment, in the building that I had seen.

Joaquin looked at me and said, 'Vicky, I told you, you should have bought that apartment, you and Sarah have a very similar flair and a nose for business.'

I thought to myself, *if Sarah had not bought, it would not have been the same at all.* On our way home via Miami, I rang the developer and said I would buy, and instructed him to fax me all the papers to Spain.

Talk about destiny, there I was the proud owner of a condominium in the Cayman Islands. A fabulous beach, pool with jacuzzi and a view over the sea to die for. Now I had to decorate it once built, and find the right furniture. Sarah was a great help, and we joined together to bring down a container from Miami.

At this moment in time, I was in Spain, as Joaquin was not well, and had to go at various times to his urologist. Absolutely horrible, he had to have various small operations, and then to Madrid to have sessions of radiotherapy. So up and down to the city, to the radiologist. I kept him company all the time, but it was very depressing. I kept on trying to con him that it was not cancer, and that they were doing their best to eliminate it. By now, he was getting savvy, and started to get really depressed and thinking he had it, getting furious with me and Dr Flores for not telling him four years earlier.

'What difference would it have made? You would have worried and suffered for nothing.'

He was getting mad that he had not had chemotherapy but Dr Flores had told me categorically that chemotherapy was no use on a soft tissue, and radiotherapy was the only answer. Similar to the cancer that Maria Rosa had in the peritoneum. Joaquin was very sick, and looked awful; we travelled up and down to Madrid, and he spent half the time in bed, as the treatment left him exhausted. His friends came to see him, and his business partners, but he was not enthusiastic to see any of them.

Realizing I was not going to be able to return to the Caymans, I asked my god-daughter, Louise Balfour, to arrange to meet Sarah Churchill in Miami, and buy the furniture that I had already chosen.

She was free at the time, thrilled to get paid to do this job, and took another cousin with her. They had a ball; learnt to dive, and profited to travel to Mexico. Sarah looked after them, and gave them lots of ideas.

I designed the whole apartment around a huge mural, painted by an Irish friend, with palm trees and sand dunes. Good stools on the bar, the rest pale blue and cream. Modern and useful. Three double bedrooms, two bathrooms and a big terrace.

After Louise and her cousin left, I rented it out very easily through various agencies. I went back once to check it out for literally a week. I did not dare leave Joaquin alone, as now he was very depressed, and angry at the urologist and me, for keeping him in the dark. He knew that he had it, one could not hide it any more. He was losing weight and looking very grey in the gills! Whether I had made the correct decision, only God will decide, but to me he had had four years of complete innocence, and no worry. Travelling and working, he had been through a good time and had been very positive.

Another lovely cousin of mine, Alison Holmes, and her boyfriend, came to stay with us; she was a very young doctor specializing in tropical diseases, with extraordinary stories about her homosexual patients, and what they got up to. Joaquin was fascinated. Later, alone, she told me to get morphine through the national health system of Spain; as long as I registered it, I could apparently get it easily.

'Oh! Vics, he is so adorable, what a crime he has the damn thing, but no way must he suffer, start giving him morphine in small doses and don't panic if he starts having illusions. He won't remember them.'

At the end of the summer, in September, Luis Modet and his mother came to stay. Arriving in Algeciras at our yacht club, Joaquin insisted on driving Luis's mother home. We all got angry and told him somebody else would drive her but when he was stubborn, he was stubborn. We don't know what happened, but he was very tired on arrival at Las Pilas, and the very next morning, could not move, with terrible pains in his legs and joints. He could not even get out of bed.

From that day on, he went downhill. I upped the morphine discretely, and one day during the winter, when he was having an x-ray, we changed his bedroom to the ground floor. It had become impossible to get him up and down the stairs, he was a big man and weighed over 90kg, though from then on, he lost weight continuously.

I brought in oxygen, and arranged for the male nurse from our village to visit him every day, and inject him with pain killers. That and his daily morphine kept him comfortable. So sad though, to watch such a formidable character decline and deteriorate, and knowing there was nothing one could do, heartbreaking.

His family came to see him a lot, but sadly, in the meantime, his brother Jose Maria had died of cancer as well. Joaquin and I had written out his will, where he had insisted he wanted to leave me everything, and I had insisted he left all his shares in Sur de España, the family company, to his nephews and nieces, as well as the family land.

He was as stubborn as a mule and said, 'No, you, Vicky, have taken care of me and given me fun, and good company, memories of travelling together in these last years of my life, I want you to be comfortable and happy, as long as you don't give anything to another man.'

I will never forget those words.

Joaquin continued, 'You will be very independent, but very lonely.'

His nephews made a mess of what he had planned, by bringing in the notary on almost his last day, and terrified he had left the shares to me, rewrote the contract in reverse. Silly twits. They were so money orientated, scared stiff he was leaving them to me.

Joaquin sold La Zorilla to his nephews, as naturally he could not keep it up and said it was too much work for me in the future. I was sad he had made this decision, as it was a very special *finca*, and we had had great illusions to build a big *cortijo* there.

Slowly he got worse, and I had to have two nurses in rotation, to sit up with him at night. He was so strong that he kept going for another month. Come 10th May, I had sent his secretary to Sevilla to pick up the *gallega*, Carmen, as she was very fond of him, and wanted to be with him his last few days, and I had no idea when that would be. She arrived, and sitting by his bed held his hand, while I and the secretary changed the oxygen mask. As I was doing it, I kissed him on the forehead, and frightened, felt it was cold and damp. Quickly I asked the night nurse to come, as she came into his room, he gave a big sigh and died on the spot. The four of us were left, in complete shock. It was just after midnight.

Horrified, I did not quite know what to do; I sent the young man down to the cottage of Colmenar, where the other nurse was staying, and started telephoning his brothers and sisters. They had all just left to their homes an hour earlier. Crying, I had to tell them all that Joaquin had just died suddenly. So one and all came back to Las Pilas, bringing their children with them. Luis, his younger brother was always great in an emergency, and arranged the undertakers and the paperwork there and then. The Spanish navy paid for it all, now I was a widow of the navy, and much to my surprise they arranged everything, and I am still collecting a pension today, tiny as it is.

The family sat around the dining room table, all staring at me, I presume to see my reaction. Carmen and her husband, Paco, came from Los Barrios. I told them to offer the family drinks, while I disappeared upstairs to cry on my own. Paddy, Luis's wife, a Gibralterian, followed me.

'Vicky, don't upset yourself, you could not have done more for him, he was going to die anyway. You have done your level best, to keep him well looked after, and tried every medicine in the book.'

She was very sweet and kind, while the Spanish sisters were just thinking of the social side of the following day. By Spanish law one had to be buried within 24 hours.

Joaquin had wanted to be buried at sea, in the straits, where he loved to fish, and with his brothers and sisters, and his doctor, Jose Maria Romojaro, we sat around the dining room table, discussing this. Being very Roman Catholic, the family all argued with me, as it was no longer allowed. The only compromise was to have him cremated, and that was only in Malaga, and then put in a niche in the family chapel, as the family insisted it had to be in consecrated ground. The doctor, a good friend of ours winked at me, and then waited for the family to disperse.

'Vicky, don't argue with them, it is not worth it. Sadly, Joaquin is dead, and they are alive, and you have to live with them.'

So it was, and the staff sat up all night in mourning, and told me to go to bed. Joaquin was already in his coffin, with my black Labradors sleeping underneath it. The priests all came early the next morning, and his brothers, and insisted yet again to have a mass in the drawing room.

'What another one?'

Thank goodness some of my friends from the riding world came to see me, and we were able to have a drink in honour of Joaquin. Then the relations from Madrid turned up, and friends from Sotogrande and Jerez. News had travelled fast. I knew this was going to happen, but somehow one is not prepared, and I lived through a haze, not believing that Joaquin was no more.

All the locals, farmers, and workers from the right of way behind Las Pilas, came in their masses to the back patio, and when the hearse turned up, they all helped to load the coffin, then lined the drive, one and all removing their caps in respect.

The funeral was held in his charity school at Rinconcillo. I had asked his nephews to be pall-bearers, and had permission from the navy to cover the coffin with the national flag and place his naval sword on top. We had a posse of young sailors from the naval base, singing *Ave Maria*, it took hours for the crowds to disperse, and kiss the widow and all his sisters. Then eight of us left for Malaga to the crematorium near where we had to stay the night. Luis had chosen a hotel in Torremolinos. It was awful, the whole scene was ghastly, and felt all wrong. At the crematorium, we were late, and they refused to handle the coffin, and left it on the ground outside.

I could not believe my eyes, and pleaded with Luis.

'This is not possible, you can't do this; you cannot leave Joaquin on the ground, just like that.'

'Vicky, don't be silly Joaquin has gone, that is just the coffin.'

Sorry, but I did not believe that, and felt Joaquin to be very close, and very shocked. As they were all having dinner, I walked out of the restaurant and back to the hotel, thinking how superficial they all were. Later that night, I had a certainty of his presence in my room, I just knew he was horrified to be burnt, and was screaming at me. I had to get up and walk for half an hour to stop my heart beating, as I was saying to him, imagine that you are closed in a hole in the wall and covered with cement. The way you are buried normally in Spain.

Since Joaquin's death, there have been two more brothers cremated, Luis included, and two nephews.

The next day, we picked up the ashes in an urn, and drove back to the family chapel, La Ermita, and I handed it over to the priest, wrapped in the national flag. His nephew, Javier, had made a hole in the wall under the model of the Baleares, dedicated to the cruiser and all her crew, that blew up at the end of the civil war. It was a short personal service, with only the family, and, of course, the staff from Las Pilas were there.

They took me home. I didn't want to see anyone.

I left the family to gossip amongst themselves.

# *25. Selling Marigalante II*

After this horror in Algeciras, and so quick, my family, bless their hearts, turned up. Sheila and my godchild, Louise, had come all the way by train, as flights were full; then Andrew Prendergast, my Irish cousin, none could believe that the funeral was finished so quickly. They all adored Joaquin, and had enormous respect for him. They kept me company and it was lovely to have them. Andrew came with me to Madrid, where we held a memorial service in the church near our apartment. Typically women on one side and men on the other, poor Andrew with Joaquin's brothers was in the shaking hands line, and no *madrileno* knew who he was!

He was very naughty and picked out of the crowd two of Joaquin's nieces-in-law, the pretty ones, and brought them back to the flat, and with Anichi and Santi, we all went out to dinner. Better than mourning in the apartment. I never had a group of friends in Madrid, so always felt very lonely there, as Joaquin's business friends were all so much older. We never spent enough time for him to introduce me to society as it was, and he was always busy.

23rd June was my mother's birthday, and as I had been looking after Joaquin intensely for the last year and a half, I had not been with her at all; so flew to Malta and took her to Gozo for ten days to a lovely hotel on the cliffs, Ta'cenc. It was a divine rest for me, and when she was in a good mood, quite a giggle. Which was not every day. I knew various old friends on the island, and they all had quaint old village houses, with a lot of charm. Being with them unloaded the strain of having Mother on my back every day. She refused point blank to move to Sotogrande.

Back in Spain, I turned my attention to Miles and Caroline, now I had time to dedicate to them. Of course, it was difficult caring for

Joaquin and worrying about the children but after Joaquin's death, I was able to organize a proper holiday for them and the distraction was welcome to me as well. I booked them onto an Outward Bound trip in America with a group of university students and teenagers. I had to go to New York to visit Sarah Churchill anyway, then with Louise to the Caymans to finish up the details of the condominium.

I thought this would be a huge eye-opener for them to visit the States, the whole excursion was out in the wild west; canoeing, riding, climbing mountains, camping out, the works, in Wyoming. While they were doing this, I went to stay a few days with Sarah in Connecticut, settled our accounts over the furniture, and went to join Louise in the Caymans. With her, I went diving for my first time, and in three days obtained my diving certificate. I was a bit nervous over having had double mastoids as a child, but a doctor told me to ventilate all the time, while descending, and if I had ear ache or pain, to re-ascend slowly, before descending again.

I took to it as a duck to water! And simply loved it. The water was so clear, and the reefs and coral gorgeous to swim over and under. I invited the instructors for the weekend to Little Cayman, Louise had already left; to a beach lodge run by a mad Texan, but most amusing. It was full of Americans, but we had planned a night dive with the resident dive master. Taking his jeep we arrived on the beach, put on the sidelights, and left the front tyres in the edge of the sea. We walked into it carrying our fins, till it was deep enough to swim. We all carried special torches. Swimming out we crossed two reefs, and descended to 60 feet and more. The lights from our torches picked up millions of plankton and tiny bugs in the water. As we crossed the third reef, a huge mass of black came swimming at me; I quickly swam below the dive master and hung on to his belt. He turned and gave me the thumbs up signal that all was OK; watching with fascination, I realized it was the famous manta ray, Matilda, named by the locals. She swam at us attracted by the little bugs in the sea that were caught in the light of our torches. She was huge, and with her mouth open, one felt one could disappear into the hole. We literally played with her, rolling over and under her belly, she swam back with us over the reefs, until it was too shallow for her. With one big swish, she turned and swam off into the dark.

On shore we were all on a high, laughing and yelling with joy. We knew the yanks in the lodge had come especially to see Matilda, and we had found her on our first dive. Two bottles of vino down the hatch, and we roared back to tell everyone of our amazing experience. We had been so lucky. The Americans at the lodge were furiously jealous, and complained to their dive master, poor fellow, just bad luck.

On the following day we went diving off Little Cayman, down a sandy slope and through a hole, or rather a tunnel, out onto the wall, a huge dark blue space. I got nerves, feeling quite dizzy, the dive master realized it was a big shock for me, and sweetly hung on to my arm, turning me around to concentrate on the actual wall, pointing out lobsters, and eels, crevices and heavenly corral. I soon relaxed swimming with the current, and got over the fear of the space. We were right over the famous Jamaican trench that was thousands and thousands of feet deep. Bottomless.

On our way up the wall, we came upon three or four huge fish; they looked like sharks to me, and getting in a tizz again, I started hyper-ventilating too quickly, which sent me up towards the surface too fast. I was pulled by my leg back down, and with hand signs they told me they were dolphins. Oof! What a relief, as sharks are not funny. When I had more experience, I used to swim with the nurse sharks and huge terrapin, cruising in and out of the corral reefs without turning a hair.

It is the most lovely sport, every day we dived at a different site, and one of the specialities was on the north side of Grand Cayman, just inside the reef, where the fishermen cleaned their catch; it was the playground of the sting rays, the southern grey. One could literally pick them up, bringing them to the surface and stroke their soft white under-bellies. As the sea here was not deep, we all had to add weights to our weight belts to keep us deep enough to swim with the rays and under them. One big mistake is to stand on one, as then in fear they could turn in a second and catch you with their tails, embedded with their sting. Now the site has become so famous, it is packed with boats and tourists off the cruise ships, even with glass-bottomed boats!

Meanwhile I obtained my Cayman residence, rented out the condominium and returned to New York to meet up with the children and the Browns, who they were staying with in Connecticut, very old friends of Quentin and Sue Agnew. We toured the city, took them to Planet Hollywood for lunch, ice-skating at Rockefeller Plaza, down to Greenwich Village and to the top of the twin towers, which were swaying in the wind, not a very nice experience, into the stock market on Wall Street and then the Statue of Liberty, where there was a queue a mile long.

We finished our day at the Plaza Hotel, having drinks in their famous bar. All part of their education. We all flew back to Spain the next day. Thank goodness they were with me, as Las Pilas was very empty without Joaquin. I was up to my eyes with the paperwork, lawyers and notary, papers in the banks, all sorts of headaches. One of his nieces, Patricia, who was out of a job, offered to help me. She was adorable and helped me ply through all Joaquin's papers. Some of his shares in companies in Madrid were non-existent. The two executives of his will, Ramón Casado our lawyer and José Maria Soriano, assistant to the notary, were very clever and both switched on; they had helped me a lot in the past, through complicated deals.

His family were naturally mad that Joaquin had left me everything, and they all rushed round to the notary to read the will. As he had thought it through very carefully, and we talked about it openly, he had said, 'Vics, if I leave my nieces and nephews, for example, land, they will pay 65%, if to my brothers or sisters 45%, plus all the other taxes etc. You are such a generous person, I know you will sell what you can, and then pass on to my family everything possible.'

I was having problems with what to do about Marigalante II; to run her without a captain, was impractical, well nigh impossible. Emilio was just not up to it, and did not have the right papers. I took the kids to Marbella, and left some lovely photos with all the ship chandlers and yachting agencies. The captain of the port, a good friend of Joaquin, and knew the boat well, said, 'Vicky, she is not going to be easy to sell, she is now over 20 years old, her engine room is in a mess, she is just not up to scratch, and there are so many new boats on the market.'

We went back to Las Pilas pretty depressed, and thinking no one from Algeciras or Tarifa would buy her. I rang George Nicholson the next day, and asked his opinion; he was still in Cannes, and his business had developed enormously. Camper and Nicholson's is a huge yacht brokerage, building, and chartering business.

'Vicky, you have no hope of selling her in France or Italy, the new boats on the market are ten times better built today than when we built Marigalante II.' Bad news indeed, but lovely to chat with him all the same, as we had known each other from the '60s.

Talk about destiny; the following weekend, when Miles and Caroline had gone off with the young on a picnic, the phone rang, and a German voice asked me if I was the Señora Cervera. Answering carefully, I said, 'Yes, but who are you?'

His reply was suspiciously vague, but I gathered he was a German, who was with some friends in the port at our yacht club, and asking the sailors on the quay if any of the boats were for sale? Of course, they all knew that I could not keep Marigalante II and they had given them my phone number. I granted permission to visit her, chewing my fingers that Emilio had cleaned the decks and the famous engine room. Being Sunday, of course, he had gone fishing.

An hour later, these two Germans turned up at Las Pilas, I tried my best to be polite, but found it hard, what did they want on a Sunday afternoon? Asking them into Joaquin's office, I explained it was Sunday in Spain, and no one did business on a Sunday. They were adamant, that they wanted to buy her as she was and could they take her out for two hours on trial, there and then. Holy Moses! They were prepared to pay down a large deposit, they had it in cash.

I knew this was an opportunity not to be lost, but had no lawyer, no notary, nobody to advise me. I did not know who they were, where they had come from or why they wanted to buy her in such a hurry. Taking me an hour at least to find Emilio, I accompanied them back to the port, having left the deposit in the safe, and told Emilio to take them out to Getares beach and Punta Carnero. An hour later as the sun was setting, they were already back at the anchorage.

I explained to these two men, that I did not know the rules and regulations of selling a yacht in Spain, or the taxes on the sale that had to be paid to the notary, and they had to wait until Monday morning for us to sign a contract. In their bad English, they replied something like, no way, they wished to do the deal there and then, they offered another $20,000 extra on top of the price, for me to agree on the immediate sale. I was not stupid, and realized, either they were planning on running away from the police, or were drug smuggling in the straits.

I signed a contract, shaking at the knees, and accepted all in cash, as there was no way to confirm a cheque on Sunday evening. They apparently left the next morning at dawn and were last seen in Tangiers a few days later. They had told me, they were going to Rotterdam in Holland, but I have never heard of them or our darling Marigalante II ever again. I suppose they painted her a different colour and changed her name, I don't know but I do know she is no longer registered with Lloyd's Yachting Register.

I was very sad and depressed, one loves boats, and we had had so much fun on board, with our mad trips to Morocco and the Baleares, and I hope gave a lot of fun to our friends as well. On the other hand, a huge relief and weight off my back, as I never could have managed to keep her up. I also knew after Joaquin's death, I would not stay in the south of Spain or in Las Pilas, surrounded by this huge family, all criticising me. Las Pilas was now surrounded by houses, factories and building estates as far as the eye could see. It was awful, plastic bags, rubbish and empty bottles littered the verges of the road. I used to come home crying with frustration at living in this ghastly town, so ugly; and Joaquin always replied to me, 'Vicky, I am much older than you, and by nature will die long before you. Leave me here in peace, and you can do what you want with it, after I am dead.'

This is what I did, as bless his heart, he had put it in my name, three or four years earlier. Very slowly I started to pack up the stables, sell off the good horses and put down the old ones. I will never forget putting down Hortensia, she was well over 20 and suffered from horrible arthritis, she used to groan in agony getting up from her stable floor in the mornings. We had to dig a very large hole, and Rafael my lovely vet came, gave her an intravenous double dose, she died on the spot and fell sideways into the hole, being so big the noise alone was awful. Then to my surprise he brought out his pistol and shot her three times in the head.

'*Heh! Rafael, porque tu he hecho este?*'

Heh! Rafael, why did you do that?

He admitted he was nervous the drug in the injection would not be strong enough, she weighed at least two tonnes, and he wanted to be very sure, knowing how much we had all loved her dearly.

All very sad, but I had spent days with our secretary and José Manuel Soriano going over our accounts, we had been spending far too much, with hardly any income. The board of directors had stopped paying Joaquin since two or three years earlier, he had sold Electrificaciones Nacionales S.A. the previous year, and the family business in the south, Sur d'España, had gone belly up. I had to make these tough decisions, cutting and slashing costs in every direction, cut the staff in half, Paco and Carmen, Emilio, Antonio the groom, my last lovely brood mare and foal went to Olivia Scully. Meridza I kept but leant her to a lovely girl, Cathy Gaggero, who promised to look after her.

# 26. Expo Sevilla. Minouche

Again distractions came in the form of the young. Towards the end of the summer two of Miles's friends from Glenalmond came on holiday, and I just wanted out for a few days, to relax and laugh, so I arranged to get tickets for Expo '92 Sevilla, having to pull a few strings with the VIPs and embassies. Michael and Belinda Whaley came with us, she was pregnant, and insisted that Michael pushed her in a wheelchair; with a silly English hat, she looked like a heroine out of James Joyce.

We went on ahead, and left them to join us the following day.

The three boys and Caroline, Miles, Mel Allan and Jamie Thewes and myself were invited by Jamie's aunt and uncle, the Chestertons, to stay in their gorgeous *finca* in the mountains of Extremadura, behind Sevilla. This was a *finca* just full of chestnut trees, totally different to our arable land and cork trees. Very high and cold in winter, Jeannie and Sam Chesterton ran the property as a private hotel, seemingly full of their children and their friends.

I had never been to an 'Expo' before, so was thrilled and amazed to discover I think, one of the best ones in our recent years. The city had done the most fabulous job, the whole fair was on the island in the middle of the Guadalquivir, the entrances and walkways covered in flowers and spraying fresh water over one's head. We quickly met up with Michael and Belinda, grabbed plans and made a bee-line for the British pavilion, where we had all been invited. Sam, if I remember, was a friend of the ambassador. They were very proud of the new bridge over the river made by British Steel. I asked the young, which other pavilion attracted them, that they had to study the plan, and choose four close to each other. Like that we could all stand in the queues and shout to each other, as we got to the entrances.

We had fun, and they were thrilled; France, Venezuela, Mexico, 3D film with special goggles, holograms over the lake; exhausting but very exciting. As the sun went down, I invited them all to the roof of the Mexican pavilion and treated them to tequila cocktails. The young were all hyped up and over the moon. The evening show with the holograms over the lake, taken through fountains of water was sensational. It changed its themes, from flamenco dancers, to Spanish stallions, horse carriages with six in hand, to Hispano-Arabs doing high school dressage. All of us horse lovers, were crying at the end, it was just so beautifully done.

We drove home through the night, totally exhausted, but staggered the Spanish had been capable of laying on such a performance. I don't know the statistics, but I do not know of another Expo that came anywhere near Seville.

End of the summer, kids back to school, but I felt satisfied that they had had a great summer and a lot of experiences, and they both looked happier and moved around with more confidence. I was back in the mundane routine of lawyers and paperwork. Shifting papers, which went on every working day, months on end. Patricia was a godsend, and as we could laugh, it cheered me up morally. Poor thing had been diagnosed with multiple sclerosis, the same as David. She had it as a very young child, but it was controlled and 'praise be the Lord' never developed. Now and then she got tired, and her foot turned out, and she had a terrible time controlling her bladder. A miserable disease.

She had married a young Brit by the name of Ian White, and had the most adorable baby son, called Luis, after his grandfather, Joaquin's younger brother. They bought from me, some semi-underground basements that Joaquin had put in my name, obviously to save taxes. Turning them into a language school, installing computers and word processors, they had a huge success. All the upcoming middle class were crazy to get their young fluent in English, and pass their exams for Cambridge.

Christmas, I knew I had to be with Miles and Caroline and David their father, we were now a sort of family. A great friend of Jane's, Carol Cunningham, asked us all to stay in her house in Scotland, north of Perth. Easy for the young, but not so for me. However, where there's a will there is a way. I flew to Edinburgh, rented a car and picked up Miles from Glenalmond, and we drove north via Pitlochry to the Thewes's, staying a night with them at Strathgarry in Killiecrankie, and then drove west to Carol's place in a village called Aberfeldy. I was certainly getting to know Scotland. It started snowing on the way, nasty cold and slippery roads; Miles had never been there before, and so had no idea. He and I were meant to prepare the house; David was being brought by Carol the next day, Christmas Eve, and I was picking Caroline up at Edinburgh airport.

Readying the house quickly, and decorating the tree, it was lovely and warm with central heating, we both flopped into bed; next morning we were snowed in, ice and snow on all the windows.

'Come on, fellow, good Scottish breakfast and it's Christmas Eve, we have to clear the drive for Carol and your father.'

The sun was out, so it was quite beautiful. We slaved away all morning, listening to the pheasants, chatting to the postman and neighbours; Miles eventually slinked off, lazy so and so, leaving me to finish and lay sand on the now clean drive. It was quite a slope, and I could not see David walking up it.

Leaving at 4.00 pm, already dark, we had a horrific drive to the airport, but the smile on Caroline's face was worth ten times the effort. She was quite difficult, so I was worried about her reaction to this Christmas plan. So far so good, we ploughed our way back to Aberfeldy, in snowdrifts getting bigger by the minute. Thank goodness the drive was sanded, and breathed in relief to find Carol's car at the door and David installed in front of the fire. He looked very tired from his journey, a white and haggard face, though very happy to have his children around him.

Carol, as usual, was buzzing away with her decorations and the tree. Insisting we all sang Christmas carols, I love them, so led the way, joined by her, but the kids just laughed at us. Neighbours came to see her, and say hello to David, so ice and snow were continually being blown inside. Despite having brought David the whole way from Northern Ireland, the ferry crossing and the long drive across Scotland in the snow, Carol was a ball of fire and never stopped. She had the energy of 20.

Stockings on the stairs next morning, sloppy breakfast and pressies in front of the fire. Caroline got very depressed and sad, so I sent them out with boots and jackets to collect firewood in the snow and visit the frozen lake in front. Nothing like exercise to drown the glooms. Carol and I were doing our level best to give the Craig family a happy Christmas, but they missed their mother terribly. It took some years before they slowly returned to normal. I understood them perfectly, as Christmas is a very special occasion in the northern part of Europe, and I missed Joaquin as much as they missed Jane. Anyway, we did our best and the dinner was excellent, everyone cheered up and one and all slightly pissed.

Carol took David back the way they had come, a few days later, and I drove the kids to Edinburgh, where they both had New Year's Eve parties organised. I dropped off the car and flew back to Seville, as Malaga was totally packed out. After the snow and ice, it was bliss to be back in the sun and the warmth. I had left my car there, so drove back via Jerez de la Frontera and dropped off at the Gonzalez *bodega* to wish them all a happy new year. Tio (uncle) Manolo, the eldest family member, was delighted to see me, and *copitas* of jerez were downed in their order. One always had to start with the sweet ones, and slowly they got drier and drier. In 1992 there were no breathalysers, but sensibly halfway across the mountains, I drew into the curve and had 40 winks. Returning to Las Pilas was seriously depressing, no horses in the stable, and raining. Only the dogs cheered me up, Napoleon, and Zarah Anastasia, and fiddling around in the staff kitchen as it was getting dark I heard a pathetic little miaow at the kitchen window.

'That's funny,' I said to myself, 'there are no cats in the house?' I looked around and realized there was an animal at the back window. Opened it and there was a Siamese kitten with the most enormous deep blue eyes one has ever seen. Soaked to the skin, as it was now pouring, I grabbed a dog towel and lifted her up and carried her into the drawing room in the main house, drying her off in front of the fire. She was frozen and miserable; I had no idea where she came from. Well, New Year's eve without Joaquin was awful, so cuddling my new find, I opened a bottle of champagne and went to bed and she slept on my chest between my boobs. As the staff came in next day, they found us both fast asleep, but the kitten sneezing away, she had caught my cold that I had brought from Aberfeldy.

She was so adorable, and had that square head of our previous Siamese back in Devon. We left the back door of the patio open, and waited to see if she left; which she did much to our sadness, but come evening she was back and with a quiet miaow, settled in front of the fire. Next day Maureen the nurse came to see me, and explained that she and Gordon her boyfriend, had bought two Siamese from the big new supermarket, hoping to rear them and produce babies. She had realized that the female was coming up to be with me, and went back to their cottage during the day to play with her mate. She knew I was very sad at the loss of Joaquin, and wanted me to keep her.

I said, 'Maureen, we will live the normal life and close the patio at night, and open it during the day, if Minouche, the name I had given her, comes here, fantastic and thank you, and if not, then she is yours.'

After two or three days she had made her home at Las Pilas, came out in the car with me and followed the horses, the farm ones that I had not sold. If ever frightened by something, whooooosh, straight up a tree, but she always came back, and slept in my bed every night. She was an exceptional animal, and so clever, and talk about the sixth sense, hers must have been the twelfth.

Sad, depressing time, still desperately trying to sort out Joaquin's never-ending papers. His secretary had left to go and work for our assessor *fiscale* in Seville, which meant Patricia and I had to do it all. Helped, of course, by the two executors. I moved money from the bank that was already in Anna's name but blocked, to release it to her. Funds and shares that belonged to his charity schools and the foundation were passed on to their accountants. Luis Modet, the official architect, and a very good friend of mine helped me enormously with the lands and their title deeds, and which lot belonged to whom. One paid more taxes, plus value and VAT than the actual land price. Long live the new government!

I had rented the apartment in the port of Sotogrande, but soon realized the rates and the taxes on the port were far larger than the income from renting, or at least not far off. Plus the hassle from the agencies and the continual back biting from would be tenants. I sold her easily.

Midwinter, now I was free to do what I liked, and one sport I missed dreadfully were the Alps and skiing. I had given it up, as it was not to Joaquin's tastes by a long shot; I had taken him up to the Sierra Nevada once, and he was not relaxed at all. Too many people from Madrid, and not sure about walking on ice. My bad luck, a cloudy day with no sun or he was depressed about something. Anyway this year, my dear friend, Françoise Marque, invited me to the chalet she was renting in Gstaad.

Drove to Malaga, now a minor autoroute, flew to Geneva, hired a car and drove to Lausanne, Chateau d'Oeux, Rochebrune, and Gstaad; Françoise's chalet was beyond the town and the famous Gstaad Palace, down a lane towards the river. It was a great reunion, as we had not seen each other since Joaquin's death. So gossip, gossip, we had a lot to catch up on. Françoise did not ski; she is the loveliest person, and very well read but lazy beyond imagination! As a hostess, she was great; she would get up in the mornings to make me proper coffee, lay on dinner parties for me to meet her friends, have my clothes washed and ironed, you name it. She even arranged for me to ski with her friends, sadly after 20-odd years, I had lost a lot of confidence, and took to the slopes very cautiously. Two days of falling over continuously I got it back, and was thrilled to pick up enough to ski more or less with everyone. Skiing down a mountain or jumping a fantastic horse over a big jump, are the two natural sports that are magic.

Back in Spain, after this lovely holiday and a total change, I had to start planning my life; the family were still being horrible and trying to treat me like dirt. What they were getting out of it, I just don't know. I put up the flat in Madrid for sale, as I had no intention of living there. Without Joaquin, Madrid had no charm at all.

Relations of the Goysuetas, his sister-in-law, bought it for a fairly reasonable price. They did not want the furniture and I was delighted to keep it. So had it stored in Madrid at Gil Stauffer, an international transporter, not knowing what the future would bring.

In the early summer, 23rd June 1993, I returned to Malta for Mummy's 83rd birthday; she was well installed in her new apartment having sold the farmhouse that Winco had built. It was too big for her to look after. Here she was surrounded by friends and other old ladies, and a funny little man, Tony Pandolfino, actually lived in the flat with her. She did not know it, but he was as gay as a beanpole. Very charming and cooked her a hot meal every evening. He was an ex-jockey and ran a riding stable down the road. All very odd, but it seemed to work out, and Mummy was still switched on enough to look after her accounts. Nothing dramatic was stolen.

The apartment block had a swimming pool attached, and we arranged a birthday party around it, supplying the food and drinks via another old lady's terrace.

Malta had changed dramatically in the last 20 years, and was now one seething mass of lower-class tourists. The Maltese themselves were becoming *nouveau riche*, buying boats and new cars, but nowhere to go. Mintoff had disappeared, and the new government seemed incapable of making a compromise with Europe.

Next winter, back in Spain, I had already organised it and took the young to the Caymans to learn to dive. I wanted to keep up my residency, so had to return anyway. Robert Horton, Antonio de la Campa, Mel Allan, Miles and Caroline and the boss! Two boys in each bedroom and Caroline shared with me. They had a ball, except for poor Miles with his asthma; he was not allowed to dive. Funny, as a few years later he became a dive master. That year though, he was miserable. I tried to make up for it by offering him rides on a jet ski, but no thank you Vics, he would not admit it, but was terrified to meet a shark. The others did brilliantly and within a few days had their certificates. Much easier for them, as having done maths and science studying for their A-levels, they were closer to the subject of hyper-ventilating and blowing out your eardrums as you descended to deeper depths.

The exam was all very technical, but it dealt mainly with problems if something went wrong. The everyday routine, once learnt, was easy to dominate, and ones confidence under water came very quickly. I remember watching Antonio, our Spanish nephew, turning cartwheels backwards out in the deep blue; once you were equalized, you could do anything. Each diver has a gauge showing him or her the amount of nitrogen (compressed air) left in their bottles carried on your back, and another depth gauge saying how deep one was or had been.

They were all thrilled to have passed, but poor Miles was suffering in the background, so I quickly arranged a BBQ on the beach. Sadly, as everyone was under 18, no alcohol was allowed in public. It was a seriously boring island. I had to buy the beer on the quiet, and lug it to the beach, and then took them to the Holiday Inn nightclub. Again not allowed in, they all looked so young. Anyway, the diving was heaven, and we chose a different spot every day, so they went home with a great experience under their belts. At Miami airport we separated, and Miles and Caroline came back to Las Pilas with me.

One last excursion before they left for school, we took the Mitsubishi four-by-four, and drove over to Kabila via Ceuta, to stay with Najat and Assiz and their children for a few days. Beautiful weather at the end of August, fun parties on the beach, couscous galore and they took us to the Club Med at Cabo Negro, which my young adored. Caroline was still very shy despite all the fun she was having, as everyone in Morocco spoke French. It was too much for her to break out, and chat back in English.

This is life; we all talk the language that is common to the group around you, and never make the effort to speak another one for the sake of the minority. We are awful, human beings, and we are all selfish.

# 27. Finding the Ruin in the Provence

Having sold the Marigalante II, the flat in Madrid, and most of the horses, I was feeling certainly lighter, and slowly the papers were falling into place. Luis Modet and Tony Cottrell were keeping eyes open for an investor, for Las Pilas. We all knew she was ripe for development, as it was inside the boundary of the municipality of Algeciras.

I hated Algeciras and its environment, the port now had tripled in size, with container ships at every angle, the charm of the old harbour had long ago disappeared. Even Gibraltar had filled in, new yacht clubs, and vast building sites right up to the runway, and the frontier.

Caroline was now at university, Writtle Agricultural College in Essex; so she had much longer holidays than Miles, who was still at school. We planned the excursion to France, dropping off Miles at Malaga airport. Maureen, the nurse, with Gordon, her boyfriend, Caroline, three dogs, Minouche and myself. Quite a car full! Caroline had been very quiet on the drive north, and very silent during dinner. We simply could not get a word out of her, despite pointing out all the historical sights. Thinking she must be mad at me, I asked Gordon and Maureen to take her for a walk on the beach and give her a drink in a bar to cheer her up.

I found out much later on, that she and Miles were very sad to leave Spain, where literally we had brought them up from being babies to adolescents. Poor kids were so unsure of themselves already, they didn't need a mad aunt who changed houses every three years, and they were too young to come to grips with why I wanted so much to return to the South of France. Give them time and they would appreciate the beauty of the coast, the mountains, the Alps and the funky little bistros, even the smell of fresh bread and coffee in the mornings as you drove through the villages. Even though, one cannot expect children or friends to have the same affinities as one's self. We are all on different planes of thought, despite their admiration, respect and sometimes love, they are on a different planet, and one cannot expect them to feel the same way. Maybe with time and coincidences, and understanding, they will learn to love and appreciate the same values, beauty and art, space and colour that affected me in my inner soul.

Feeling very sad for Caroline, I drove on to our first rendezvous, just below the lovely old town of Grasse, where they make the perfume. Lavender and roses and wild thyme covered the lower mountain slopes. Our hosts, my friends Antoine and Anne D'Assche, greeted us with open arms, a bit horrified about Minouche, though the dogs they knew about in advance. Where will she sleep? The chairs were all covered with Grandmother's something or other.

'Don't worry, Anne, she does not know she is a cat, and will sleep anywhere.' Thinking to myself, she will be in my bed immediately.

Thank goodness they left, and we had the house to ourselves, and a divine pool, surrounded by olive trees, which Minouche adored climbing all over.

Relaxing for a couple of days, after our drive from the south of Spain, catching up on the sun, we started exploring the little villages between Grasse and the coast. I just could not recognize Mougins, Castelleras, Valbonne; roads, apartment blocks and parking lots surrounded them all. This was exactly what Jacques and I, back in the '60s, ran away from. We drove down to Cannes, one hour and a half, bumper to bumper traffic. Once on the Croissette, one could glimpse the sea and the islands in the distance. Holy Moses, just to come for a swim, took us half the day to get here. We drove along the coast, so the others and Caroline could see the Carlton Hotel, the Martinique, the Blue Bar and the casino, all my old hunting grounds of the '60s; I had to give them an idea of what I remembered 30 years earlier.

We went swimming just for the pleasure to get into the sea, but swamped amongst the masses, ghastly oiks and typists from Paris, fat old couples from Lyon, every sort. We drove to Monte Carlo, and hung around the port, showing Caroline, the Prince's Palace, and the city of Monaco and the casinos. She was still too young to go and gamble properly, and none of us had the right clothes with us, so we took her to the border with Italy at Ventimiglia, and looked over the river at the frontier. I showed her the port of Menton, where I had found Sable, and told her the story. I did not want to buy land or an old house in Italy, so we returned to France, and drove inland to discover all the little villages up in the mountains, above Monte Carlo. The mountains were very steep, and no wonder Napoleon had an impossible time crossing these southern Alps.

Next day we drove back towards Grasse, where I had seen on the map valleys, that wound their way into the Alps, and landed up in the loveliest countryside. Staying the night in a hostel, and talking to the locals, we discovered all the information we needed. I knew all this back country, from the '60s and it was gorgeous to find it unchanged, but it was still very wild, and miles from anywhere. I kept going, discovering every valley and every village, most of them empty. We turned north towards Auron, one of the skiing centres. An old friend of mine owned the most up-to-date chichi resort. We made a plan and took the right road, found her hotel and had the most gorgeous three days there.

I was still not convinced, beautiful as it was, as an all-round residence, I was not ready to buy, it was miles from Grasse, and even more from Nice and the airport. From here there would be no swimming in the sea at all. On our way back to the D'Assche's, we took a different route and passed via the village of Saillans, stopping in the village real estate office with the most lovely old *mas* in the window.

The site was lovely, but the village seemed a bit sad. We went back the following day for a viewing. The agent directed us out of the village back towards Cannes, and then north up the mountain. Thank you very much, a steep incline with stones and rocks; as we slid and bumped upwards, I asked the agent, 'Is this the only road to this property?'

'*Oui, Madame, c'est l'unique, il y a quelques annees c'etait mille fois pire, et que les ans et les mulles arriveraient au Moulin.*'

'*Ah! C'est un vrai moulin?*' I asked.

'Yes,' she said changing into excellent English. 'It has its own river and a little lake and was a working mill until ten years ago.'

Immediately mentioning water, I became even more interested. As we rounded a curve amongst weeping willows, we saw this lovely old pink house, with small square windows and shutters. An elderly woman came out to greet us, and I realized she was the owner. The agent had already told me, that she was recently widowed, and now felt too isolated living up the mountain. Shaking her hand, I told her that I too had just lost my husband. The house was lovely, but with very small rooms and totally rebuilt, and my fingers were itching to start building again. Wandering around the land, we saw the lake and the river, it was really very pretty. We thanked her and left, thinking to myself it was well worth the visit, but it was isolated, and no one I had ever heard of living close. We had three more properties to visit, all Hollywood, superb, but miles over my budget. The Lloyd's crash had hit London, and I imagined these were the millionaires selling off their assets.

Caroline had to leave for her university, so I took them all out to my favourite restaurant in the port of Antibes for a farewell fish dinner. They had all fallen in love with the *soupe de poisson*. Stinking of garlic, we staggered exhausted to bed; then to the airport to see her off. By now, she was much happier and gave me a big hug and said how she had loved the adventure of discovering the real South of France, that she had never imagined the back country so beautiful and unspoilt.

Our next port of call was the village of Grimaud, just outside St Tropez; I had rented the house of friends for two weeks. On arrival, Madame la Marquise was also horrified at Minouche and said the dogs could sleep in the garage! Gordon was great, and told her how clean they were, and that they always slept in the car, especially as it was still summer in the south. The house was an old *mas* and much smaller than the D'Assche's, but it had an olive grove and a pool and was only 15 minutes from the centre of St Tropez.

As we had a drink around the pool, the husband was very curious as to my plans. They all knew through the bush telegraph, that I had lost my husband. After asking about property prices and showing him on the map the areas that could interest me, he asked me did if I knew St Remy de Provence.

He told me that St Tropez was dead in winter, everyone went back to Paris, shops closed, restaurants closed, even the cinema closed.

'Vicky, before you make a decision about a house here near the coast, I advise you to visit St Remy. It is the centre of the Provence, near Avignon, a big city, Arles and Aix en Provence to the south. There you have a year-round resident population of all sorts of nationalities, writers and artists and a fun-loving community. Antique dealers abound, with their centre at l'Isle sur la Sorgue, just the other side of the Rhône. It is the centre of southern culture, and today very much the fashionable place to buy a property.'

It all sounded very interesting, the owners left for Paris, and we settled down to enjoy our stay in St Tropez!

The weather was divine, and the mass of tourists had left, September and October are gorgeous, except for the evenings that get shorter by the day. We spent the mornings in the port, reading the papers and sipping coffee, wandering around the little back streets and La Place de Lice, for me to remember the mad days of the '60s, playing boule in the place, and always having dinner in the secret back room of the Bistro de Paris. Midday on the beach, Club 55, and visiting the vineyards early evening.

We understood our host's remarks about the farms. There were no ruins that needed restoring within hundreds of kilometres in every direction. Frustrated, one day I remembered my old friends from Geneva, who had bought the Muneca in Cuarton, had a house in St Remy. I rang them, and asked myself to stay for the weekend.

They were over the moon, so leaving Gordon and Maureen with the animals, I grabbed my map, and took off over the Estoril Mountains towards the Autoroute de Sud. At Cavaillon turned left straight to St Remy, and I found Rosalyn and Marcelo d'Honnincthun's house on the outskirts of the town. She loved to gossip and wanted to know where and with whom I was, and where I had been? What was I up to?

They were adorable, and drove me all around St Remy and its surrounding, and then up to Les Alpilles and Le Baux de Provence, where we walked around the battlements and the old village, still packed with tourists, but with the most fabulous views of 180 degrees. One could see the Camargue, Marseille, the Luberon Mountains, and north to Avignon.

We talked non-stop about my ideas and projects, and I repeated what our friend told me in St Tropez. Yes, they agreed.

'Here you are inland, but with very easy access to the coast, swimming pools replace the sea, and they are quiet and private. The whole atmosphere of Provence, is based on music, art, sculpture and design; esoteric thought and Nostrodamus. There is a new influx of artists and writers, and Caroline of Monaco with her horses and children, who go to school here. They all add to the ambience. Music festivals all through the summer, two big antique fairs, not to mention the local fetes in each village, where they have bullfighting, running the bulls, and herds of Camarguaise horses galloping around the village. Funniest of all, the bulls in rubber swimming pools, attacked by the local boys trying to tackle them and throw them down into the water!'

I returned to St Tropez, my head buzzing with ideas, and retrieved everyone and the animals, back to St Remy a couple of days later. Gordon and Maureen were delighted with the ambiance, the boutiques and stalls in the main square, glasses of wine and foie gras; Provençal skirts, knick-knacks of every colour. Stalls of olive oil, breads of every kind, pâtés and even Spanish ham. I looked all over for *boudin*, black sausage, but sadly could not find it. Cheeses yes, of every type and colour, we could have gone on discovering the market for hours. I suggested, though, to go up the fashionable bar of the time, Café des Arts, where I was recognised by the owners, as having dined there the week earlier with Rosalyn and Marcelo. So we were wined and dined and introduced to all the locals. It was a charming atmosphere, with attractive people coming and going. In those days, Madame ran an excellent cuisine, whether at lunch time or at night.

I began to have the shivers in my shoulders, and felt someone was calling out to me. I did not want to make quick decisions, but somehow this whole area had a very special feeling. I felt already that I belonged, that I was part of the scenery, something I had never felt in Algeciras.

I looked for somewhere to stay, not wanting to be a guest of friends, as I needed my independence and to be free to make my own plans.

We made our way to the hostelry above the town, it was freezing, with a howling mistral yet again. Minouche went wild amongst the trees, but managing to catch her, we all landed up in front of their fire. Delightful people, and they were fascinated to know where we had come from, and what our plans were.

We explained that I was a widow, and wanted to come back to France in the south and was looking for a property in the area, preferably a ruin, 16th or 17th century, that I could buy and do up.

I had quite a few contacts in the Luberon, so we started by looking them up, asking questions non-stop, and driving miles in every direction; the weather was gorgeous and the colour of the mountains and valleys superb. The only sad fact, no sea; such is life, one cannot have everything, but we were very lucky to have this chance to know the Luberon.

Visiting houses and land every day, we were tired of the strain, and decided to leave for Spain and come back the following year. On our way west, we spent a night in l'Isle sur la Sorgue, my old base when I was an au pair kid learning French. The following morning the phone rang early; it was Edward Lifran, over the moon and totally hyped up.

'Vicky, come quick, I have found the ideal place for you. It is you, and I know you will be mad about it. It only came on our books this morning.'

'Edward, *tranquilo*, no hurry, I will be back next year.'

'No, Vicky, I know this is you, meet me for a pastis in the bar at Eygalieres.'

He knew my weaknesses! We met this charming young agent and took off to see the property. Edward, as smart as a cookie, took me in through the back entrance, drove in front of the ruin, right up to the rim of the forest, turned his car round in a tight circle and there she was. I just sat and gaped with my mouth open.

It was immediate love, a long low *mas*, 16th and 17th century, one part for the guardian, the middle for Miles and Caroline, and the west part for me and my guests. All the walls were of stone, and the roof all old tiles, the centre part was vaulted and the west wing was so deep in sheep shit, one had no idea where the floor was.

Out on the patio, there were very old pig stalls with feeding troughs that were definitely Roman; wild roses, yucca bushes and fields of irises, and pine trees in front.

'Oh Lord, Edward, why did you wait so long? You are right, and this will keep me busy for years. How much land?'

'Twenty-five hectares.'

After a boozy lunch in Eygalieres at our famous bar tabac, I booked into the local hotel, and contacted my friend the *notaire*, Pierre Lacaille, and told him the story. The next night he joined us, and we crept into the property, hiding behind the yuccas; just as we got there, the old farmer came out and saw us both. I knew then, that he was sure I would buy the property. I beat him down, however, on his price and we landed up at a very reasonable compromise.

I was introduced to Sarah Holcroft in the bar tabac, where everything takes place in Eygalieres. She said straight out, 'Oh! Hello. It's you who is going to buy the Mas de la Rose, that sack of shit?'

I nearly hit her, I was so cross. It was so rude and unpleasant. Later we became great friends, and her husband, Harry, ticked her off, for not buying the *mas* before me. I learnt there had been three buyers before, but none of them had the foresight of how to renovate the old ruin. One was a very smart Italian with two or three decorators, who apparently had said to their employer, 'We cannot do this, it is far too big and impossible to rebuild and it would take years.'

I realized I had taken on an enormous challenge, but I was never worried, at least at the beginning. I did get quite depressed towards the end, as I never could see it finished. The first days of November, I signed the compromise, paid down a deposit, and left for Spain and Las Pilas. It was planned to finish the deal in the middle of March. I chose the 17th – St Patrick's Day.

*Mas de la Rose - how Vicky found her, 1993*

*The Queen and Prince Philip ,Georgetown, Cayman Islands, 1994*

*Vicky at Ephesus, Turkey, 1994*

*Last evening of the cruise with Olga and Nikita, off the Turkish coast, 1994*

*Luis Modet's backside, divine! 1994*

*Miles and Caroline, 1995*

*Mummy at 85, 1995*

*West Wing of Le Mas looking worse for wear, autumn, 1995*

*Christmas at Le Mas, 1996*

*Le Mas, drawing room finished, 1996*

*Le Mas, finished, 1996*

*West Wing of Le Mas, finished, 1996*

*Christmas with Edie Coulson, 1997*

*Miles and Vicky at Le Mas, 1997*

*Napoleon arrives, 1997*

*Brazilian party for my 60th, with Caroline, Amy and Louise, Le Mas, 1998*

*Catherine with sons Max and Archie, my nephews, 1999*

*Aerial view of Le Mas, 1999*

*Doneraile Court - family home, 1999*

*What was left of Bonaca after Hurricane Mitch, 1999*

*Luisito and Cristina (baby), 1999*

*Maria's 90th, Co Gallway, 1999*

*Millennium NYE party, Le Mas, 1999*

*Minouche, 1999*

*The bird sanctuary on the Saltees Islands off Co Wexford, 1999*

*Diving off the Caymans, now an advanced diver, 1999*

# 28. Mas de la Rose

We returned on March 3rd 1994, leaving behind a young couple to look after Las Pilas in the interim while the negotiations for its sale were being controlled by Luis Modet. We drove back to a house that was very close to the Mas de la Rose on the outskirts of Eygalieres. Maureen was going to look after the house we rented, cleaning and shopping, and bring us a picnic lunch to the *mas* at midday, leaving us free to get on with the work, and provide us a hot dinner in the evenings.

Come 17th March, having already met the notary of Orgon, we agreed to meet and sign the deeds with the farmer. It was hilarious, he came with his sister and brother-in-law, and argued every little point. They were fighting between themselves, and asking for more money. The notary shut them up, saying they had already signed a compromise. After an hour, finally we signed the bill of sale. What a miserable deal, not even a glass of champagne to congratulate ourselves. As we walked out of the notary's office, the farmer turned to me and asked, 'Well, at least you are not going to sleep in the old stables.'

I replied, knowing he was talking about the west wing, and the sheep shit, 'Well, you will never know.'

Months later, he came back with his ridiculous wife, on a Sunday afternoon; we were all half asleep and topless, and she with no shame, came down the line of sunbeds, looking for the owner. I hid behind a Herald Tribune. No control, I threw a wobbly, covering my boobs, and asked this idiot what on earth did she want at 3.30 pm on a Sunday? Do I come to your apartment and barge in and disturb you. I was very cross. They were obviously dying to see what I had done, news travels fast in the Provence. They were spitting with jealousy, but *tant pis*, they never had the intuition to develop the property.

It was still March and wet and cold, so first thing was to get the young men waterproof jackets and tools, spades and shovels, pickaxes and wheel barrows etc. We found an amazing store of old army vehicles, and everything they wanted. I made friends with the owner, and she was fascinated to know what I had done. She knew from years earlier the Mas de la Rose and knew all her old history, lived quite close, so I invited her over to come and see it again. She told us all the history of the *mas*, how the owners back in the $17^{th}$ century owned all the land in the valley, and their signature was engraved on one of the stone windows. We found it on the back window of what I had planned to be the dining room: 'WHB Reille, 1687'.

The first big job was to drill for water, and clean out the sheep shit from the west wing. In the meantime, Odette Cottrell, the agent, introduced me to her builder, Jean François. A charming young fellow from St Remy, who had built, or rather renovated, three farm houses for her. I had seen them all, and saw that he was passionate over old stones, and had excellent taste. I showed him the *mas*, and my rough plans that I had already drawn in Spain, explaining how I wanted to start with the guardian's house, so I and the children could live there, while we continued with the rest.

We had to have an architect, to be able to make the plans official. I chose Hugo Bosch from St Remy; he had an excellent team, but once the plans were legalized, I told him I did not need an architect on site. 'The rest I will do, and if there are problems, I would contract an engineer.' He was a bit miffed, and said it was too difficult for me.

I explained I had already built a *cortijo* in Spain, apartments in the Marais in Paris, and four more old buildings in Spain without an architect. Naturally he was cross, as he lived off the commissions from the artisans and workers, plus his fee.

'I will surely need you, when I have to fit bathrooms under the roof, and make an inside terrace to give light to the bedrooms, so don't panic, I will contact you immediately.'

'What about the staircases and fitting the doors and windows etc?'

'I can do those with my eyes closed, don't worry.'

I hired a driller, who was certain there was water at a certain depth. Sadly, he was just a local working with his son. His machinery was very limited. He did his best, but no result. I then called in a geologist, a pain in the arse and he told me there was water near the road. 'OK, but who pays for it to reach the house?'

Then I employed a wizard, who came from the higher alps, with special twigs; he danced when his twigs started shaking. He simply asked me, 'Where is the nearest water source, that has a serious debit?'

'It is two kilometres beyond the *mas*, towards Orgon the village, there is a spring with masses of water.'

We walked down the old lane to the left of the property, and I pointed it out to him. He told me to leave him alone, and go back to the *mas*, which I did. An hour later, he came back and walked very slowly through the grass in front of the ruin towards the yucca bushes. Stopping just in front, his twigs started shaking like mad, we were all there watching. He loved an audience; we thought he was quite mad.

'Madame,' he said grinning, 'here is your water, it runs from the spring you showed me, through your field, missing out by two metres your drillers marks; then turns and runs here in front of the building, then it turns again and runs under the forest.'

Well, believe it or not, we marked the site, painted white stones on the spot. We congratulated our wizard, and prayed he was right. He had already told me, that we would find it at 120 metres, and that there was enough water for a huge garden.

Jean François was doing a great job in the building, using the small amount of water in one of the old wells, but warning me, that there was very little left. He was already halfway through the middle house, windows and doors outlined in old stone, and matching up the old tiles on the roof. Through friends I found a water engineer from up country near the Mont Ventoux, who had a huge drill and all the accessories. I phoned him and explained my predicament; he was interested and came south to see me. He took his time and followed me to the original spring, and back again. He had heard of my wizard, and said he was very well known. We settled on a deal, and he agreed to come the next week with his drill.

The driller began wearing waterproofs and a hard hat, the workmen on the roof watching fascinated, knowing I had no more water. Every half hour he was covered with clay and swearing at his machine, every evening he had to close in the hole. Three days later I was out searching for something, and whoooosh! He hit it, and it poured into the air, just like an oil geyser. What a shame I did not see it. As we have the same problem in Africa, I know what bliss it is to find your own water.

We had found 6,000 litres an hour, in an old *mas* that was known to have no water. What modern technology can do!

As all this was going on, I took the maximum amount of time to visit the antique dealers and their yards. These were like Spanish *rastros*, old stones, doors, beams, fountains, pedestals, you name it. I went to a very big one near Apt, where I found beams for the drawing room, fountains and old stones for the garden, many more at l'Isle sur la Sorgue, and St Remy; old chimneys at a special place near the Pont du Gard. I discovered the most glorious parts of the Provence.

St Remy de Provence was becoming very well known. Everyone met at the Café des Artes for pre-lunch pastis, especially on Wednesdays, market day, when the town was thriving. Art galleries and boutiques, bistros and cafés were two-a-penny; often when wandering around the tiny streets, a local policeman or woman would be leaning against the doorway. One would know immediately that Caroline of Monaco would be on a buying spree. I have met her often in the town, or at horse shows with her children, and she was always asking who I was. I am stupid, I should have walked up to her and introduced myself, as she seems a very nice person. Having met Rainier and Grace in Ireland at the *Bal des Petits Lits Blancs*, I should have taken the plunge but somehow too shy to take the first step.

The town was booming, and every week we heard of new arrivals and the buying up of property in or near St Remy, it was very much in fashion. Hugo Bosch was very much in demand. He and other friends were always turning up at the *mas*, and we had fun picnics near the pool. Telling me the local gossip, and saying there was not another old *mas* left on the market that was original and authentic; I had literally bought the last ruin. One day he brought with him an

American couple; a very tall distinguished woman and a charming little fellow companion. Dee Caperton and Cary Guy.

They lived in Paris, but wanted to move south and had bought the Mas Mireille on the old road from St Remy to Avignon. A delightful pair, and we became great friends, swapping building stories and antique hunting. Dee was impossible, and changed her ideas every day, moving curtains and furniture from one room to another. Cary was similar but outside, one minute an avenue of trees, next a rose garden and then a forest of bamboos.

With a water supply, more guests started to arrive, Dini McConnell and her huge ridgeback, came to see what I was doing; she was an old friend from New York, and the step-daughter of Terry Pantz. She immediately loved the Provence, and started looking at property. Then my god-daughter arrived, Louise Balfour, Hugh and Sheila's daughter. She had helped me a lot with the plans, the complicated cross sections and levels for the upstairs terrace. She saw that I was exhausted, and wanting to see as much of the Provence, encouraged me to take a few days off the site, heading to the Fontaine de Vaucluse, St Remy, and the Camargue, laughing non-stop.

As the work on the site continued, Gordon was having a flirt with Sarah Holcroft's nanny, and one night brought her back to the *mas*. Maureen found out, and, very cross, said she was going to leave. I asked her to stay, as I knew I could not feed them, shopping and running the site. Both Gordon and his friend, used to go boozing in Eygalieres, and came home plastered. The lorry with two containers had arrived by then, so the garage was piled high with my furniture from Las Pilas and Madrid. One evening his friend got angry over something, and threw a glass at my face, it missed me by inches, I thought then it was time to slowly get rid of them. Maureen was determined to leave, so I told the boys we would have to get two portacabins and live on the site. A small one for me and a large one for them, and finish with the rented house. I just could not manage it.

We had an old second-hand van, that they used for carrying tools and materials. I gave a lunch in the middle house for a group of friends with a large paella, ordered from a local restaurant, it arrived so late, that the guests ate all the tapas, and hardly touched the paella. Our bad luck, it poured with rain, so everyone huddled into the vaulted room, and, of course, drank too much. When the boys left, we still had the rented house for another week, they ran the van into a pine tree and smashed it to pieces. I put the paella into the back of the Mitsubishi, and drove back to the little *mas*, where with all my strength lifted the paella out of the four-by-four. It was far too heavy, and I fell face down into the dish in the garden. Shattered, I just left it there and went to bed. Napoleon the male Labrador, helped himself, and next morning, I have never seen a bloated belly like it. He was huge, and spent the next week farting paella!

Maureen left very sadly, as she had been a great help, and the memories I had of her looking after darling Joaquin were unforgettable. I have never seen her again. The boys and I drove north to a place I had been told about near Valence, we found the portacabins, and arranged for them to come the next day. When they arrived, it was like a film, two houses on trailers. The driver just asked me where I wanted them. I chose a place slightly behind the building, but with a good view of the garage and the drive, mine at an angle facing east, so that I had privacy from the other one. The driver put down blocks, brought out a crane, pushed a button and swung the cabins over the blocks. We were amazed, he did the whole job in 30 minutes. The boys started moaning, saying, 'You promised we would live in an old farmhouse, now look what we have. You will have to pay us extra for living rough.'

'Get on with you, you are spoilt black, and having a marvellous time. Because of your behaviour, Maureen left and I cannot keep up a rented house.'

Then they moaned about washing with a hosepipe; all I had was a bucket! We set up a kitchen in the garage and space to keep plates, knives and forks, and plugged into the mains a small fridge. We camped like this all of May and June, hurrying with the work to be ready for Miles and Caroline and their friends from school, who wanted a holiday job.

I nearly went mad with Luigi, the pool builder; we had signed the contract in the bar tabac of Eygalieres, practically my office. Then he turned on me.

‘What happens, if I dig down the big rock, and find another layer of rock below?’

‘Bad luck, chum, you’ve signed the contract. What is more, you have only gone 1.50m deep and the contract is 2.50m, if you don’t follow the contract, you won’t get paid. I have the money hidden in my car, ready to pay you.’

Never have I seen someone move so fast, he climbed onto the bulldozer and drove it himself. Within three hours the pool was correct, and the wall of rock was shear to the bottom. We all sighed with relief, as no one knew for sure the contours of the underground levels.

Marie Jo Laget, the woman from the army shop, used to come over with pies and quiches in the evening, a very kind person, I certainly did not have the time or energy to think more about it, until one evening, Hugo Bosch turned up to see how we were getting on, and curious, of course, to see what we had done.

As he was leaving, he grinned his big smile, and asked me, ‘Do you know who that is?’ pointing to Marie Jo.

‘No idea, except she has an ex-army store on the road to Avignon and comes here often in the evenings just to talk to us and helps by bringing food.’

He laughed his head off.

‘She must be in love with you, she is the biggest lesbian in all Provence.’

‘Oh! Lord. I never thought about it. You are probably right. I will have to set her mind at rest, that she is wasting her time.’

Finally we finished the staff kitchen, bathroom and their two bedrooms and another godson, Jim Goodsir, came out to help. I was able to move into their bedroom-to-be, and leave him my *cabana*. Then my mother came for her 84th birthday, 23rd June. I put her up across the road in a hotel with a pool, and the rooms were all on the flat, so she had no steps. We brought her to the *mas* every morning, and had arranged the terrace with shade, so she could sit in her wheelchair and watch the goings on. It wasn’t easy, but we managed it. She thought I was as mad as a cracker, but then she always did.

The 11th July, I was waiting for the kids, they were driving out, Miles and Caroline, and Neil, Charlie and Alan – Miles's friends from Glenalmond. I had calculated they would arrive around midnight, so I accepted a dinner with a lovely hostess, Miette de Villeyre, in Les Baux de Provence. She always offered me a bath before dinner, knowing I was filthy from the site and had no bath. Coming home, to which now felt was my home, day-dreaming, I had the fright of my life, from round the pine trees, whooping and shouting came the young. They had seriously scared me. They had arrived, found their way at least two hours earlier.

Later a very pretty girl joined us, Rachel from Hong Kong, Miles's girlfriend. Old fashioned, staying at a friend's house, I tried to keep them sleeping separately. A big joke, as giggle, giggle, they came up from the garden. Apparently all the school sixth form, now mixed sexes, were sleeping around. What we did at 21, was now the norm at 16.

They worked like skivvies during the day, but had great fun at the weekends. I arranged to take them on outings, first canoeing on the Sorgue, and Alan playing football in the square of Avignon, broke his leg, silly twit. Then we rented a boat in St Tropez for the day with water skiing, next a picnic on the beach in the Camargue.

They were all very amused at the St Tropez atmosphere, the yachts backed up three in a line, the bars and bistros along the quay, and the Club 55 on the beach. They ogled the naked girls, or at least topless, disgusted and horrified at the men. Early September was a gorgeous time in the Med and the light in the evenings on the vines and the pine trees is unique. The kids wanted the nightclubs, so we did St Tropez by night, an expensive past-time; I was just there to foot the bill, feeling sad and with my memories of the '60s and '70s, which were fun and crazy.

Marie Jo Laget insisted on organizing a picnic for the young in the Camargue on a private beach that belonged to friends of hers. I had a quiet talk to her a few days previously, saying, 'Marie Jo, I like you very much, you are a good kind person, but you must know by now, I am totally straight, and my partners in crime have all been macho males. So delighted if you come to the *mas*, but I won't go out with you in public, but we remain friends.'

I don't know what her reaction was, but it was never mentioned again.

Caroline turned 21 on the 31st August, so we had a cake hidden in the picnic baskets and champagne in the cool box. After the beach, which was divine and totally empty, we had planned to stop amongst the vines and pines and have the birthday dinner, a night picnic beside a canal. As it was a surprise, and the moon full, they all thought it was great.

End of summer, the young headed back to university and school and I had paperwork up to my eyes. I wanted to finish the first third and the vaulted middle house. I pushed on, and once over the worse, planned the garden, then let the bank relax and returned to Spain, living in Las Pilas with one bed and a small sofa.

# *29. Miles's 21st. Helicopter*

Over the winter I was getting depressed, as I couldn't see an end to the construction. I'd had enough and never thought I would see it finished, but actually 1996 turned out very positive, with all the details falling into place; the garden was growing, and the shutters on the guardian's house and the kids' middle part were all painted with the famous *bleu charrette*. My roman troughs full of flowers and the *micoculier* came out with all her leaves; baby green frogs jumping in the windows and, thank goodness, out again. The garage was finally clean and tidy, with central heating and pumps installed, racks of wine and booze in one corner. The dogs' kennel was now ready, with a stable door that opened into the pantry, and steps for Minouche to get out via a high window.

Summer came in like a bang, and when it's hot in the Provence, it really is sweltering. I decided to give a big party mid-July for the tennis tournament, turning the garage into a nightclub, and the billiard room into a restaurant. Sarah, 'the one-armed bandit', St George, who also had gone through a building saga near St Remy, had invited the Kents to stay; HRH Prince Michael of Kent, his wife, Marie Christine, and their two children, Freddie and Marie Gabriel. They arrived when the party was in full swing, it had rained during dinner, pretty miserable, but by midnight it had cleared up. Typical Sarah, she can never be on time, thinks it's funny to turn up four hours late. No one paid any attention, but I did my best to introduce Prince Michael to other interesting people and pretty girls. Miles took the two kids off to meet the young. I, dropping half a curtsy to Marie Christine, asked her, 'How are your lovely German warm bloods?' Knowing she had a stable full, and used to hunt in England. There were many things

I knew about her, but kept my cool. If only I had the courage to call her Mrs Troubridge, as I knew she had been married to one of the brothers, but never sure if it was the marine general or the admiral who had rented Furze Tor in Devon after we had gone to Malta.

At four in the morning, Lord Frederick Windsor (Freddie), demanded a comfortable bed and a TV. Miles told him, 'Vicky has a full house, and we are all sleeping on mattresses and sleeping bags in the pool house.' He threw a wobbly and insisted on being driven home. Yours truly had to do it, there were no men left, the parents had long gone, and there was no other solution. I took him home, a good 30 kilometres. He jumped out, and struggled with the gate, as an upper window flew open, and Maxime de la Falaise stuck her head out, shouting, 'Who is there and what on earth do you think you are doing at this hour in the morning?'

It was well after 5.00 am; Freddie, like all of us, was terrified by her, he slunk through the bushes in the garden and disappeared, while I drove home with a pale grey sky of dawn.

We were going kayaking, a few days later at the Fontaine de Vaucluse, and they wanted to come. I arranged lunch at the Partages des Eaux, and to meet them in the old hotel in the town of l'Isle sur la Sorgue (the Venice of France with the river dividing the town into islands) and then to lunch beside the river. Again Sarah came three hours late, she was impossible. Five, six phone calls to find out what on earth she was doing. I took them eventually off to my lovely restaurant on the river, where Miles was sitting beside HRH Marie Christine, and during lunch kept fiddling and looking nervous. We found out later, she was stroking his legs under the table. Poor fellow he was so shy, he should have pinched her back!

Prince Michael declined later to kayak with me and one black Labrador, and preferred to go with the guide. Tough for me, as it had rained and the river was in spate. He obviously had no confidence in my rowing capabilities; I was delighted, as I could not think what we would have talked about for two hours on the river.

Come the next summer, we moved in the furniture, cleaned and polished the woodwork, hung the curtains and installed the music, all the millions of details. We had a lunch for the end of the building site, inviting all the locals who had been kind to me. Some of the farmers who bred Camarguaise bulls and Spanish *toro bravos* were simply amazed at what I had done with the old ruin. They all said it was the prettiest old *mas* in the region. Jean François, the builder, was very chuffed, and felt very proud; but turning to me, said he would never again take on such a huge project. I agreed with him!

The young arrived again for their holidays with friends; Caroline first to move in a friend to the west wing, in an adorable room under the eaves, called a *radassier* in Provençal. They were rooms used by the boss of the household, where he could play around with the prettiest maid and have an accompanied siesta undisturbed! Horrified it smelt of stinking drains, I quickly realized the septic tank was done badly, and the smells were coming backwards up the drainpipes. We had to re-dig, literally in front of the main entrance, another smaller tank with siphons and chemicals to let the gasses escape through a separate pipe. We had it done just in time, thank goodness.

Miles was now 21, and as his birthday was in April, when the weather was very unreliable, we planned his party for 27th – 29th June. A monumental job of hiring tents, portable loos, a band, and bulls to be run in and out of a plastic pool.

He had already booked a bus to travel from Edinburgh, where all his school mates from Glenalmond lived, or were now in universities. Thirty-five 21-year-olds, and I had to find the girls! So difficult, as French parents keep a tight rein on their young, and I needed 17/18-year-olds. The only way to get them to come was by asking the parents as well. The bus arrived on the 27th evening, and the boys and three young girls rushed to reserve their tents. I had them all lined up down the drive, with the opening flaps towards the field. Naturally they all tried to open the back part of the tent, shouting, 'No, no, they are opened on the other side.'

A small panic, but finally under control. Miles nervously said, 'Vicky, leave them be, please don't get annoyed, they are so happy to be here.'

My three women were in charge and had a barbecue well underway. I had already arranged a house in the village of Orgon for my guardians, so they could sleep, knowing how these 21-year-olds would stay up all night. The dining area was just under their windows, the band and disco alongside. After their arrival, one and all in the pool, fed them, and that night only the hardliners stayed up late. The actual party was the 28th; they slept in their little tents, borrowed from the boy scouts, and only appeared at noon. Miles took them all off to Eygalieres for pastis and sandwiches, some walked up the mountain, while others lazed at the pool.

Come evening, the boys were all looking very smart in their kilts, and evening dress, some in dinner jackets. Neil Campbell was in a panic, as I had put him on the gate to serenade the arrivals with his bagpipe, and someone had played a joke and hid his kilt. A very cross young man. They found it finally, he and Sandy, almost a professional bagpiper, dressed to kill, went and stood at the entrance to the garden, and saw in the cars. The French were very impressed. The dinner was excellent, but halfway through, down came the rain, what bad luck having changed the date from April.

The Ambassadrice, Anne Cox Chambers, was with a priest, so naturally I had to put him on my right. I had previously warned her, that they were all very young and being from Scotland, drank heavily, that it was not going to be her scene at all. She insisted she would love it and wanted to come. Together with Andrew and Gilly and two or four of the parents, we made up a table and kept them amused.

Thank goodness they left before the serious drinking began.

The more it rained, the more they drank, I was worried stiff about the tents, they were going to be waterlogged, as the ground near the field sloped away from the upper drive. Come 2.00 am, it suddenly stopped and out came the stars, as it was warm, the end of June, everything dried up within no time. I went to bed shattered, and as my room was the other end of the house and upstairs, I did not hear a thing. I knew, though, they had gone on until 6.00 am.

The next day I had arranged *une ferrade*, contracted out from my neighbour, who bred Camarguaise bulls (a smaller breed to the Spanish fighting bulls), to bring a portable swimming pool and six bulls to my second field in front, and put up a portable ring, so by the time the young awoke, everything was installed. Headaches galore, and not to mention *capotes anglaises* chucked into the bushes, with three French girls forgotten by their parents!

Coffee in mugs and aspirins all round, they finally managed to walk to my second field, where I had laid on another barbecue, with pastis to wake them up, while Sandy had climbed our mountain, playing his bagpipes in a mournful wail.

They could not believe their eyes when they saw the ring and the first bull let out of his lorry.

'Heh! Vicky, what is this for?'

'You go in the ring and fight the bull with its horns, until you turn him onto his back, if you do it well you earn a prize, a large glass of pastis.'

It was hysterical, half the boys were huge, tough rugby players, and flipped the bull over immediately, so much so, that the farmer said to my guardian, Sylvain, and Sonia, the cook, 'I never knew the Scots were so strong, I will have to take my lorry home and bring back much bigger bulls.'

Which he did, plus this plastic pool full of soap, the whole thing was hilarious, added to by the arrival of French parents who had mislaid their daughters. Of course, they stayed and joined the fun. Then other neighbours complained about the fire of the barbecue, the typical person who finds fault with everything. My staff answered the phone, and replied, 'To begin with, Madame has here in the bush an extinguisher, second an officer from the *sapeurs pompiers* (fire brigade) is on duty until the party has stopped, so snoots to you.'

Thinking they would all be exhausted, as they had to get into their bus at 6.00 am, I had told Sylvain and his wife to move back into their house, that tonight they should be able to sleep. Not a hope, they went on partying until the bus left at 6.00 am.

Miles told me afterwards, on arrival in London, they were stuck in traffic jams, Sandy got bored, stripped naked and went streaking down Oxford Street.

I heard later the comments on Miles's birthday: the best 21st they had ever been to. At least one felt the work arranging it was worth it. Certainly very memorable.

As Miles's party had demonstrated the *mas* was an ideal house for entertaining and I enjoyed sharing it for house parties large and small. The following year I held another fete for the tennis tournament, planning the seating for the adults in the garage, and the disco next door in the old barn. Just as they all arrived, down came the rain in sheets, the young rushed for the tables under cover, and left their parents and friends outside. I grabbed an umbrella, and one of the cheeky Parisians remarked, 'Hrrrrgh, you have an enormous house, why don't you let us into the dining room or the large entrances?'

'Because you are all spoilt Parisians, and you will muck up my new house, which is not yet properly finished.'

To give themselves more space, Miles and Caroline relented, opening the billiard room to turn it into the disco! Slightly dryer than the garage, where the adults were boozing the night away. The young threw themselves into the pool, then danced until the morning. Someone in the early hours grabbed my cousin, Andrew Prendergast, and threw him in as well, fully dressed. He took it very well, but not to be forgotten. The next day was horrific, mud and sand all over the new floor. I had to employ two extra fellows to clean the place up, and that took them two days.

The rest of that summer there were parties and picnics, kayaking and camping out in the mountains. We spent a lot of time with Dee and Cary, they were adorable and great fun, and loved my young. Mark Cresswell came on holiday; my godson, Marcia's second son, spent his time in the pool playing with Minouche on an old windsurf.

Andrew and Gilly and their two sons were staying with me, and three days later, thank goodness sunny with no mistral, I had planned a surprise. Louise Balfour my god-daughter, and Amy, her little girl, and her sister, Catherine, were all staying. As they sleepily came down to breakfast, I told them all to wake up and eat up, that something very special was arriving in about half an hour.

The kids were all peeing with excitement, trying to guess what mad Auntie Vicky had up her sleeve. A deep-sounding roar came over the mountains from behind the *mas*, just over the roof, and my friends from Avignon, two young pilots, brought their helicopter over the pool, swinging it in circles over the garden, gently landing on the grass field in front. The whole house rushed out, mouths gaping, 'Look, look what has she done now.'

Screaming with excitement, they rushed to the field, following them and the dogs barking in horror. I shouted, 'Don't go near until the props have stopped turning.' We brought the pilots into the house, and offered them coffee.

'Vicky, we've made it on time, we'll have a drink!' Laughing and giggling they persuaded Andrew to get them a pastis and whisky.

'Hey, you can't drink and fly these kids!'

'Rubbish,' they replied. 'We'll fly even better!'

Andrew, who was Daddy to the little boys, didn't seem to care two hoots and poured them a couple of large slugs. Then the children were taken three at a time for half an hour's flight over the *mas*, and the valleys around us. Andrew wanted to throw Louise out, he was always up to what he thought were funny tricks! After all the children, they offered me a ride, and I accepted, as I was fascinated to see the new quarry of Omya (a German consortium that had a factory near Orgon, our nearest village) digging out our mountain in front, a horrible white chalk, which is produced from a very refined limestone. It was a local scandal, and myself and all one's neighbours were up in arms over it. We later formed an association to fight it, and get it stopped. From the helicopter, I had a marvellous view right into the craters, horrified to see the damage they were doing to the Alpilles, her pine forest and vegetation.

For the last expedition of the summer I took all the young to the Gorges du Verdon, plus the Lane-Spollens, Hugh and Patrick. It took us hours to get there, as these mountains were above Nice, and nearly on the Italian border. Simply stunning and very exciting. We spent the nights in a hostel in the village of Verdon, as couldn't be bothered with all the camping gear. The first day we went white-water rafting, all in a huge rubber zodiac, but like a twit I kept falling into the river. The guide was very quick and dived in twice to drag me out.

The next day was worse as we had planned to go 'hydro-speeding'. We hadn't got a clue what that entailed; we soon found out, wetsuits on, flippers in your hand and crash helmets on your head, we were all issued with plastic boards with two handles. Into the river, flat on your boards face down having put on your flippers. It was great fun, except I kept turning upside down, poor Miles was worried for me, as I banged into rocks, got caught up in whirlpools and disappeared out of sight. I did eventually arrive at our rendezvous, but said to myself, 'Vics, you're too old for this, *basta*.'

I had an ache in the back of my neck, as I was always twisting to gaze at the beautiful scenery above us; right at the bottom of this gorge, the sky was miles and miles above us. On the third day we were taken even further up the gorge, and I watched as they were all rigged out in the same gear. Order of the day, 'canyoning' – was I glad to have let this one pass, as they went down steep rocks into the river; jumping across it, hanging on to ropes, swinging on hooks attached to it, then sliding across, and jumping into hidden pools. I used to love this kind of outward-bound adventure, but sadly all things pass and there is a time for everything, and a time to stop.

A bleak shadow was cast the following year when the houseguests arrived. Miles and Caroline came for their holidays in August as usual, as well as a very old friend from Madrid, Kit Pinto Coelho, widow of the Portuguese Ambassador, and dear friends France and Ricardo Tutino, from Paris and then, darling Hugh Balfour and Sheila, my cousin, with their daughter and granddaughter, Louise and Amy.

After an active life Hugh by now, though, was a very sick fellow, having been diagnosed with non-Hodgkin's disease, same as Jackie Onassis. Sheila was very naïve about his illness, and I think just did not accept it. The moment he arrived at the *mas*, I could tell immediately that he was dying. Thin in the face, bags under his eyes, he just looked haggered. Appalling for a strong, very positive man, just like Joaquin was. What a filthy disease. I did my best to give them a lovely holiday, and showed them the Provence from every angle. Kayaking, he insisted on being left behind with his granddaughter, Amy, very sensible.

My mother was another occasional visitor, coming in June 1998 for her 88th birthday, as always, accompanied by her little queer, Tony Pandolfino, the Maltese man who looked after her with much love and attention. This was the last year she could travel, as she kept on falling and breaking her hips; subsequently an agonizing decision, but I had to put her into a home, where she was looked after round the clock, in the lovely old town of Medina, the ancient capital of Malta. If she had stayed in her apartment, with the maids ripping her off, she would have needed a hoist to get her in and out of bed.

She had a nice time at the *mas*, and loved being there, but the stairs were hell for her. An old friend from London came to join her, Claire

Delahunty, and a retired naval officer who was a hoot, Captain Sir Edward Archdale, and her stepson, Colin Smythe, son of Winco, who had died in Malta some years earlier.

Sitting on the pavement in St Remy, watching the *Transhumance*, an annual event in memory of the shepherds and their flocks, when they left the lowlands and the valleys, Edward, bolshie as usual, stuck out his cane and his gammy leg and tried to stop passers-by from blocking his view. He thought the café-restaurant where we were was now his! The shepherds and their sheep, baby lambs galore, paraded around the town, the men were dressed in their old-fashioned Provençal costume, followed by their faithful sheepdogs, dodging in and out of their flocks. Traffic, of course, had been banned from the centre of town.

Events such as these went on in St Remy all summer, herds of Camarguaises horses were galloped totally free, and running of the bulls up and down the side streets, and in and out of the cafés. Now, sadly, like everywhere else, ruined by mass tourism, it has become too popular. One has to park one's car miles outside the town, and forget about getting one seat, let alone five on the pavement.

I did my best to keep my guests happy, and at the same time to show them as much as I could of this fabulous part of France. The Provence is unique, not only the heat, the cicadas, the pine forests, but the people themselves; real southerners, always laughing and talking, drinking and smoking, but surprisingly, the locals and peasants have a sound knowledge of political history, and affairs of the state. Quietly listening to them over a coffee, arguing away, they were far more knowledgeable than the average Spaniard from the same background.

Autumn in the Provence is always lovely, the colours of the trees, and the soft light was lovely, all the *fetes des villages* were finished, and everything became quiet. Time to visit Avignon, and go to the cinema with Dee and Cary. We had the most charming cinema inside the old ramparts, right underneath the spotlights of the Palais des Papes, with a good bistro and bar within the walls. Incredible films, with four programmes all in original languages. All of us foreigners living in the area, met there, whenever a special film was on. We were spoilt, the coast was a two hours to the south, and Paris a TGV every couple of hours from Avignon. Also, we entertained each other, whenever we felt like it. I used to go up to Paris quite a lot, it was naturally my old village, not only lovely old friends, who lived there, but the memory of all that had happened in my youth, bistros and *quartiers* that held nostalgic memories.

# *30. Honduras, Roatan, and India*

Come September 1998, Miles had to make up his mind what he was going to do, he was just fiddling around at university having fun, but not passing too many exams. I had a serious chat with him.

'If you are not going to work and study, then I will send you round the world, and you can work your way from one country to the next, in the hope that you might grow up.'

He was quite shocked, but I reassured him, I would pay his ticket to Los Angeles, he then had to get hold of my contacts there, and pay his way from there on. I would pay his return to Europe only in an emergency. That or go back to university. And work non-stop to pass his exams.

Caroline was the total opposite. She passed her equine and management exams in two years, then went on and obtained a BA in agriculture in one year. Record time. She was and is very clever. Why today are the girls so much more studious than the boys?

Miles accepted my proposition, so I sent him off to get his ticket, visa and vaccinations, and booked him on a flight at the beginning of October with a filofax stuffed full of all my contacts' addresses and phone numbers. I sweated, thinking of this young lad, naïve, having lost his mother, and father with multiple sclerosis, off on his own in the big wide world. I had to be strong, as I knew he just wouldn't grow up if he was not pushed into being responsible and using his brains to get jobs in each country, so he could move on round the world.

I had given him all sorts of addresses in LA; Hollywood directors, actors and producers; what does he do, goes straight to the Malibu Beach where the hippies hang out, and never contacted anyone with clout. He got a part-time job, then moved on to Mexico, ringing me reverse call in a panic as he had lost his filofax! Oh! La! La! And wanted again the addresses I had given him of my friends who live there. Typical; so frustrating.

Before I could breathe, he had arrived in Guatemala at the old city of Antigua, which I knew well, and got himself a job running a business in the mountains of Atitlan with a *soit disant* friend, who naturally later on, took him for a ride. He screwed him up, stole his money and left him penniless. Another long-distance phone call to please bail him out.

I needed little excuse to escape the French winter, so this time I thought I would go and see him myself. I first enjoyed a diving holiday in the Caymans and then I took a trip to Belize where I met up with my impossible friend, Jacqueline, who joined me in visiting Guatemala.

Arriving in Antigua, we met Miles and he took us to his house in the old city, simply gorgeous with enormous pillars with a flat roof around the courtyard and that evening we joined his friends, who were thrilled to see us. He was managing a bar and restaurant, and seemingly doing very well; we spent the evening with them, reminiscing all the adventures he had experienced on his way through Mexico, and what he was doing in Guatemala. I played it very cool, not asking too many questions, waiting for him to come out of himself, which he did, and seemed very happy, planning on staying there four months and then moving on to Honduras. I was delighted for him, as I had said time and time again to both him and Caroline, 'It is your life, you must live it as you feel, I am not telling you what to do and where to go.'

I travelled a lot from Provence, never needing a stronger excuse than the French winter. It was unsettling to leave the *mas* behind in the hands of others, and I was constantly checking emails on the move to ensure all was well. In 1999, whilst in Honduras, to my horror I received an e-mail from my step-brother, Colin, saying that Mummy had died suddenly. I cannot explain the shock I had, there in the jungle in the mountains of Honduras, with no one around me and feeling awful. Her doctor had never told me that she had a heart problem, though she was 88. What should I do? Caroline was halfway across the Atlantic, and Miles with his latest girlfriend on his way from a small island south of Roatan.

I phoned Colin, and heard the sad news first hand. He said, 'Vicky, there is nothing you can do, she's died, I will take care of the papers and we'll go to Malta for the funeral, when you are back.'

I knew he was right, but felt dreadful.

She had always made me feel guilty, and I had spent years building divine houses for her, trying to make her life more agreeable, but still she was jealous of my life. She had tried to dominate me, but failed miserably. No excuse, I had done my best, and it didn't work, feeling awful being in Honduras, when it happened.

As soon as I was back in Europe, I contacted Colin and made a quick date to go to Malta. Not only for the funeral, but sorting out her papers, and selling her apartment etc. We held a lovely service in the Cathedral St John's in Valetta. Previously I had gone with the naval clergyman to pay my last respects at St Luke's hospital at the morgue; it was horrific as they had done nothing to make her up. I felt sick and went to throw up in the garden. At the service, I made a speech, saying how unusual it was for a daughter to talk at her mother's funeral, but as those present did not know her in her heyday, and only knew her as a very old lady, they could not appreciate her humour and wit when she was younger. I carried it off, as I felt very strongly, as half the old friends on the island had gone already.

She had permission from the War Graves Commission to be buried on top of my father in the same grave, in the naval cemetery. In fact, it was the three services, as all the young men from the air force, who were bombed and shot over Malta during the last war, were also buried there. A lovely place with lots of pine trees and in a very quiet corner of the island.

We retired, after the service at the cemetery, to Marsascala, to a place I had found and booked out for drinks and a buffet lunch. We were not many, and the weather was foul, but we drank Mummy's health with some good naval gin! God bless her.

A few years later, to be kind, I invited Tony Pandolfino, the Maltese fellow who had looked after Mummy for so long, to spend Christmas with us at the *mas*. To our surprise he brought a lovely little boy with him who was quite adorable. Maltese but looked half Chinese. Miles and Caroline and I had our doubts about Tony long before this, and only two months later did the truth come out. One evening, I received a phone call, with a very stressed voice, saying would I not try to contact Tony ever again. I replied, 'Who are you, and why do you say that?'

Turned out to be his brother, and Tony had been taken in by the police for being a paedophile. I racked my brains, and asked what had happened to the little boy. He had been sent to a children's home and was being taken care of. He the brother refused to give me his contact details. I knew Tony had been very odd, always finding excuses to go to Cavaillon to buy videos. We found out they were all pornographic ones. Sad, as basically he was a very pleasant fellow and had taken care of Mummy for years. I have no idea where he is now, or what he is doing.

*

As it was so close and convenient, I would frequently visit the UK and Ireland, particularly to visit the young. In 1999 I was driving around the UK visiting old friends and was due at Caroline's near Wellingborough. I arrived in the pitch dark, as the traffic was horrendous, to find her house was full, all young friends sharing it, so she took me to an adorable hotel with a thatched roof just across the road. Shattered, I crept into bed and slept for 14 hours before rising the next day and calling Sheila. My God what a shock, she announced the very sad news that Hugh had died the previous day. Poor bugger I could see it was coming the last time he came to France; Sheila did not want to know, and hid her head under the sand as an ostrich. So I had to cut short my stay with Caroline, and drive back west to their home in Dorset. It was just something I had to do, I loved and admired him, he was the most super person, and they had fallen in love at our first weekend in Gozo, an island just off Malta. I had a very close relationship with them and all their children.

I stayed two days and visited the morgue, and paid my respects. I learnt the funeral was arranged not for another week, not like in

Spain or the South of France when under law it has to be within 24 hours. I went back to France for a week, and returned for the funeral. Sheila's house was packed with family and masses of old friends from the navy. A very moving and lovely ceremony, everyone had adored him. Sad for me to see his children crying their eyes out, and Sheila looking shattered.

One of my most memorable trips was to India. The first plan was that cousin Sheila and I would join Serena Fass, a supposed Indian expert, on an organized tour of northern Rajasthan.

I flew via Cairo to Jeddah, where I had to change flights in transit, shawl over my head, looking like a real arsehole in front of hundreds of poor Indians waiting to get their entry visas, into this God-forgotten country; only controlled by their mighty oil reserves. It was 1.00 am, and I was kept waiting for hours, they'd never had a lone woman in transit before in their lives, let alone to India.

Finally made Bombay at 6.00 am, and the dawn was just round the corner. Drove past miles of squatters and tented slums, a real culture shock on your first visit. Our tour of northern Rajasthan turned out to be a bus full of 19 women. Sheila and I could not believe our eyes. One male driver and a boy, and one male guide, and 19 idiotic women, and what was worse they spent all their time shopping! Great.

After this actual two-week tour, which had its hilarious moments, I finally took off south, not only to find warmth and the sun, but to be alone and travel rough with the local Indians, the only way to get to know a country properly. Also, I had made a promise to myself to find the ashram of Ama Amritanandamayi in the southern state of Kerala.

First stop Goa, to lie on the beach, and soak up the sun, miles and miles of white sandy beach, but a dirty brown ocean. Heaven to feel the warmth again, after the freezing north.

Goa was run down and dirty, decaying houses and rusty buses, and the whole place is very odd, as it is spread over a huge area. You can feel the Portuguese did not care, let it go down hill, and then left. India is trying again to attract the tourists and make it chichi, but if it was not for the weather, and the beaches, it is totally a disappointment.

I then packed up, left the suitcase in the hotel, and tried to catch the train south to Cochin. Found out there was only 2nd class, no air con and the bunks were boards or planks so narrow, most of the bigger backpackers could not fit on them! So cheated on myself and found a flight. Saved myself 19 hours of horror.

Cochin, to my amazement had a vast new airport, full of marble and glass, but once in the taxi rickshaw, I came down with a thump, as we weaved our way between thousands of people, cows, goats and kids towards the centre of the city. I was heading first for a particular hotel, that sells tickets and permits to get across to the Lachwasdeeps Islands. I had already heard they are out of this world to dive in; hundreds of atolls and vast sand dunes, but you have to obtain a permit to get there. My rickshaw driver found it, and quickly I obtained all the information for another year. Then I had a quick, excellent lunch, and went to the bus station to catch the local to Allepey, 120 kilometres further down the coast.

Fairly normal bus, with no glass in the windows, and thank heavens, not too many people, but it was a good three hours, and just arriving at Allepey, we became entangled in a huge mass rally of very red-looking communists marching in the opposite direction. I kept my head down, and very quiet, as the locals were all watching to see my reaction. Just grin at an Indian, and they grin back, but the chaps outside on the darkening road, were too serious for words. I was very happy when we arrived at our destination, and another little taxi rickshaw found the only hotel in town. Or so it seemed at the time!

Fleapit, with a bar only for men, damn it, did I need a drink and a strong one? The good news was they knew the ashram I was heading for and could book me a seat on the inland waterway ferry for the next day. A dirty looking curry, and masses of mozzies, we were very close now to the waterways, and deep inside the state of Kerala, one of the most populated states of India.

The ferry turned out to be a converted steamer, and packed with backpackers and a few Indians, but sadly for me, not many. It was really the backpackers' dream of getting down the canals to Trivandrum and Kollam, and the beatnik hang-out now in fashion, Verkala. The trip was divine, and we chugged out of steaming Allepey past row upon row of houseboats, with rush-matting tops and pointed bows. Great fun to rent, if you have the necessary, and are a group. Otherwise my ferry was an idyllic way of moving through masses of water lilies and thousands of hyacinths, so many they are blocking the inland waterways seriously.

The canals widened into lakes and then became narrow again, the flora and fauna on either bank was breathtaking, not to mention the birds. Ducks and waterfowl, geese, storks, and pelicans, all there.

Halfway, we stopped for a real Indian meal, curry served on a banana leaf, which, of course, you eat with your left hand, and then role up the leaf neatly, to show you're finished. My boat companions, who were all travelling India, were very clued up, so I watched with fascination, what they were doing, and followed suit.

I started talking to an Indian, who was part of the boat organization, semi-guide, to see we didn't get into trouble, and he asked me how I knew about the ashram? He said he knew it, and did not like it, rambling into a long explanation about how the Indians themselves were fed up with all these gurus, and semi-gods, and did not believe as much as the foreigners in their Hindu spirituality. He also told me, as a nature lover, he hated seeing their drains run into his canals!

Round a few more heavily laden bends of palm trees, past a fishing village with the most amazing nets, huge big arches hung up on sticks, soaring red-coated eagles, we entered a narrow channel, and this fellow laughed and said, 'There you are, the Ashram is ahead of you.'

To my utter amazement, I saw a huge red skyscraper, or rather a modern tenement building, rising above the palm trees. I turned to my new friend, and said, 'Wow! Do you really mean to say, that's it? How can anyone build something so ugly in these beautiful surroundings?'

We came to a crunch at the landing of the ashram, a few backpackers got on, and I got off, waving goodbye to all the clean-looking westerners, and feeling a bit sick with apprehension, as I had never been inside an ashram in my life. A very tall, thin white Finn, dressed all in white, looking like a ghost, met me by chance and helped carry my two bags. We wandered through, what looked like a building site, with scurrying little men, and sacks of cement and gunch everywhere, round the hideous building, to the centre of what turned out to be an island, and came upon a huge monolithic Hindu temple, with the most outlandish heads, garish in colour, of all their gods, staring at one from the roof.

Off with one's shoes and up the steps to fill in forms and papers. The Finn gave me a key and said, 'Go and collect your mattress, and find your room, then come back for the evening service in the temple, after which is dinner and *seva.*'

I looked totally perplexed, and a very nice American, also all in white, saw I was lost, and said, 'Hi! I'm Harry, what's your name? Let me help you.'

Very kind, he took me to where the mattress store was, and then to find the room. Up a lift in the hideous apartment block, floor 16! I thought to myself, being a builder by trade, *this damn thing will fall over, at the first hurricane!* The room was concrete, two-by-three metres square, if that. Two other women, Germans, were already installed on the floor. No cupboards, no hangers, one chair for three, and one tap and a hole in the floor, as are all Hindu loos.

I quickly changed out of my pants, and found something that looked a bit more holy, and followed Harry outside. He filled me in on all the goings on, and when I asked him about the yoga lessons, and learning to meditate etc, he looked blank. He told me, as Ama, the guru, was not there (this I did already know), that all her disciples or devotees, as they called them, had left either with her to the north of India on tour, or had gone back to their homes on holiday. I was shocked at hearing this, as I had come specially to learn as much as I could about Hinduism, yoga and meditation, and to learn more of what an ashram is all about.

He said there is nothing to do but *seva*, which turned out to be any job you can do to help the community, peeling potatoes, cooking rice, cleaning the floors, you name it. Feeling very low, I went to the evening service, and found I could not bend my knees the way they do, the lotus position; too old and stiff. The service, though, was moving and it was interesting just to watch the people. One youngish man with beautiful hair, sat in an upright position, and never bent his back for an hour and a half, how I was jealous! Another red-haired woman, obviously a foreigner, swayed and clapped to the music, drums and pipes, and a castanet-type of instrument. It went on for ages, very monotonous, especially with a sore bum, on a concrete floor.

Food was at the back of the temple, in another huge open building with a tin roof; you found stainless steel plates, washed them in dirty water, and went to get what you were offered. Boiled rice and sleeky, sticky green-looking vegetables; I was so hungry, I had to eat what there was, on an even dirtier mat on a filthy floor. A charming English woman came and talked to me, the others all around were Indian, except for two youngsters off the ferry. She explained that I must bring my own drinking water, and buy biscuits, and fruit etc from the shop for the westerners, and not to wash the plates where the Indians did. I felt as if I was back at boarding school; at the same time, it was mind-boggling.

Harry turned up with his wife, and both sat in the lotus position and he told us how he had left everything in America to come and follow Ama, that they were devoted to her and her work. He ran all the building sites, and problems that related between engineers and the locals.

He told us that normally, when Ama was in residence, there would be 400 to 500 westerners at the ashram, and literally thousands of Indians, who all slept in a different building, and the young we saw having dinner, were students in a computer school set up by Ama. He also told us how her head-follower was a doctor, who had also abandoned his life in Delhi, and now lived like a monk, had given all his money to her causes: donations to widows, building hundreds of houses for the poor, leper colonies and three ayurvedic hospitals already.

Ama was invited as chief guest to the United Nations peace organization in 1998 and many other world societies; one must read her books, and her biography.

Harry told me to go further south, where the yogi from the ashram was staying with a healer at Verkala, in an ayurvedic centre, not to waste any more time here. I groaned at the thought of more travelling, but having sussed out the ashram, thought I would be very happy for any excuse to move on!

So next day, I was up at 5.00 am to see the sunrise, and return the mattress, after a night of tossing and turning and sweating in the humidity, and watching, on the roof top, a lot of very young people, meditating and praying. Very moving. No ferry, so I had to get another rickshaw taxi to the station, where Harry had told me there would be a train at 8.30 am to Verkala. Arrived and a lovely big black station master looked me up and down, grinning again, no train. 'What do you mean no train?'

'Train broken down up the line, coming tomorrow. Perhaps!'

Off again in a rickshaw to find the bus station. I found it with literally thousands of other people, one milling mass of humanity. No one understood a word of what I wanted, until I found an office-like place, and some surprisingly well-dressed officials in perfect British uniform; it's the contrast that hits you. In broken English, they explained there was no bus for Verkala, but some other town with an unpronounceable name was near enough.

I got into the appointed bus; it was unbelievable, dead dogs on the ground, and a dead donkey, plastic bags all over the street, but thank goodness I found a window seat with no glass in it, plenty of air was a must. The bus next door was full of young girls, who all stared at me in fascination and started giggling. I must have looked very odd? They never stopped laughing until they took off, with a cloud of black soot, and clanking bangs and grunts.

We followed suit, and the bus was already full, I had no idea where I was going, and could only trust the officers' pidgin English, that at least it was in the right direction.

I had kept my haversack on the seat beside me, but soon had to have it on my knees, my bag was over my head in a locker space. Thank goodness for the window seat, as I had a series of companions in the other one; no legs, a leper, purely black, one arm, you name it. I did not look too closely. When we reached the next town, there were at least 300 humans on the bus, and I could see there was no way I could get up, collect my bag and get out. People came in through the windows, the women stared and laughed. It was actually hilarious.

I asked the conductor very slowly the name of where we were going, and again, unpronounceable. He spat through his teeth, and said, 'Go sleep, you end stop!' I noticed all the Indians fell asleep immediately they sat down. Impossible for me to copy them, and far too fascinated watching their world go by.

Finally people began to get off, and one could breathe again. We stopped at the unknown town, and the last three of us left said goodbye to the old rattle-trap. Caught another little taxi and shot off to Verkala, to find the medicine man was an emaciated Indian with a sarong, and a long beard, grinning and bowing, delighted the ashram had sent me. To my surprise, the yogi was another emaciated fellow with white hair, who was an American! I don't think either of them had seen a decent meal for years. Found out very quickly in the ashram, everyone down in Kerala were vegetarians, with a few eating some fish.

I found a room in a private house, and thank goodness it had a fan, as now it was 42 degrees in the shade and 100 percent humidity. Very clean and a good shower, owned by Germans, of course. Fabulous cliffs very near the house, and tiny shops and restaurants all along its edge; soon I became orientated with Verkala, and it was full of charm and unsuspecting surprises, plus a lovely beach with big breakers. What a relief after the tenement building in the palm trees.

Spent hours with our friends, discussing philosophy and religion, studying meditation and learning the basic necessity of it, and the calming effect it has on one's being. They would not teach me yoga at the same time, or they were too busy. Their house was like a clinic, and there was a young Australian man, poor thing, who was full of skin cancer, and another American woman with her family, who had breast cancer and refused to have it removed, so was going through the ayurvedic treatments, and natural oils etc. Very, very brave people.

I stayed as long as I could, as time was running out, but I really profited from the experience; reading their books, swimming, and meditating; very good for hyper-active old me. I came away with a deep feeling of humility, much calmer in myself, less aggressive, and with a greater understanding of the human psyche.

One last excitement, there was a holiday especially dedicated to elephants in a village nearby, and as I adore these creatures, I decided to go, whatever the cost. The Australian came too, so we found a taxi friend and bartered our price, and off we went. Another experience, a town packed with more humanity; we had to walk for ages, thank goodness the taxi fellow was charming and took us in tow. There must have been 10,000 people; one cannot believe the crowds until you see them, and feel them and hear them!

There was nowhere to get a drink, so we sat on the pavement until midnight, and then the ellies arrived, led by *matouts* carrying burning candles. Huge big bull elephants, females and their calves, and three or four six-month youngsters. There were police everywhere shouting and, I imagine, swearing, trying to keep the crowds away. It became so dangerous they had to line the elephants along the pavement, facing into the road, and manacled their front feet to the back. This I did not like, but as taxi-man explained, there had been too many accidents not to do so. Most of them looked unhappy and sick, with big sores in their ears. How I would love to open an orphanage for them, in some lovely green grassy mountain hideaway. Their noble characters and their knowledge is far beyond our understanding. Imagine when the Maharajah of Bikener died, his 600 elephants were lined up at the station to say goodbye to their master, each one lifted its trunk and roared, and tears ran down their eyes.

# *31. Burglaries in France*

Although always having been a committed winter traveller, I started travelling more in the summer for the simple reason that I was renting the *mas* out to guests. In June and July of 2000 I travelled to South Africa, Zambia and Zimbabwe; alone because Mugabe had recently arrived on the scene and scared off my potential travelling companions. Firstly I had a leisurely two weeks in South Africa, where I boarded the famous 'Blue Train'. It was an experience, the service and the food exceptional, but not terribly amusing, except for the most amazing collection of black queers, who fawned around one like butterflies dressed in black and yellow uniforms. From there I went on safari and canoed down the Zambezi River, picking out a path between sleeping hippos.

The reason I was renting the *mas* was because the costs of rebuilding it had been horrendously high, and as much as I hated to do it, and maddening that it was always the best months when people wanted it, letting the property was the only way to recoup the expense.

My first clients were in June 1997; very rich Americans, who had booked the house and invited all sorts of grandees, including, Beatrice the Queen of Holland. My staff laughed as she came downstairs in the mornings, with her hair perfect, carrying her two dogs under her arms. She walked straight beyond the lavender into the forest, as her security guards were caught out, and had to rush partly undressed after her.

I had a horrendous experience with another American. One day my mobile phone, now we had them, rang. It was from my house with the staff in a panic.

'Madame, what do we do, the tenant, this very odd American is allergic to Minouche and insists we clean the curtains and the beds with a professional Hoover. And send her to a cat's home.'

'Holy Moses. Minouche belongs to the house, can you not keep her in the guardian's wing?'

'Well, we will try, but as you know she wants to go out hunting at night.'

I telephoned the agent, who was in a panic and did not know what to do, and in the end the client took another house. Thank goodness I had insisted that they paid up front, a big row as he wanted his money back. I had replied via the agent, that the client had not said he had an allergy to cats. He should have stipulated this in the beginning.

When not dealing with irritating tenants, another bore was that robberies in the area were becoming more and more frequent. The first happened during the day; they had broken through the French windows of the drawing room, leaving horrible big scratch marks on the lovely stone floor, and tyre marks over the back rough grass, right up to the house. The police from Orgon came and checked for fingerprints; they had been looking for money and valuables, finding nothing, they grabbed four or five statuettes in bronze on their way out, my trophies that I had won at horse shows, sickening.

The insurance paid up as I had proof of the break-in, by the damage to the floor and the broken French windows. The alarm must have gone off, as all the doors were open into the boiler room, where the alarm was always set.

The police were charming and knew me well; they made their report, and advised me to photograph the interior, if ever the buggers came back, which I did. They also told me the gangs from Marseille were getting worse and were now full of gypsies from eastern Europe, who made their way up into the Provence. They worked their way from one village to the next, stealing cars and ransacking any house they found empty. Always when the guardians had their day off. These chaps must have been watching the house, as we had gone out only for a short time.

Six months later, I was on my own and drove home from the back lane via the forest and the back entrance. As I approached the house, I saw the big double doors of the garage were open. I drove into it, and saw the door to the boiler room was open and the connecting one to the interior. With my heart thumping, I screamed like mad, to frighten anyone inside, and went out via the children's wing, where I found their kitchen door open and broken. Phoning the police as I ran. They came in five minutes, flat out in one of their fast cars. As they drove in the entrance, two officers jumped out and the car did a circle on the lawn and went out again. I did not know why. The other two told me not to move from the garden, they were going to search the house. They saw I was very frightened, as I thought the buggers were still upstairs.

In no time at all, their car returned with the head sergeant, asking me if a little black box full of paperclips was mine?

'Yes, it's a souvenir I keep on my desk for saving paperclips, nothing of any value.'

'Madame, that is enough proof,' and he turned his car again and went back the way he had come. I was totally confused. The police in the house came out, talking on their walkie-talkies, told me to relax and that I had caught them in the act and they must have run away through the garden, when I came into the garage.

Together we found the alarm still screeching at the bottom of the pool, vibrating like mad it had scratched the paint away, leaving horrible marks on the bottom. The sergeant came back, and told me he had seen a suspicious car parked in the woods just before the house, when he returned to it, two fellows were getting into the car. He had held them up with his pistol, handcuffed them, then searched the boot, found my little box. Once he had the proof, that it was them who had broken in, he radioed their station and brought in another vehicle to take them to the jail.

They all accepted a pastis and we sat round the kitchen table, I was still shaking. Once relaxed, we went through the house taking note of what else they had taken. The second alarm had been ripped off the wall and smashed to pieces. The police came to the conclusion that I had arrived just at the time they were doing this in the children's wing, and had scarpered out of the kitchen door, breaking it as they went.

I was asked by the police to go the station and make a statement, and help with their interrogation of the two fellows. Not very pleasant, as we had caught them just in time, nothing else valuable had disappeared, but the police wanted to know exactly where they had come from, and what they were doing in France. All their papers were false, no ID cards nor passports; they said they were living just outside of Avignon, which turned out to be a slum area, where all the gypsies hung out from Romania and Bulgaria. I wanted to know how they knew my house was there, as you cannot see it from the road. Were they tipped off? How did they know the way through the forest, there was no path? They told us ridiculous stories, none of which was true.

I had problems with the staff, as well. I had to sack Sylvain and Florence, after some jewellery had disappeared. I had gone to Paris on the TGV, and on arriving at Mouchy, Philippe, the Duc de Mouchy, a very old friend, said, 'Vicky, as we are late, your luggage is in your room, so leave it, and come and have dinner as you are.'

When finally I unpacked, I realized my two beautiful rings were missing from their pouch, one sapphire and one ruby, both my engagement rings. I felt quite sick, thinking it could be his staff, on the other hand, it could have been on the train. On the train though, you don't open luggage, and then a pouch, take out two rings and close it again. A thief would have taken the whole pouch and shoved it into his pocket. I could not ask Philippe or Joan, his wife, it would have been too ghastly, to accuse his staff, if they had been taken from the train.

So I went for a long walk in the morning through the park, thinking what on earth should I do? Suddenly it came on me, that it was Florence, damn her, who had packed my bags at the house before I caught the train. All this I told the police, and they agreed with my assumptions.

My trip to Paris was ruined, not only were they valuable, but very sentimental. I could not claim the insurance as I was out of the house, and stupidly had not included travelling in the policy. I learnt the hard way, always add a clause to cover travelling, when in Europe. When seriously abroad, I never took them. I hated the idea of going home and facing her. A nasty cup of tea, but very bright and excellent at her job. It had to be done, I asked them to leave and I was well rid of them.

With the burglaries, staff problems, and complications of renting the *mas*, it was here that I seriously started thinking about selling. As time passed, all my lovely old friends, artists, designers and fun, swinging, nutty people disappeared. Darling Dee was dying, and Cary her boyfriend, was out of his mind. We just did not know how to help him. One day he rang us all, and that was it, Dee had died quietly, during the night. An appallingly sad end to a perfectly lovely person. She did not want to die, and tried to fight it every minute. She was unique, and we all loved and admired her.

The cost of running the house and keeping up the garden was tremendous, and the approaching quarry along the mountain ridge in front was eroding the capital value. I had had enough, so I put the house on the market, and initially had a great number of interested buyers, but as soon as another agent became involved, they were put off by saying, 'Don't touch any property near Orgon, the Omya quarry has permission from the government to extend towards the south west along Les Alpilles.'

It was not true as we had been fighting it non-stop with our association, and it had been put on hold. This is how the agents pinched their clients and took them elsewhere. Naturally as the quarry of Orgon became more and more known, the price and the fame of a perfectly lovely *mas* was dropping. I had clients who wanted to buy it from Grenoble; she was smart, and as hard as nails. She refused to meet my price, whilst I kept on refusing her offer, meanwhile the husband hung around in the background, saying nothing. This went on for at least two years.

The spring of 2003, I had planned to visit Mallorca and Menorca, looking for a base in the Mediterranean that was fun, with the weather mild all year round. I was invited by Claudine Cumberlege to her adorable village house just outside Palma de Mallorca. I had known her family for donkey's years!

Very curious to see the island today. Of course, it was totally changed from the '60s, overgrown is a good description, and Germanic to the end of your fingers. I was stubborn, and sure there were beaches and coves, that were still wild. I drove through Soler, the north coast, to the east. I took the ferry to Menorca, much wilder and some good properties for sale. I rented a small house in Pollensa, but from day one just got the wrong vibes, just something one could not put one's finger on. There were some very nice people, but the majority were nouveau riche or nouveau poor. The famous Formentor, which I remembered with Joaquin, was very disappointing, the sand washed away, and two and a half metres of beach left, more or less. The actual port of Pollensa had one decent place, the yacht club. The nearby beach was inaccessible, packed to the edge. Even to the north, at Soler up on the mountains, there were some lovely properties, but one would have to live inside it, and never go out.

I gave up, not a suitable place for me long-term. A damn shame, as the island is lovely, and the sea and beaches to die for, but the people are far too middle class, too boring and there were too many of them. Menorca had some charm left, and a few wild beaches, but come the 15th September, it emptied and stayed empty until May. One had the feeling that you were on a very small island, with a limited horizon, and so be it. I did find a lovely old farm, which had large possibilities, and I could have made it very pretty but the only beach close by was another tourist rat-trap, and not an elegant restaurant in site.

I returned to Provence disappointed, but to think again, and leave the Baleares to the plebs.

# 32. *Safari to Africa.*

I was fed up and sick of studying Mediterranean islands, not finding an ideal place to lay down my ageing bones. Either they were packed with mass tourists, and come September were as dead as dodo through the winter, or were so inaccessible, it took three flights to get to them.

I knew flying west or east to the hotter climates, was no solution, as I suffered badly from jet lag, and the older one gets, the worse it is. Further from Miles and Caroline too.

The winter of 2003, I had long talks with the family of our lawyer who was helping us fight Omya. His mother-in-law, a very charming old lady, told me she spent all the winters at her son's outside Nairobi. She suggested I should come and stay and test the climate, that the flight was direct north – south.

Joaquin and I had always adored Africa, and found every excuse to return, the call of the wild is something born in your guts. So again in January, I went to Nairobi invited by these lovely people, Jonathan and Sylvie Campaigne. They had a lovely house on the outskirts of the city. I was whipped off to lunch at the Muthaiga Club, where part of the film, *Out of Africa*, was shot, when Karen Blixen walked into the bar where men only were allowed!

I had masses of contacts in Kenya, and I contacted first Tristan and Cindy Voorspuy. They invited me to their superb property north of Nakuru National Park, Deloraine Estate, once the home of Sir Francis Scott, family of the Queen Mum. Driving with Cindy and her two children, we drove north, the main road to Uganda. Passing huge lorries rumbling over the holes in the road, she would be passing these monsters and waving her hand out of the window, shouting, 'Vicky, zebras to the right, impalas to the left.'

It was very sweet of her, but I had seen masses of these in the Serengeti, Tanzania, and was much more terrified of passing lorries going flat out. Finally we arrived at the town of Nakuru and eventually turned off the main road towards Deloraine. The road was only a track, and we bumped our way up to the big house. I can never understand why people don't make up their roads, I presume being on a slope, quite a hill, that when the rains come, they all get washed away yet again. The house was enormous, set in a park, with lovely gardens and a big pool. The stables were behind the house, and I nearly died when Cindy said, she employed something like 60 grooms or *sykes*, as we call them in Africa, a leftover from the Raj.

Their main business was called Offbeat Safaris, they organised riding safaris all over Kenya, but very upmarket. I joined one in the north; Waterford glass and silver, with damask tablecloths, was the order of the day.

Cindy, knowing I had been breading horses, riding and judging in international events, insisted I came out with her and her children the following morning. I had retired from the equestrian world, once I was in France, a good ten years. If one carries on past 50, one begins to look like one!

I insisted I hated early mornings, and put it off for another day, but could not refuse twice. I felt an absolute idiot, out of practise and riding muscles not in form, on a horse I did not know. Her kids were very condescending; don't blame them. It was a good way to see the surrounding country, and I was only surprised to notice the kids did not salute the locals, who were walking to the road, or catching a bus. I mentioned this to Archie, their son, after having passed various Kenyans, and noticing no good morning or 'Hi! How are you?', something.

Cindy said, 'Ridiculous, as they see them every day and as Archie plays football with their kids, there's no need to say hello each time they pass in the early morning.'

Knowing the Spanish attitude back in Andalusia, where my grooms were horrified with the English riders, who did not say, '*Buenas dias, que tal*,' or '*Adios, muchas gracias*.' when they left.

We all have different habits, and the English in Kenya are a race apart. They are very lucky still today, to live a colonial life with delusions of grandeur. I adored the bush and the land around Nakuru and Naivasha, and very nearly got caught up to buy land there. Very glad I didn't, as in Tanzania, the people and the residents are so much more natural. I had enough pomposity and snobbishness in Paris to last me for a lifetime.

Tristan very kindly organised a Landover for me, and a driver, George, to take me all around the bush to the north of Mount Kenya, Laikipia. So off we went on a mad adventure, with the final destination in the middle of nowhere, Tristan's main base for his safaris. Passing the equator, we climbed the side of Mount Kenya through very thick forests until finally the tarmac ran out and we stopped for gas. A young white man came up to me, asking for directions to Kuki Gullmann's *shamba*, the woman who had written *I Dreamed of Africa* about her Italian husband, who died in a car crash on his way to Mombassa, and her son who died of snake bites. His best friend as a kid, Charlie Mason, now lives in Tanzania, up our mountain, Mount Meru. He and his wife Serena, decided to move here after having various horrible incidents in Kenya; she had her car stopped by thugs, and her two sons were kidnapped for several hours. Thank goodness they abandoned them a few hours later in the bush. She had been terrified they would rape her in front of her boys. After this horror, they moved here to Tanzania.

Driving now on the rough tracks of Laikipia, the scenery was breathtaking and very rough, but sadly not many animals. George told me that they roamed so far to find water, that the distances were enormous, so the game dispersed. I was not convinced, but thought the poaching was so bad, from the Somalis to the north, that the game was being killed off. Arriving at Tristan's outpost, we were greeted by the South African manager and a large kudu, totally tame, in the courtyard.

After a quick shower to remove the grime of the road, I was taken back into the bush, now dark, to find their American clients who were on their riding safari and had set up camp along the river. On our way there, we passed a female elephant and her young, baboons galore and various antelope.

Dinner round the fire, with the famous tablecloths and glass, all his clients were very curious, very American. 'Who are you? Where did you come from? How did you get here?' As always, the yanks have to put you in a box, square you off, and then normally ask you what you are worth. It's amazing how they cannot be discreet. I remember once at a dinner in the Caymans, this American kept asking me questions, including, 'You say your father was an admiral in the British navy, we all know they do not have business brains, therefore always poor, and your husband in the Spanish navy, they must be worse! How did you land up in the Cayman's and with a condominium?'

The cheek of the fellow! My hostess was appalled and very embarrassed.

'It's none of your business,' I replied. 'We are Europeans and we do not discuss in public, one's personal finances.'

I think in the Kenyan bush, my reply was slightly sharper, laced with humour, and I turned the conversation quickly to their ride, and the game they had seen on the way. They admitted there had been very few. They were all very relaxed and fun, and were obviously having a ball. After dinner, on our way back to the ranch, on the track mummy giraffe with the most adorable baby loped very slowly into the dark, two minutes later we spotted a pride of lions just off to our right, all looking very sleepy. I felt so sorry for the Americans, who had to stay in a group, and missed these beautiful creatures in their natural habitat.

George and I left to cross Laikipia straight through the bush in the direction of Lewa Downs, a huge reserve of rhinos run by the Craigs, relations of friends in the UK. It took us hours, crossing dry riverbeds, and sliding over huge rocks; how George did not miss the track I can't think. Finally down in a valley, we passed a very modern-looking building and I asked what it was.

'Mama Vicky, I don't know its official name, but it's full of scientists, studying the flora and fauna of the region.'

I took in what he said and stored it in the back of my memory. The road turned into a building sight, with a double highway in construction, after hours of bad road, were we delighted to finally join the tarmac road to the north.

We had made it to Nanyuki, a pleasant small town on the edge of

Mount Kenya. We drove around it, and discovered the office for the 'protection of rhinos'. A very nice man was in charge, who told us of all the rhino projects, Lewa Downs was the main park and Samburu to the north west. We decided to stop there, as we were both exhausted after our drive through the bush. Next day, we drove north on the tarmac road to Lewa Downs, stopping as I had planned at Fuzz and Bimby Dyer's Borana Lodge. We got hopelessly lost and turned in circles, as Fuzz had refused to put up any signs. No one normally drove there, but flew in by baby planes from Nairobi to their airstrip, or were picked up by the lodge's four-by-four and the driver naturally knew the way. We landed up at his brother's farm amongst herds of Borana cattle that were being driven into pens for the night. His foreman gave George directions, and as we turned round and headed back the way we had come, we were surrounded by masses of giraffes, Northern and Rothschild. We could watch them easily as the bush here was not thick.

Arriving at the lodge, beautifully built with large thatch roofs, on a slope with a water hole underneath it and a pool to the side. All the rooms were delightful with enclosed bathrooms and a chimney, each one an individual cottage. The thatch fascinated me as it was done by a group of Welsh thatchers that had migrated to Kenya 100 years earlier. Each band of thatch was tied onto a beam, like a knot, it was so neat and clean, almost too chic.

A lovely bunch of clients, all of different nationalities, gathered in the salon before dinner. Quite a few had contacts with me, via friends or connections. The VIP was a tiny bush baby that lived on Fuzz's shoulder, when he jumped off onto a sofa and disappeared. Panic all round to find him, as he was so tiny. Dinner was upstairs in the dining room, and Fuzz's brothers joined us, I could not quite capture the relationship between the family members. I wandered around the next day, and photographed the thatch from all angles. Met up with Ben Jackson, who was then building the last cottage along the hill, especially jazzy for a honeymoon couple or film stars.

As I had told Bimby that I wanted to visit the rhino sanctuary, Lewa Downs, and visit the Craigs, she arranged a second guide to show us the way through the bush directly. A gorgeous drive, passing the *shamba* of Fuzz's parents, Tony Dyer, who lived in a bush farm beside the river. A lovely character and a charming fellow. As we crossed his property, we arrived at a game fence and a big gate, the rhinos were here.

We drove for miles through flat undulating country, and saw lots of ellies, buffalo, wildebeest and giraffe. Finally, we spotted the rhinos in the distance, very tranquil and paid no attention to us at all; they were all much more interested in their grazing ground. All wild animals will only attack, if protecting their young, or very angry because they are being annoyed. If you leave them alone, there's 90% chance they won't go for you!

I found the Craigs in their office, but he was flying out that minute and left us with his manager. We watched him run to his bi-plane, throw in his briefcase, jump in, start the engines, whip the baby plane in a circle, and accelerate down the airstrip to take off; flying over us, wiggling his wings in a salute. I thought to myself, *what a life, if only I had known it 30 years earlier.*

With the manager we talked about conservation, and the wildlife and the future of Kenya, then he sent me to William Craig, who ran the lodge on the edge of Lewa. A charming younger brother, who immediately asked me to lunch, together with a bunch of clients, who were already there on safari.

We passed the tented camp of Abercrombie and Kent, a permanent fixture, on our way out, surrounded by trees and close to the only river. Elephants were meandering amongst the tents as if they owned it, for my liking too close to the track and the office buildings of the estate. An American, who I had met in Nairobi, had bought a large piece of land near the entrance, and was planning another rhino reserve. George and I agreed that very soon, there would be no more animals completely wild, they would all be in reserves or parks, behind wire. The elephants were fabulous, and used to join up in a herd and make their way through Nanyuki at night, on their way up Mount Kenya, leaving their droppings as proof.

Saying our goodbyes, we headed back to Nanuyki, planning to visit the Mount Kenya reserve, owned by Tiny Rowland, with the animal orphanage of Don Hunt and William Holden attached to it. Cheetahs and bongos, a very rare antelope and an amazing cross between donkeys and zebras, and a very sophisticated lunch.

We followed on my plan and left the main road to Sweetwater, another reserve, with a very touristy hotel; I had my introductions to a Swedish lady, Annie Olivercrome, who was passionate about chimpanzees. Staying the night in a tent, I found my way to her house and her chimps some distance from the hotel. We made friends immediately, and I was fascinated how she handled the babies. They climbed all over her, playing and loving her presence, I was not too keen to cuddle them, but they were adorable. Before we went to lunch, she put the smallest to bed in a cot, with his nappy, in her bedroom!

Afterwards, she took me to the enclosure, where the big chimps were enclosed; we walked into their sleeping quarters, and saw how these grown-up babies coped with their lack of freedom. They were happy enough, as the enclosure was enormous, and they ran very free in this big space. They also loved to show off, so when the tourists came to their fence, they would crowd onto it, demanding attention. It was totally forbidden to feed them, but despite notices all around, an odd banana made its way through the grill. There was one huge fellow, who stood on his hind legs and slapped his chest. Annie told me the story, how she had been called to Uganda to save him. He was in a cage so small, he could not stand up. He was shown to the clients of the bar, where the owner collected money for showing him off. Poor fellow. He now stood up all day, stretching himself.

I met Annie again at Peponi's, Lamu Island, but was very sad to hear her contract had been terminated at Sweetwater. Never have I met someone so dedicated to the chimps.

In Nanyuki I bade farewell to George and paid him off, flying back to Nairobi and on to Lamu, now the famous island off the north east coast of Kenya, where I had booked into Peponi's, having heard so much about it through various friends and especially Dee and Guy from the Provence. Arriving at the airstrip, one is shuttled across the waterway to the island, not to Lamu town, same name as the island, but to Shela, the village at the end. It was divinely relaxed; luggage picked up immediately and into the bar, served mint tea and vodka and Lars, the owner, was very welcoming. My room was on the ground floor giving onto the beach. A whole mish-mash of people from Nairobi and Europe.

Next door was the newly built house of Ernst and Caroline

d'Hanover, Princess of Monaco. He was already in the bad books of the islanders; having got very cross with the owner of the nightclub in front on Manda Island, he had lost his temper and slugged this fellow on arrival at the quay. Bad luck he fell backwards onto the gunwale of the boat and into the sea. Ernst was had up by the local police, and a court case followed, to my great surprise in Germany not in Kenya. He is so fed up and returns to Lamu very rarely. His children love the island and return frequently.

I thoroughly enjoyed the beach, which went on for ever, but was very disappointed in the sea; snorkelling, one could not see one's hands, the sea was murky, with very little visibility. The only diving was off a boat, and miles out to sea, and if it was rough, it was very unpleasant. I had fun, and adored the village, winding one's way through tiny little streets. Patsy Schryver had a plot in the middle of the village, and had asked me to help sell it. Finally when I found it, I worked out half was missing, with a hideous abandoned hotel in front, blocking her view. The rest of her land was a donkey garage and a vegetable garden.

I visited Maryjka Beckmann's house on the beach, and thought it would be great to rent it over Christmas. I was now determined to see as much as I could of the coast and the islands. I had treated myself to four days on Mnemba Island, a very exclusive island owned by CCF Africa, off Zanzibar, with good diving on the reef. As I did not know the island, I arranged to stay in Stonetown, the capital, for two nights; friends had put me in contact with a dear little man as guide, Twalib. His head only came up to the receptionist's desk, peeking his head over the top with a huge grin. Very nearly missed him, as I could hardly see him. He turned out to be delightful and took me in hand, showing me round the Sultan's palaces, the slave market and all the tiny streets of the town. At night the quay came alive with hundreds of locals cooking fish over braziers of charcoal, Twalib told me to look, but not to eat there, as I would get sick. He showed me a fish restaurant on a pontoon, which looked clean and safe.

The next day I hired a Suzuki and we drove south to see the red monkeys. I went out on a boat to watch the dolphins, but Twalib stayed ashore as was frightened of the sea and did not swim. We went round the south coast to the east side and then north to the land of the spices. Sadly, they are not producing them as before, when one could smell them from a boat miles out to sea. Up to the northern point via a little village, full of kids playing in the sand and huge white beaches on the western point, Ras Nungwe. Further south I found a beach bar over-jutting the sea, had another swim, as it was very hot, and invited Twalib to some lunch. There was an island just in front of us, and he told me it was full of 'voodoo' and never to go there. Of course, I immediately wanted to go.

'Come on, Twalib, show it to me, we can ask a fisherman to take us. I would be very interested to watch voodoo practicing their art.'

'No way, Mama, I won't go and the fishermen neither.'

Twalib was Musulman, as are 90% of the inhabitants of Zanzibar, and very strict with their religious beliefs.

I had to get back to Stonetown, as I had a reservation for dinner on the roof of Emmerson and Green, an old hotel in the middle of town, that had become famous for its charm with two queers as owners, who always have marvellous taste. They had built up a reputation that had reached as far as Paris, so I was very curious to know it, but as it was full and I could not get a room, I booked a table for dinner. Climbing the stairs I arrived at the roof, to find it full of diners sitting on the floor on cushions. I found the one place kept for me squashed between others. The dinner started coming, plate after plate, delicious. All *musungos* – this is what the locals call us white foreigners – chatted up my neighbours, and then arrived a group of negro dancers. It was a miracle how they found the room to dance.

The following day I was picked up by the Mnemba Island's Land Rover; in it was already another couple from South Africa, John and Sue Dovey. I was very lucky as they were charming, and fascinated to know who I was and how I knew about Mnemba. Driving north again, but this time passing the spices, we went north east and headed towards the beach. It was low tide so we had to walk through the sand quite a distance to climb onto a boat, which took us across to the island. The sea was turquoise, dead calm and the island was simply superb. We were met by the staff with large pineapples full of juice. They carried our things and walked us through the bush on a little path, to the main area. It was beautifully built; so discreet one could not even see the bungalows. A good bar, well-stocked, and I was delighted to see backgammon boards laid out on little tables. The dining room was open to the sky and surrounded by the bush. All the tables were laid out for two or four people, and I thought, *oh damn, honeymooners or families of four*. John and Sue immediately asked me to join them. A great mistake for hotels not to have a central table, most travellers want to meet others or talk to newcomers; married couples don't know what to say to each other, and honeymooners in today's world have normally been living together for a long time before they married.

Finding my bungalow, I discovered tiny little deer, sunnis, even smaller than dik-diks. They lived on the island and were practically tame; the most enormous eyes one has ever seen. After a good siesta, swimming and walking, I joined my new-found friends at the bar to play backgammon before dinner. Both agreed how sad we had no sunset, as the sun dropped to the west behind Zanzibar over the mainland, the only fault of the island, otherwise paradise.

I went diving the next morning and the reef was spectacular but fairly limited, and realizing this was the only reef off Zanzibar, so full of boats from all the hotels. More people arrived and we joined various tables together, finally having a fun crowd. Time went like a flash and I had to leave, to head to Mafia Island. I already had a rendezvous with Peter Burns, a good-looking white Kenyan, a pilot and owner of the only lodge on Mafia Island, south of Dar es Salaam. Thinking he was piloting us, I was very disappointed to discover he was too busy, but would join us later. Mafia was disappointing, quite flat, no mountains and the coast unreachable, except in special places. The only lodge was Peter's, very pleasant, but full of mosquitoes and bugs. One could not sunbathe on the beach without being bitten alive. It made up for it in atmosphere, a very special group of clients and hurrah, a host's table; bachelors, single women, dive masters, and other white specialists. As well as some geologists, and scientists, who were studying the larvae on the next-door beach.

The dive master was a German, and obviously lurching after one of the German clients. We were taken out in a *dhow*, and had to throw ourselves, once tanked-up, backwards into the sea. Once we had equalized and swum to the bottom, he disappeared, following his lady around the reef. However cross one gets underwater, one cannot shout in anger, just have to go with the flow. Another day we went out to a sandbank, with a tent and all the paraphernalia, so the clients who didn't dive could enjoy the sea. It was lovely, the diving not very exciting, but the lodge was delightful.

Now the serious part started, this time Peter flew us back to Dar es Salaam, where I connected with Precision Air to Kilimanjaro. Michael Leach met me at the airport, and I was delighted to return to his lodge, Ngare Sero, up on Mount Meru. On our way from the airport, all new, we had a glimpse of Kili in the moonlight. After a week at the lodge, I had itchy feet again, as I had finally made the huge decision to sell the *mas* in France, and move to Africa. Always the call for adventure, and to live here was so much less expensive.

*Elephants with their mahouts at Amber Fort, Jaipur, 2000*

*Gate of the suttees at Meherangarh Fort, 2000*

*El Mansour found in Cairo, January 2000 (he actually recognised me)*

*Marwari champion stallion at Dunlod, 2000*

*St Leger reunion at Chateau d'Eu, 2000*

*St Leger reunion in the church, 2000*
*Vicky on the far left next to Count & Countess de Saint Leger, who are standing next to the Countess de Paris*

*The old man at Jodphur, 2000*

*The Taj Mahal, from the village behind it, 2000*

*Vicky micro-lighting over Victoria Falls, 2000*

*Vicky on a quad bike on the Makghadighadi Pans, 2000*

*Canoeing down the Zambezi River, we met this hippo head on! 2000*

*The wedding of my godson, Edward Mitterand, July 2001*

*La Ermita, 10th anniversary of Joaquin's death, 2002*

*Wild boar ripped up the lawn, Le Mas, 2002*

*Snow at Le Mas, 2003*

*Rented cottage in Tanzania, October 2003*

*Caroline at her wedding, with her Aunt Inez, 2005*

*Miles at Caroline's Wedding, 2005*

*Beginning of construction on my site at Dolly Estate, Tanzania, 2005*

*Caroline's kids, Iolo and Cara, 2007*

*Floods at Dolly Estate, 2005*

*Foundations of the house, 2005*

*Finished house at Dolly Estate, December 2006*

*View from the veranda looking at Mount Meru, December 2006*

*Swimming pool is finished, 2006*

*The swimming pool at Le Mas when I returned to visit, 2007*

*My friend Sarah Henderson watching out for crocs during a picnic in the bush, 2008*

*On safari in Ruaha with Miles and Fiona (now engaged), 2009*

*My house with Kilimanjaro in the background, 2007*

*Miles and Fiona's wedding. 20th August, 2011*

# 33. Finding Dolly Estate

I had to move my arse and start looking at land, sussing out prices and what was available. Michael took me up to Momela along the ridge to meet David Reed, agriculturist and author. The road was so horrific, it put me off ever buying land that far from the main road. I went to stay at Rivertrees Country Inn, advised by friends. The owner, Martina Gehrken Trappe, a charming German lady, who has turned out as a great friend; always pulling her leg, I say she is the nicest German I have ever met. Rivertrees is a huge garden, with enormous trees all along the Usa River. I had a lovely bungalow, and an outside bath. She returned from a safari, and we made friends immediately. A bit cold; one is so unused to cold in Africa, especially in August. Buildings are not designed for warmth, as nearly all year it's boiling.

I went to find a Dutch woman, Edith Brinkers, who lived next door to the old polo club, a friend of Patsy Schryver. She told me all about a place called Dolly Estate, further on beyond Usa River. I laughed and said why did they call it after a London tart? It had been bought by four young men, and apparently the original owner, who had turned the estate into a sisal plantation, named his land after all his women friends!

To begin with I was not interested, too far, too hot, and I felt the owners who had bought it, were not clued-up enough to develop it properly.

Somehow I met Jerome Bruins, a Dutchman, and his wife, Zsuzsa, a Hungarian. He was a passionate polo player and ran the stables at the polo ground, and managed various flower farms. No fool obviously. In the back of my memory, I think Patsy had mentioned them back in

Europe. I started to meet the polo players, and asked one young man what he thought was the better country to live in and make a base, Kenya or Tanzania?

'Tanzania, without a doubt. The people are charming, always smiling, and we have lots of friends here, who are great fun. No tribal nonsense, Nyerere got rid of all that.'

This was a very quick conversation but I remembered his remarks. Going to bed that night, I mucked around in my brain all that I had heard, tossing and turning, thinking of Africa and all she represented.

I had always said to myself, that I would end up with a thatched-roofed house in Africa; talk of destiny, here I was.

I met up with Jerome the next day. He drove me around Dolly Estate and showed me all the plots of land that they had marked out, only 500 metres from the tarmac. No bumps. Or few at least. I fell for a plot of 130 acres with a lovely valley and hills at the bottom, with its own hill on which I could construct the house, and an amazing view of Mount Meru in front, and Kilimanjaro behind. I calculated that I could keep enough acres for me and the kids, and sell off the rest to pay for the building.

Jerome and his three associates had bought the old sisal farm for peanuts, and now were selling sub-divisions of various acreage. It immediately reminded me of El Cuarton. They had planned two polo fields, tennis courts, and a pool and in the future, a golf course. They invited me twice for a sundowner on their plot, as each shareholder had kept 40 acres each. I thought to myself, *well, this is the ideal place for my thatched roof.* An added incentive was the whole estate was going to be a game reserve. For this reason no fences were allowed, so the game could roam free. I returned various times, wandering around the land, looking, feeling and dreaming. It was a huge decision, the climate was right, or so I thought there and then. I was not told how cold it is in July and August.

Dolly Estate seemed a perfect compromise, between being miles away in the Serengeti, or in West Kilimanjaro, or a town such as Arusha, or down on the coast where it is a continuous humid heat. I had already decided that Tanzania was far nicer than Kenya; nicer people, seemingly safer, with a direct flight from Amsterdam or a quick hop to Nairobi and plenty of connecting flights to the rest of Europe. The Chinese had moved in in droves, and are rebuilding the road via Namanga to Nairobi.

Also, I now knew the coast and the islands, and how easy it was to access them. Being such a creator, the idea of watching Dolly take off would fascinate me. I made up my mind. I rented a cottage in the flower farm Hortansia, very close to the estate, and an ideal *pied-à-terre*. I told Jerome I would pay him a 10% down-payment there and then for 130 acres, and the rest when I came back in October.

I flew back to Europe, and got on with selling the mas; heartbroken, but I knew it was the only solution. The couple from Grenoble who had been fiddling around for two years, making very low offers, finally came back with another low but slightly better offer. The other clients were messing about, not making up their minds. In the middle of these negotiations, a very strange fellow turned up out of the blue. He was dressed in velvet, with incredible shoes, I could not make up if he was Arab or Jewish. He wanted to see the house, and I took him on a tour, after which he made an incredible offer in cash, and said he would meet me in Geneva in a week's time to clinch the deal. I contacted my lawyer, Bertrand Lapeyre, and we were both very doubtful, thinking this was a crook; the offer was too good, and he looked too sleazy for words.

Making a rendezvous in Geneva, Bertrand organized a specialist from Lugano, who accompanied us, to verify and check the cash that this fellow was offering me. The meeting was in their lawyer's office, very James Bond. We were ushered into an office at the back of the building, where I sat down at a long table, winking at Bertrand; we waited a good 15 minutes. Finally they arrived, staring nervously at our man with his machine to count the notes. In the meantime, our security guys were outside on the street, each with his revolver in his belt, and a top security guy on the corner. Our buyers, who were obviously crooks, realized that we were protected from every angle; frightened, I imagine that they could not cheat us, they backed off the deal, making excuses. Thank goodness, but what a pity, as the price they offered was over the top. Poor Bertrand had come for nothing. At least we took him for an excellent lunch at the Hotel Rhône, on the other side of the lake.

Back in the Provence, I understood I would have to accept the offer from the couple from Grenoble. We argued non-stop, but finally came to an agreement. I hate these deals, but once decided, I want to go ahead, and can't stand the arguments over money.

We signed the sale in Avignon at Bertrand's office, and I started the enormous job of packing up the house. All the furniture and paintings, the contents from the billiard room I gave to Miles and Caroline, as half of the lot belonged to them anyway. I had to arrange transport to the UK, with all the fuss with the paperwork. Certain valuable paintings that belonged to Joaquin's family, I sent up to Paris to a great friend, an auctioneer. He sold them in one of his auctions three months later and darling France Tutino went to check on it, and to her great surprise, the one painting none of us liked raised a very high price. I gave the benefits to two of Joaquin's nieces, Patricia and Cristina Cervera Cottrell, the daughters of Luis, his youngest brother.

I arranged a transporter to ship two containers out to Tanzania, one to be delivered to the cottage I had already rented very close to Dolly, and the other to be put in storage. It was murder despite the help, to load the containers, remembering this is what I need to live in the cottage temporarily, and this can be stored for later, in about two years; calculating roughly the time it would take me to design and build my thatched cottage.

It was hell, and I think I was ripped off by the people helping me, as many items disappeared. It was impossible to keep my eye on both containers.

The time arrived to leave, and a lovely friend offered to take me to the airport, Eugene Lane Spollen. Pouring with rain, we loaded the dogs' cages, and a little blue bag especially from Air France for Minouche. We stopped before arriving at Marseille, so the dogs could pee and I injected them with tranquillisers. Crying, but determined, we saw them off to Amsterdam, Minouche in her little bag at my feet.

Arriving in the freight hangar in Amsterdam, a delightful young man had already let them out of their cages, and put them on leads. As soon as they heard me, they tore away, totally hysterical, poor things they had been in their cages since 6.00 am. Walking round the parking lot, they had a pee, and jumped into the van I had rented. The driver was terrified.

'Don't panic, they are big and black, but wouldn't hurt a flea.'

Arriving at the hotel on the canals, they rushed to the edge, and I thought *damn, Napoleon, the elder male, will jump in.* He certainly looked down into the water with great interest, but it was four metres at least to the water level.

Miles and Caroline had come to Amsterdam to see me off; it was adorable, as they were there on my arrival, loved the animals and helped me enormously.

We walked around the canals and pushed the dogs under all the trees, followed by Minouche – nothing! Fed up, I said to the young, 'Come on, time for dinner and discovering swinging Amsterdam.'

We locked the animals in my room, with a marvellous tray of cat litter, brought by Caroline. We took off for the nightlife and had a ball. Not knowing Amsterdam, I was very curious to see and feel the atmosphere.

My flight was at 10.00 am, but knowing the crowds at Schipol and the dogs etc, we had to leave at 6.00 am to get there for 7.30, leaving us time to let them out in the park, to do their business. It was a great idea, but both being black, disappeared into the dark. Caroline and I went bananas trying to call them back. When they returned, I quickly injected them with the tranquilliser.

At the airport, it was mayhem, the dogs had to go one way, and me the other. Finally sorted out, they were weighed and in their cases, I cried, thinking I would not see them again until Africa. Now it was Minouche's turn, she yelled a Siamese yell when I pushed her into her Air France blue bag. I hugged the kids, and thanked them enormously for their help, and pushed my way through the queue, a milling mass of people.

Once through all this ghastly mass of humans, and sitting in business class, I started to relax. As the flight took off, Minouche started to miaow. 'Shut up, keep quiet.'

One of the hostesses came towards me, and asked who had a cat near here, and I thought, *oops, this is the end, they will put her in the hold.* Totally wrong, she just wanted to see her. I brought Minouche's beautiful head just out of the bag, and this young woman went bananas about her. From then on she was fed on cream and salmon and allowed to sleep in my arms. I had a little collar and a chest brace, which I could control her if she got frightened.

# 34. Moving to Tanzania

Arriving at the flower farm, Hortansia, where the cottage was that I had booked, we were met by the manager, Joseph, a French Corsican. Scrambling out of the Land Rovers, dogs going ballistic to be free and haring round the lawn, it was pitch dark so I could not see any of the work that I had planned with Joseph before arriving. He had not answered any of my e-mails. I was too tired to start asking him questions, and just unpacked the vehicles and went inside. The cottage was very empty, except for one table and four chairs. One bed in each room, but thank goodness, thanks to Martina, the fridge had some picnic food and two bottles of white wine.

Saying goodnight to all our helpers, the young Oriental man, who had joined me at Amsterdam, sent from Paris by Vigdis, and I, sat on a suitcase and viewed the scene. It was pretty miserable, clean but horribly empty. We were so tired, so I took Minouche to bed, which was as hard as a board, and put the dogs in the salon on a blanket. I woke up to the most awful noise, banging and scraping at 7.00 am – back into another building site. I was so exhausted after the sale of the *mas* and the removals, I needed to rest for at least a week, to recuperate my strength.

Walking around the cottage, I quickly realized that all the work that I had planned with Joseph was not only unfinished, half of it had not even been started. I began to understand the total lack of efficiency, and hopeless building ethics, that the Africans were capable of. Such a shame, as the Tanzanians are charming people, but utterly incapable of sticking to a plan or organizing their working day. The foremen were totally incapable of giving orders and never had the authority to sack workmen on the spot for laziness or bad workmanship. I did not need this at the time, I just wanted peace. I was mad at Joseph for getting me into this mess, without an apology.

As the four-by-four had not turned up at the airport as promised, the first thing was to go to the town of Arusha, and rent a Landcruiser, buy a mobile phone, get a chip and do some shopping. Robert, Martina's driver, drove us into town, a good 45 minutes. Traffic became much worse in the latter years. We drove along the side of Mount Meru, and turned into the town, through a huge avenue of jacarandas, and gardens of flowers. Crossing the old German quarter, the Corridor, we made our way to the centre with its clock tower, marking the middle of the distance between Cairo and Cape Town. Finding Barclays Bank, just off the Corridor, very new, I met the manager and set-up my accounts, before returning via Rivertrees to have some lunch and thank Martina for all she had organised for our arrival. Without her pushing Joseph I don't know what we would have done.

I could not leave the dogs, as the fence round the garden was nothing like finished, it meant either shutting them in the house and locking it, or taking them with us. No garage, it was not even started, and what was meant to be the staff cottage was non existent! A very unpleasant few weeks, except evening walks around Hortansia in the company of hundreds of Vervet monkeys. The dogs went wild chasing them, the monkeys used to watch, then tear up the trees at the last minute, screeching with anger. The property had a lovely stream in the middle, with huge ficus trees growing on the banks. Very quickly I met all the whites who lived nearby, as Martina had a pub night on Thursdays, where they all congregated.

I found a dear little maid, Asha, who was adorable, and pushing like mad, the workmen finished her room and a loo and shower – before it was just a hole in the floor – and my office was wired up for the computer and the desk. Finally the containers arrived, having taken 12 hours on the road from Dar, and days to clear customs. Was I glad to see them rumbling down the tracks of Hortansia. Thank goodness it was sunny, and I was able to off-load all the furniture; getting back into my double bed was heaven, and I moved the hard local ones into Asha's room. I had calculated exactly the salon, with my old kitchen table and dresser from the Provence, they just fitted.

The clic-clacs, that were sofas and spare beds for the young above the billiard room in the *mas*, made up the sitting area, a bit of a squash, but it looked pretty.

Yago Casado, a Spanish friend from Lamu, a painter, came to stay. Very good looking, but never got up in the mornings, typical Spanish. I had already made friends with George and Jo Cooke and Annabel Ross, all from Dorset, Donhead St Mary, same village as Sheila, what a small world. Annabel, a lovely young woman, and fun, daughter of a Marine general was working in Tanzania, so I took Yago to dinner with her, they hit it off, and she went to Lamu to stay with him. She has an incredible energy and could not stand the laid back artist, who would not move his arse until lunchtime!

I was a nervous wreck planning Christmas, as Miles was coming, and Nikita and Olga a few days later. December 2004 was amazingly hot. Miles and I spent Christmas day with Martina, eating turkey in 42 degrees. Miles was fantastic and carved the beast pouring in sweat. On arrival, I showed the land to Nikita and Olga, still totally wild, no tracks and thick bush. I had to back the four-by-four up to get out of the property, and I'll never forget, I left the back doors open to let in some cool air, as the a/c did not work. Absolutely stupid, as all the dirt and dust swirled round and came in on us, covering us in mud and brown filth. Olga who is very chichi, was simply horrified, and spent the afternoon trying to get clean.

They thought I was quite mad buying this property on the hill, but in 2004 it was so wild, one needed a huge imagination to see what it would be like in a year's time. I was fascinated to see the development and watch it grow. BCW Limited were the owners, comprising of two Dutch brothers, Jerome and Bas Bruins, an English banker, John Warren, and a Greek coffee farmer, Tony Christianakis. I knew I had to connect my own electricity, but had insisted they provided water, which they duly tried to do via two bore holes, sadly producing only saline water.

In the meantime, Nikita hired a private bi-plane, and we three flew to Lamu for the New Year, having rented Maryjka Beckmann's house on the sea very close to Peponi's. Normally Ernst Hanover and Caroline gave a big party, but this year, because of his court case, he had not come. So we all went to Katy Barker's new house, just finished, further up the coast. We dressed up as Arabs with masks. I borrowed a black slit veil, so no one knew who I was. Very funny for half an hour, wandering between the other guests, everyone guessing who the Arab lady was, though the joke wore off pretty quickly, as it was so hot. Katy was a photographic agent, for models and film stars living in London, and was widely known amongst the media. Her party was great, and somehow we all landed up on the roof to watch the fireworks. A very large Frenchman, who was trying to flirt with the bird next to me, sat on me. I threw him off, suggesting he went back to his wife, who, poor thing, was downstairs looking for him.

We left discreetly and found our way to the village square, where all the action was taking place; a large crowd, most of them pissed, it had the atmosphere of a Spanish *feria*!

Lamu is a very special place; the whole island is one huge sandbank, like Manda Island in front, surrounded by mangrove swamps. It has become an international playground for what is today the jet-set, or rather what is left of it. Peponi's always attracted a fun crowd, and with the arrival of Ernst and Caroline d'Hanover, the snob angle was on the move, and attracted Europeans and Kenyans looking for somewhere special.

Nikita and Olga loved it, and I am sure we will return, but sadly not to Maryjka's house, as it has been sold, I think to more French.

Nikita and I were swimming off the beach further down towards the point, the day before we left; suddenly the sea was in turmoil, with a big current going in towards Lamu town, then it turned and started to sweep us out to sea. I shouted that something was weird and not normal, and I had not the strength to swim against the current. I swam to the beach and found the gentle slope of the beach was now a steep bank. I hauled myself out, and yelled at the kids who were near the shore, to get out quickly. As we walked back towards Peponi's, we saw all the *dhows* anchored in the creek, turning on their anchors, losing only 1 'o' their chains, hauling in their sails and there was a general panic amongst their crew.

It was the tsunami. We were all ignorant, Lars kept running in and out from in front of his TV set, and shouting the news to us on the beach. No one could believe what we were seeing. Once again I was there in the thick of it. Four drowned in Mombassa, hundreds to the north in Somalia, but as Lamu was an island, the current went in, and then went back to the open sea, we were very lucky.

Back in Hortansia, I started looking for the ideal contractors. I had by then lots of contacts and lots of advice. A lovely young man, Philip Ashby, offered to help, and pushed me to get started on the house in Dolly.

The first job was cutting the bush on the hill; I was determined to build my house on it, to get the best view. I planned the foundations to face Mount Meru, and behind Kilimanjaro. Once the bush was cleared, with a way for cars to reach the top, I had a site-warming party, which finished in the dark. Everyone here drinks like a fish in the evenings, but are shocked if they catch you having a slug during the day! Wow! In France one never stopped all day!

That evening was warm, a heavenly sunset, and the bush around one was cracking and creaking with animals and insects. The night air of Africa is magic, and the land I had bought, 130 acres, was enormous, but my plans were to sell the minimum allowed 10-acre plots to pay for the building. Now four sold, three to go, but I did not know, the problems ahead of me.

We started off digging trenches from the bore hole up to the hill and across the valley to two water tanks, so the girls I had employed could water the trees I had planted on the far hill, to block off the village. Philip had hired manual labour to dig the trenches, a group who he knew of, very tough young men, who we paid according to the metres they dug in a day. They were all just out of prison! We lowered a submersible pump into the borehole, and finally were able to get water up the hill to the building site. There were shouts of joy as the water arrived, Philip came up and sniffed the air, looking horrified, he said, 'Where is the salt?' He cupped his hands and tasted it, spitting it out, 'This is *magadi*, bad water. Where are the results of the water test?'

I looked horrified, saying, 'I don't know, we have never received them.' A complete cock-up, the secretary of BCW had never delivered them. Apologies all round, as when they were found, the water contained 45 milligrammes of fluoride and 2,048 milligrammes of alkalinity, and was unfit for human consumption. Useless, too, for a garden. A local expert told us, as the soil was full of salt, if we added this water to it, it would make it worse. He was right, as the hibiscus and bougainvilleas just wilted away. We used it for the building, having made a big tank up on the hill where the centre of the house would be. The indigenous trees and the local grass did not seem to suffer.

The foundations, when finished, were solid enough, I hope; though every year we have to treat the cement with anti-fungus, as it peels away in layers around the base and the lower walls.

Once the foundations were finished, a few classic mistakes were easily rectified, I gave a 'watering the foundations party', one of the best I had given. I hired a disc jockey, covered the water tank to make the bar, and we danced until the beer ran out. My staff had turned up all beautifully dressed and once the music started they all joined in; good music to the Africans is irresistible. It was very funny watching them intermingle with my guests, the disc jockey was fantastic and kept everyone pumping and jiving until dawn. One young man from a nearby lodge was screaming for more beer. 'Sorry chum, it has run out,' I replied.

Come May, I had to go back to the UK as Caroline was getting married to Dylan Roberts, her boyfriend. They had been together for years and were having their wedding at his family home in Wales. I flew to Edinburgh to be with Miles for a few days, hired a car and drove south, getting hopelessly lost in Liverpool, a part of the UK I had never been to before. Miles had started a business hiring marquees and put up the most fabulous tent for Caroline. Louise came with Amy, as the bridesmaid, and we all stayed in a hotel nearby. Poor Caroline never got any sleep, as other weddings were on in the hotel. The whole place was jumping. We organised the pub next to the church to stay open, but the silly buggers closed. They lost out on good business, as a lot of guests had driven miles to get there.

My cousins from Ireland all came, and we sat in the pews right at the altar. Miles gave his sister away, looking very smart in a tailcoat and Scottish trews. Dylan's family were charming, lots of brothers and sisters, and very grateful for me having brought up and looked after Caroline through her early years.

A great wedding, 28th May 2005.

Catching up with all the news from Ireland, and friends I had not seen in ages. Caroline looked lovely, and Dylan always funny and amusing. They went off on their honeymoon to Mauritius. So correct, they had not allowed me to help financially with the wedding costs, as they said they were too old and had been together for ages, but they allowed me to pay for the honeymoon. At least something.

Back in Africa, the building went on, and the walls went up, the contractors were delightful, but Philip and I had to be there every day, as they had no idea how to follow my plans. Getting to the plumber, he put the pipes back to front, with the baths facing the inside walls, they had to be changed to face the windows.

Meeting him twice walking down the track, I asked him, 'Antonio, where are your tools?'

He simply replied 'Oh! Mama, today I did not bring them.' I went quite potty. A charming fellow, but his technical capabilities, were certainly lacking. Very sad, as these locals probably had never seen a bathroom in their life, but he had to change all the plumbing, so one's guests could have a bath and look out over the bush. The workers were all delightful people, but so disorganized. The actual contractors were worse, charming and kissing my hand on arrival on the site, very gentlemanly, but they had no idea how to organise their workmen.

Now I started planning the roof, as I was determined to have my thatched roof in Africa, having made friends with a delightful fellow from Zimbabwe, Hugo Titley, who, poor fellow, had lost everything in his home country, thanks to Mugabe. It was an enormous job, but he did it, bringing up the grass from Pangani, and I had an excellent carpenter, who did all the woodwork, screwing in the beams.

We hit bad luck, as 2005 was a wet year and it never stopped raining. We laid out the grass every day on the slope in front of the house to dry it as most of the transport in local lorries forgot to cover it with plastic tarpaulins. I had to find huge plastic covers to try and keep the roof dry.

Hugo did a fantastic job, and despite the rain, we slowly progressed, and when we were finally under cover, we could start the technical side of the building: plumbing, electricity, drains etc. I had made a deal with the three neighbours to the north, two Indians and a Brit from Nairobi. We put in a line from the local village, Maji Ya Chai, and two transformers. Terribly funny, they all agreed and arrived with their boot just full of cash, opening it to show it to me. 'Shush, the guards are watching,' I whispered.

Very embarrassing, I quickly closed it, and took them to my site, showing them the transformers already installed. You cannot believe it, since then I have not heard a word from them. It was a fabulous idea, as we now get our power on a separate line all down the outside of the fence, and only have to put in an underground cable to the houses. BCW was quite right not allowing overhead wires to run across the properties and made it an obligation to lay armoured cables underground.

By October I had started the pool, parallel to the guest cottage. I had contracted out Dania Ventures, managed by an ex-pilot, Ian Gregory, and I drew up the plans and the curved shape, so I was eyes wide open coming back to the site after a few days away, seeing that it was all wrong. I was furious with Philip, who had not followed the plans at all. The head workman, Omari, shrugged his shoulders and said he had never seen them.

This is what went on non-stop through the winter, summer below the equator.

Then there was the horror over the doors and windows. I had ordered through the builders, white eucalyptus, but old wood; Hugo, now my neighbour and a great friend, lifted up a door and nearly dropped it, it was so heavy. It was full of water, had not been cured at all. I now have window frames made of one wood, the doors another, the actual windows a third, and cyprus planks as the floor of the veranda. I thought I would go barmy. With all my building experience from Paris, via Spain and then the Provence, not counting the apartments in Paris, I had built six big properties, but never have I had so many problems. Lack of the language was a great negative point; I thought I would learn it quickly. Since Joaquin and I were here in 1985, the vocabulary had tripled in size. Twenty years earlier, *gwaheri, asante, karibu san,* were enough to get by. Now, in 2005, it was totally different. I was just too old to learn another language, my French and Spanish, which are fluent, I used in the Provence, chatting to my lawyer in Spain and answering the contractor in French. I suppose I am just too lazy.

Very stupid as I miss out on a lot, and have never done a big project without knowing the language, but on the other hand, one keeps a private life to oneself and can remain apart from the everyday yak-yak.

The house was still a mess of cement, doors and windows all over the place, and at the same time I was planting trees and bushes, but at least I could throw myself into the pool to cool off, taking care not too many of the workmen were hanging around.

Adam, my driver, like an idiot, had pinched Philip's motorbike, when he was in town, and raced it around the property showing off. Turning the corner too quickly towards the garage, he keeled over, twisting the handlebars and the front wheel. When Philip came back to the site, he saw some Africans wandering through the lower *shamba*, jumped on his bike and raced after them. Immediately realized his bike was not straight, and something was seriously wrong. Was he cross, as this was some special bike. Finding Adam was the culprit, he yelled at me, 'Either he goes or I quit, I won't work with this fellow again.'

Philip stayed, Adam left. He was a very cheeky fellow, and knew he had been wrong, but he was full of charm. He is now a tour driver, and his sister, Saada, is my cook. Philip and I were still going slightly mad with the workmen; we would disappear to the garage, have a smoke and a stiff gin and lemon, thinking nothing of the lifestyle. I had seen the heart specialist in London a year before, as Daddy had died of a heart attack back in Malta. I wanted a check-up before starting this African project, and the doctor said to me, 'Vicky, how much do you drink?'

'Oh! Three gins at lunch-time, then some wine, and vodka at night, probably finishing with another bottle of wine.'

Of course, I was joking, but he took me seriously, and gave me a good verbal thrashing, saying, 'If you don't stop, something serious will happen to you.' He had tried to frighten me. Losing his papers back in Africa, I never thought more about it. And then I had my stroke.

# 35. The Break In

Finally the house was finished, it took ages and getting the details done was agony. I was now pretty lame, and hobbled through the rooms, encouraging and criticising. Philip had to leave, as he is a white hunter and had a new contract. The water problem was temporarily solved by pumping water up from Usa River, above where the *magadi* water ran. Moving into the house was typically mayhem, but fun and after two or three days she looked fabulous. One's friends were adorable, and everyone helped. Two Jack Russell puppies arrived, Kimo and Keva, just too adorable, except the female, Keva, became very cross if picked up, and snapped at people. Kimo, very sadly, we ran over in the Landcruiser two months later, and killed him instantaneously. I was heartbroken. Serena and Charlie gave me a present of one of theirs, not blue-blood but the most adorable character. I called him Kiko. He sleeps on my pillow every night.

Waking up the first morning, I looked out of my French windows over the green bush of the valley and up to the Momela range of mountains, with Mount Meru to the left. Bliss to have it finished, despite the details and closing my eyes to the faults. Planting the lawn on the slope in front, flowering shrubs and masses of bougainvilleas, I created a garden that was very simple, with the most amazing view over my indigenous trees to Mount Meru. I could actually see two or three houses of friends on the mountain on clear days.

I was trying to finish the details in the house, it was hell as I could not move around easily, and there was so much to do. I had to manage alone, as Philip had gone and Adam also. I employed a new driver, Francis, a very good-looking fellow, who drove well, but he turned out to be dishonest, pinching the batteries and my old beloved tape measure of 20 metres that I had since the El Molino days. I put up with it, trying to keep an eye on him. He was disliked by my other staff, so the atmosphere was not good.

The weather can be a problem, so very changeable. You just don't know the weather pattern here, there are two rainy seasons, short rains normally in November and the long rains in April/May. Nothing has been normal for two years.

One's life is all marked out, telepathy and destiny is a part of one's existence. If I had the stroke in France, I would have had two steep flights of stairs to get to my bedroom, and no ground floor bedroom existed. Here, the staff take me for walks, wash my hair; get me in and out of the bath. In the beginning they even put in my contact lenses. I have taught myself to be as independent as possible, sitting on the loo; I dress myself and wash with the left hand.

Living here definitely has its advantages over Europe, though slowly they are changing. I was very lucky to have built my house four years ago, as since then the costs have sky-rocketed. Salaries are now double, cement too, and all building materials, not to talk of diesel. I have installed an inverter for three lights and my computer, anything to economize the generator. I keep driving my eight-seat Landcruiser, inside Dolly Estate, and to the local gym, only three kilometres on the main road, but it sucks up diesel. I don't dare to drive at night, as I can't see my foot, and more than once could not stop. My right foot slips between the pedals, thinking I am breaking, but nothing happens, as my foot is on the floor. 'Heh! Vicky, you're in too much hurry to get to the bar?'

Our local village, Maji Ya Chai, Water of Tea, is named after the river that borders the estate, which when in spate is the colour of strong tea. Many friends have bought land next to the river, but all complain and say it's filthy, *magadi*, which means it is full of alkalinity and fluoride. Unfit for human consumption.

The only clean water comes from Usa River, which is at quite a distance. Apparently, we are in a zone of *magadi* which runs up to Kia airport. Usa River, our nearest big village, is actually a dump, despite the pretty name, it has horrible sandy streets with bumps everywhere, dirty little shops and one petrol station. The owner, a charming fellow, had dreadful trouble with the girls he employed, they were all ripping him off, and so the whole lot have been replaced. Francis, the ex-driver, was involved, I think. He certainly stole the car batteries, and my building equipment, a very smart but sleazy fellow.

Now I have a lovely Masai, Eliudi; a big fellow, and he helps me everywhere and does a great deal on the *shamba* (country property), while my two maids look after me, Saada and Christina. I have taught Saada to cook, like Asha in the cottage. Their memories are nil, always saying, 'Sorry, Mama, sorry, Mama, I forgot.' Teach them a recipe today, and two weeks later they have forgotten it.

One has to be very democratic, I am Irish and sometimes lose my cool, and get angry with them; they get upset, as basically they are lovely people, and cheerful. Getting angry doesn't help. You do sometimes go potty, as lying to them is a way of life, so you know in advance that what they are saying is not true.

Once I pulled the leg of Adam, the first driver and brother to Saada. 'Why do you bother to go to church for three hours on Sunday, when you lie non-stop during the week?'

You can't get an African to blush, as you cannot see it! Forty percent are Christian, forty percent Muslim and the rest, nothing.

It's a lovely life here, peaceful and quiet, if, like me, you are privileged to live on Dolly. Three and a half kilometres from the main road, and I have built my house on the only hill, with views to die for over Mount Meru and Kilimanjaro behind. We have the polo club below, with two fields, the swimming pool, gym and tennis courts. Now they are building a golf course on the lower land. Our only big problem is the lack of water as one day Usa River may dry up.

When I bought my land, 130 acres, I had calculated to sell plots of 10 acres, the minimum allowed, keeping 60 for myself, more or less. I have sold 40 already. I was told that wild animals were going to be released, and we were not to build fences around the property to let them roam free. It has taken a long time but now we are very spoilt, and having cut back the bush, I have every kind of antelope at my doorstep. They have decimated my drive, and eaten all the flowers, but well worth the joy of seeing them each morning: Grant's gazelles, Tommies, impala and gerenuks. Fabulous. Just now, this minute, a herd of eight zebras, literally here in the parking area. They all love the short grass, and now that I have had slashed a huge area, they are here every day.

Hugo and Lizzie, now my neighbours, have built their house just down the hill under my pool. He did not want to look into my kitchen back yard, now we look into his! Lovely, though, to have them as neighbours. She is working for Nomad, a safari company next door to Rivertrees Lodge, which is just across the river. His second marriage, her first, and they have had horrendous bad luck, as their first child, a boy, was born brain dead. Dear Lizzie had to go from Nairobi to Cape Town, having scans and tests, poor little boy is growing, but cannot talk or walk. It's heartbreaking to see him.

The white community here are all charming, much younger than I, and all working, either in the safari business, or lodges. Whilst the Tanzanians are tour guides, drivers, cooks, or specialized in building projects. The country is growing fast, and each year you can see the developing improvement. Maji ya Chai has quadrupled in size in the last two years, with houses mushrooming on either side of the main road. The centre of the village is a muddy, slushy track, with Muscovy ducks wandering in and out of vegetable stalls. The people are charming, and very friendly. I feel a right fool not speaking Kiswahili. The first country in which I have built a house, where I have not been fluent in the language. It is much more difficult than I thought.

Being lame and feeling pretty miserable, with spasms like electric shocks down my right arm, I don't go often to Arusha, as it means all day in the car, let alone to the capital Dar es Salaam. Arusha has developed enormously in four years; it is now categorized as a city; one huge new hospital, belonging to the Lutheran church, five new hotels and masses of new restaurants. They are now talking about a double highway around the town, and tarmac the side streets. We'll see if it's true.

For me, it's always fascinating to live in a country that is developing, one can feel the buzz and watch the Tanzanians changing their attitude and their clothes. All the school children in uniform, their heads shaved, both boys and girls. Secondary school kids are taught in English, I have helped many to further their education, and quite a few to get in to universities, plus looking after an orphanage for street children, putting in electricity, buying them blankets, sending up carpenters to fix the dormitories, and food every month.

The kids are adorable, especially the young ones. Again though, we are surrounded by dishonest people trying to make money, instead of giving. Two fellows were caught stealing, and one took some of the kids away with him.

Another project was laying pipes of water from the mountain down through Kitefu, my next door village, rebuilding a water tank and trough for the animals. Once finished, the villagers cut the pipes, and siphoned off the water. That is why one gets very fed up helping them.

One night, on waking up at 11.50 to men talking on my veranda, I sleepily thought it was my night watchmen talking to my driver. My dogs, two Jack Russells who sleep on my bed, were twitching their ears and their hair bristled. They started to bark hysterically, followed by the two Labradors in my den next door. The phone rang, it was my lovely neighbour Lizzie Titley, saying, 'Vicky, don't move there are nasty thugs in your house, I am contacting my security'.

Terrified, I started pushing the panic button next to my bed, the alarm went off, which set the dogs' barks to a higher pitch. Then came loud banging on the door to the den, and I realized whoever they were, they were trying to break into the house. Then a shot rang out near the pool.

Suddenly there were more men outside my bedroom, one long brown arm and a huge stick broke through the corner window, screaming for money.

I shouted 'Get out you buggers, I don't have money here you fools, it is in the bank!' while still pushing the alarm.

The men at the French window to my room were still desperately trying to break it; and *smash bang* the others broke through into the den, and suddenly a big tall guy with a huge panga appeared above me, standing on the dividing wall. I turned and pushed the button again, as I did this, he jumped down onto my bed and slashed my left arm with his panga screaming for money. He kicked me onto the floor and ripped up the mattress looking underneath it. At the same time other thugs broke the door of the den open – silly twits, it was not locked. They emptied all my drawers onto the floor, took all my costume jewellery, plus three or four good pieces. At the same instant a gun went off, a sawn off shot gun, which broke the glass and their bullets smashed into my cupboard, missing my head by 20cms. The tall guy dragged me backwards by the arms through the broken glass. They tried to panga the two puppies, who were very frightened and dashed between their legs out to the bush. My old Labrador Vegas had run into my bathroom and hidden in the shower. At this instant the thugs bolted out through the kitchen and down the hill at the back of the house. They had run thanks to a young professional hunter, Keith Charters, who had heard the first shot and lived on the far side of Lizzie.

He had said to his girlfriend, 'Shit, that was up at Vicky's.'. He left the car running, grabbed his gun and a sack of ammunition and in two minutes he was here; the thugs must have seen him coming as he walked across the lawn carrying his gun. One minute later the two security companies turned up, and drove to the staff quarters, but by then the buggers had escaped. His girlfriend, Francie Travers, came into my room and got me dressed, I always sleep naked! We were all shaking with the shock of it all.

Vegas was so frightened she would not come out of the shower for ages. The security guys found my two private guards tied up, one with an arm broken and the other with a slashed head and face. Their button alarms were found by my gardener the next day in the bush below the pool.

Mini Trappe came with his gun and Will Powell with his. They went off into the bush to the north west and hunted these guys all night. We found their tracks the next day to the east, where they had jumped the fence towards Kitefu the local village. Slowly we took stock of what they had taken. Having smashed all the doors and broken windows, they obviously did not know the layout of the house.

They were drunk on my booze, and probably already on drugs. They obviously were here quite a time before breaking into the den. They had already broken into the sitting room, tried to rip out the wires of the TV and music equipment, they took the decoder, my camera, the jewellery, my mobile phone of course, and two plate warmers that we imagine they thought were solar plaques. Last but not least, my husband Joaquin's naval ceremonial sword – that made me cry. I had put it on his coffin at his funeral. I put out a reward of 300,000 Tanzanian shillings if anyone could find it. Very recently it was returned to me by the police, thank goodness.

Now the police are doing their best to catch the gang, but it is very difficult. Two of them had guns, but there were at least eight or nine altogether.

They should be prosecuted for attempted murder, as I was very nearly hit in the head. Later they did find them and were dealt with accordingly.

I have had burglaries before in France and Spain, but never anything so frightening, have never been shot at before, or had rough men breaking into my bedroom, screaming at me and emptying my drawers in total abandon. Now I am installing an electric fence around the house, and an iron door into my den.

Despite these horrors, it is lovely to live here, away from the masses in Europe, and their bureaucracy, traffic jams, and over-crowding, not to mention the pollution and the cold. I love living here in the bush, with the animals around me, never ending space that stretches mile upon mile to the south and the Masai Steppes. Mount Meru in all her glory to the north, not to mention Kilimanjaro to the east. Of course it has its dangerous moments, and anything can happen, but being inside Dolly Estate has a certain security. We are all among friends, surrounded by an electric fence and guards. Not like South Africa, which is too much, but there is at least some protection from the unknown.

Destiny raises its ugly head, and we all live day-to-day, hoping for the best, treating the Tanzanians with respect and kindness which we hope will pay off in the long term.